White Ler
on Brown Sl

White Lens on Brown Skin

The Sexualization of the Polynesian in American Film

MATTHEW B. LOCEY

Foreword by Ed Rampell

McFarland & Company, Inc., Publishers

Jefferson, North Carolina

ISBN (print) 978-1-4766-8918-0
ISBN (ebook) 978-1-4766-4744-9

LIBRARY OF CONGRESS AND BRITISH LIBRARY
CATALOGUING DATA ARE AVAILABLE

Library of Congress Control Number 2022057302

Front cover image by Alan Poulson Photography (Shutterstock)

Printed in the United States of America

*McFarland & Company, Inc., Publishers
Box 611, Jefferson, North Carolina 28640
www.mcfarlandpub.com*

In Love

To my dearest wife, Mele Kaye Todd,
for her patience and sacrifice for me
and our children.

In Reverence

To my mother, Eleanor Kawehilani Kanahele,
whose life as a widow raising five boys,
as a businesswoman, and as a hula dancer
inspired me to write on this subject.

In Gratitude

To Naomi Noelaniokoʻolau Clark and
Pualani Kanakaʻole Kanahele,
women who inspire me towards
higher education and Polynesian values.

In Memoriam

For Merata Mita and Haunani-Kay Trask,
women I immensely admire, women I so wish
could have read this book.

To all the women above, who are of Polynesian descent.

"Most of the work shows that you are capable of doing
something and all other prejudices of race and sex now
perhaps fall away."—Merata Mita, from the documentary
Merata: How Mum Decolonized the Screen (2019)

Also to this noble effort.

Table of Contents

Acknowledgments

Center for Pacific Islands Studies (CPIS) (UHM)—Thesis Committee

Alexander Dale Mawyer, professor and graduate chair, Pacific Island Studies, is mentioned first for having made the highest contribution to this book. He was a mentor of research and thesis writing and one of the nicest, most supportive, positive, and encouraging people on earth.

Noelani Arista, professor of history, for valuable assistance and advice about my direction in writing.

Vilsoni Hereniko, professor of creative media and former chair of CPIS. His Indigenous Filmmaking and Pacific Islands Studies wisdom had a large impact on my *na'auao* (knowledge).

All CPIS graduate student faculty, staff, and fellow graduate students (with whom I shared research, uplifting discussions and debate).

Dr. Terence Wesley-Smith (chair) for accepting me into graduate school and for mentoring my research.

Tarcisius Kabutaulaka (professor) who filled my mind with Pacific knowledge.

Family

My contrasting grandfathers:

Frank Harrison Locey, a successful businessman and man of the world who owned a private zoo and from whom I received my sense of humor.

Clinton Joshua Kanahele, a wise, serious, devoted church member, father of 14, and educator, who was the first Hawaiian high school principal. Hawaiian was his first language.

Agnes Kalanikauanakikilani Sanford, beloved grandma, master hula dancer and master cook, and also my Hawaiian etiquette *kumu* (teacher).

My uncle, Dr. George Hueu Sanford Kanahele (Hawaiian scholar and author). When my educated elder uncle wanted to have intellectual one-on-one conversations with me, I knew I had finally come of age. I enjoyed those moments immensely, and I learned a lot from them.

Uncle Edward Huihui Kanahele—even after his passing at an early age, his short writings on Hawaiian epistemology have enriched my knowledge and educated many others.

I have over 50 loving cousins in my Hawaiian ʻohana (family). I would love to mention all of them, but I'll mention just one, Nicole Kanahele Stutz (associate professor of English), who also helped me copy edit my early drafts and encouraged me to publish. She is also a female hula practitioner and instructor, so her opinions did strengthen my pursuits. *Mahalo nui* (a big thank you), Nicole.

South Seas Cinema Society

This film society is a huge resource for this book, and I'm happy to be associated with this group. Many years of research, reviewing films and ephemera, data collecting, and documenting have been shared.

Robert C. Schmitt was a founding member of the Society, former Hawaiʻi State Statistician, author and valuable researcher of early and silent films about Hawaiʻi.

DeSoto Brown is a founding member of the Society, former archivist and now historian for the prestigious Bishop Museum in Honolulu, also an author and collector extraordinaire.

Ed Rampell, a founding member of the Society, is an author and a film and stage critic.

Caroline Yacoe (M.A. Pacific Islands Studies with an emphasis in Melanesian Arts), Dan Long (collector, Society host), Steven Fredrick (film collector, film historian), Roger Meeker Atty (collector), Doug Mossman (actor), Don Stroud (actor), Joe Hill (collector, TV historian), Ernest Carvelo (film collector), and Benny Chapman (actor) all have contributed in so many ways to this book directly and indirectly by sharing their South Seas cinema ephemera, films, and personal histories.

Libraries and Staffs

Hawaiian & Pacific Collections—Hamilton Library UHM, Stu Dawrs (Co-head Librarian)—quality and quantity research took place here in a prestigious and limited-access collection. Thank you, Stu and your staff—good memories. I love research, and that place was nirvana for Pacific research.

Wong Audio/Visual Center—Sinclair Library UHM. Their huge Pacific film and video collection was highly beneficial when reviewing hard-to-find films out of New Zealand and other South Pacific Islands. Helpful and friendly staff.

Hawai'i State Library. Valuable collection of state and national historical items from government records, historical books, and newspapers. Mahalo to a very experienced and knowledgeable staff.

Other Miscellaneous Contributors, Mentors, Example Makers and Friends:

Dr. Elizabeth Kapu'uwailani Lindsey (Anthropologist), David Hanlon (PhD, Chair–UHM Department of History), Glenn Mann (Professor of Literature, Film and Narrative Studies, Dept. of English-UHM), Norman Douglas (Professor Pacific Cinema–Australia), Houston Wood (Hawaii Pacific University Indigenous Pacific Cinema Professor and author)

*Titles are as when I was associated with these individuals. Some have moved on, retired or have deceased. Bless them all.

Foreword by Ed Rampell

I first met Matt Locey in 1989 during a meeting in a classroom or office at the University of Hawai'i's Mānoa campus. Also joining us at the gathering were author DeSoto Brown, a Bishop Museum archivist and historian, and the late Bob Schmitt, longtime State of Hawai'i statistician and author of the groundbreaking *Hawai'i in the Movies 1898–1959*. The four of us had two main things in common: We were film buffs who were all interested in and entranced by—some may say "obsessed" with—movies and TV programs set and/or shot in Hawai'i and the Pacific Islands.

Together, we formed the South Seas Cinema Society, a fan club devoted to collecting, analyzing, studying and enjoying Pacific pictures. Over the decades, our informal film society grew to include monthly get-togethers (usually at Dan Long's *hale*, which included a state-of-the-art home movie theater) where likeminded aficionados of Oceanic imagery on the big screen socialized, devoured a potluck luau, kibbitzed and watched a production featuring Hawai'i, Tahi`ti, Samoa or some fictionalized island, such as Bali Ha'i in 1958's *South Pacific* or Ami Oni Oni Isle in Betty Grable's 1942 *Song of the Islands*.

With his energy and insatiable interest in the subject, Matt emerged as the heart and soul of the South Seas Cinema Society. More often than not, Matt notified members about and programmed our monthly screenings, introducing the titles we'd see and then presiding over the good-natured discussion that followed, sharing insights, observations, jokes and critiques of the tropical tropes "*Haole*-wood" often depicted in these frequently goofy flicks, which sometimes include monkeys and snakes, although none are actually found in Polynesia (except, perhaps, at the Honolulu Zoo in Waikiki). During the 1990s, Matt also co-presented and co-organized a South Seas Cinema Film Festival at what was then the Honolulu Academy of Arts. As the backbone of our fan club, Matt acted as our president, or, as we unofficially dubbed him, as the "*Ali'i Nui*" (high chief) of the South Seas Cinema Society.

1

Now, Matt Locey's *White Lens on Brown Skin: The Sexualization of the Polynesian in American Film* is being published. This book is literally the fulfillment of a third of a century's worth of work, viewing, reviewing and analyzing how Pacific Islanders and their isles are pictured on the big and little screens. Since the 1989 founding of the South Seas Cinema Society, as one of those co-founders, it can honestly be said that *White Lens on Brown Skin* is the culmination and fruition of, and arguably the greatest achievement of, what the four of us set out to do when we first met at the UH, lo, those many moons ago.

White Lens on Brown Skin is quite possibly the best film history and analytical book ever written chronicling and critiquing South Seas cinema, a distinct film genre that began in 1898 but a category of cinema/TV that has remained overlooked and neglected by scholars, critics and filmmakers alike—until now. I myself co-authored three books exploring the genre, all published by Honolulu's Mutual Publishing—1995's *Made in Paradise: Hollywood's Films of Hawai'i and the South Seas*; 2001's *Pearl Harbor in the Movies*; and 2013's *The Hawai'i Movie and Television Book* (now in its third printing). But I can candidly tell you why Matt Locey's work, which I had the pleasure and good luck to read in manuscript form, is far deeper, more insightful, and better researched than the books I co-wrote or any of the others I've read on the subject.

Matt is a movie/TV industry insider, an assistant director who is a member of the prestigious Directors Guild of America. He began working on sets at the Diamond Head Studio and on location throughout the Hawai'ian archipelago starting back in the *Magnum, P.I.* days, when Tom Selleck played the title role in the 1980s. Matt's extensive screen credits, which can be seen on IMDb, went on to include the largely Kauai-shot Harrison Ford 1998 feature *Six Days, Seven Nights* and 2001's O'ahu-shot blockbuster *Pearl Harbor.* Thus, Matt has the penetrating perception of somebody who has worked up close and personal in the movie/TV biz for decades.

On the scholarly front, in 2016 Matt earned his Master of Arts in Pacific Islands Studies at the Center for Pacific Islands Studies, in the University of Hawai'i at Mānoa. This rigorous academic training has endowed Matt with the scholastic skills and background for conducting research and analysis. Therefore, he is far more qualified than I (who earned only a BA at Manhattan's Hunter College with a major in cinema) to comprehensively, theoretically write about film studies (although he does so here in a way to appeal to academic, film fan and general audience readerships).

But the factor that best qualifies Matt Locey to authoritatively write about South Seas cinema is that he is of the *koko*—that is, he has the "blood" and traces his lineage directly to the Hawai'ians or *Kanaka Ma'oli*, the original Polynesian inhabitants and discoverers of Hawai'i who lived there before the arrival of Captain James Cook. Matt has also spent most of his life in Hawai'i, and he is culturally imbued with the Kanaka Ma'oli lifestyle and worldview.

As someone who has Hawai'ian heritage, Matt is authentically empowered to scrutinize, probe and put into perspective how his people and ancestral homeland have been depicted by (usually) others onscreen. In terms of culture, "self-determination" means the self—not outsiders—determines how it is depicted. Put into its proper historical and societal context, *White Lens on Brown Skin* must be viewed as being part of the Racial Reckoning America is currently undergoing. Especially since Matt is shining a spotlight on a smaller, usually overlooked ethnic group, the Pacific Islanders, whose lives and depictions also matter.

Furthermore, as the book's subtitle—*The Sexualization of the Polynesian in American Film*—indicates, *White Lens on Brown Skin* is also influenced by the #MeToo and #TimesUp movements that oppose sexual exploitation in Hollywood and beyond, as the book tackles Tinseltown's tropes depicting nubile, naked, pneumatic nymphs inhabiting a Native Nirvana, eager to sexually please (usually) white, male Western interlopers. As I have noted in the past in a reference to a now "cancelled" racial caricature, "South Seas cinema without interracial sex is like Aunt Jemima's pancakes without the syrup." Matt grapples with these celluloid stereotypes much as New Zealand anthropologist Derek Freeman challenged a social science classic, 1928's *Coming of Age in Samoa*, purportedly debunking and setting the record straight in Freeman's iconoclastic 1986 *Margaret Mead and Samoa: The Making and Unmaking of an Anthropological Myth*.

Here's an example of one of Matt's original, acute insights: a recurring motif of South Seas cinema's is that while the genre indeed portrays many mixed-race characters, biracial children are rarely depicted together onscreen with their biological parents. Part-Polynesian *dramatis personae* usually appear without their birth mother and father, who are typically kept offscreen, perhaps because they have already conveniently died.

Now, this by itself is a completely uniquely observation. But with his extraordinary perceptiveness, Matt goes on to link this repeat plot twist to the fact that for much of Tinseltown's history, parts of America practiced Jim Crow and segregation. Matt then ties this into how this impacted the Hollywood Production Code, a form of self-censorship carried out by the motion picture industry. Thus, interracial romance and, in particular, the ensuing birth and raising of children, was an extremely touchy subject full of anxiety that had to be delicately finessed in mass entertainment in a country where a form of apartheid widely existed when much of South Seas cinema was being filmed.

In addition to Matt Locey's philosophical framework, *White Lens on Brown Skin* also has the virtue of probably being the most comprehensive, up-to-date chronicle of South Seas cinema, from Thomas Edison to Jason Momoa, Jon Hall to Dwayne "The Rock" Johnson, Dorothy Lamour to Auli'i Cravalho, Robert Flaherty's 1926 *Moana: A Romance of the Golden Age* to Disney's 2016 *Moana*. In addition to the aforementioned sensitive issue regarding miscegenation and families, Matt extensively explores other classic *Kanaka* clichés that recur throughout this genre that stretch back to the origins of the motion picture medium. They include:

The Canoe Greeting of the Westerners when their ships appear; the Lagoon Swim Scene with scantily clad *vahines*; the "hip-notizing" sensuous Indigenous dance; the First Kiss between Western newcomers and Natives; the feasts featuring foods, such as poi, that are strange to the European palate; and much more. Matt puts these Tinseltown tropes into the context of Hollywood's oversexualization of Pacific Islanders.

But Matt is, by nature, an optimistic individual, and he holds out hope for the decolonization of the South Seas screen image and the creation of more culturally accurate, sensitive Pacific productions. Like his Hawaiian ancestors of yore, Matt is a pathfinder, navigating a course to making more truthful, respectful productions. One small, but significant, new example of this development is that the Academy Museum of Motion Pictures, which opened September 30, 2021, in Los Angeles, devotes much of its galleries, displays, etc., to the legacy of racially insensitive onscreen imagery. The Museum—which is operated by the Academy of Motion Picture Arts and Sciences, the same organization that annually bestows the Academy Awards—is also stressing the importance of inclusivity and diversity. As part of this emphasis the Museum's exhibitions include a recognition of Native films, with a screen playing on a loop part of the 2009 documentary *Reel Injun*, co-directed by Cree filmmaker Neil Diamond, Jeremiah Hayes and Catherine Bainbridge, with clips from Indigenous productions, including the 1994 New Zealand/Aotearoa Maori movie *Once Were Warriors*.

Informed with the sensibility of being a longtime film/TV professional, a movie buff, an accomplished scholar with a master's degree and, most importantly, being himself a Hawai'ian, Matt Locey has written a definitive, pathfinding book about the beloved if neglected genre the four of us met up to celebrate and study a third of a century ago at the University of Hawai'i. *White Lens on Brown Skin: The Sexualization of the Polynesian in American Film* has been authoritatively authored by a Polynesian filmmaker/scholar/Native, and every page contains Indigenous insights. For creating and giving us this *makana* (gift), as one of the South Seas Cinema Society's co-founders with Matt Locey way back in 1989, I take my lei off to him.

Ed Rampell, named after CBS broadcaster Edward R. Murrow, majored in cinema at Hunter College, in Manhattan and spent 23 years in Tahiti, Samoa, Hawaii, Guam and Micronesia, visiting more than 100 Pacific Islands. Rampell co-founded the South Seas Cinema Society, co-authored three film history books, including The Hawaii Movie and Television Book, *and co-starred in the 2005 Australian documentary* Hula Girls: Imagining Paradise. *His proudest creation is his Polynesian daughter, Marina Davis, the Samoan soprano.*

Preface

I was raised in two environments, the first being in Hawai'i with a Hawaiian family. Then, when I was eight, my mother sold our big house, and we flew off to diaspora or to my second life in Washington state. There in the Northwest I was exposed to the "normal" life of a U.S. citizen in a "normal" American environment. I adapted well, but my fond memories of the islands did not leave my heart and mind. I tried to aid my recollections with any information about Hawai'i, but anything to do with the unique 50th Island State was hard to come by. What information I did receive was not from school or the library but via Madison Avenue commercials and Hollywood-produced TV shows. One day, I knew something was not right when, while watching a Dole Pineapple commercial, my Hawaiian mother suddenly threw a solid object at our TV, complaining that the hostess of the commercial (who was Asian and donned the stereotypical hula outfit with a grass skirt) was not Hawaiian. Now this sudden act of violence was not normal for an educated and "civilized" mother.

As one can imagine the incident has stayed with me throughout my life. Being too young to truly digest its significance in the overall scheme of modern life on Earth, I was more concerned that our only TV would be shattered. What would a typical American preteen of the '60s and '70s do in life without our sole form of entertainment, our teacher, and our babysitter—the TV? I guess I now understand the youth of today, with their obsession with smartphones. After eight years of life in ordinary continental America, my now-widowed Hawaiian mother thought we were exposed enough to normal American lifestyle and good public schools, so we packed up and moved back to unordinary Hawai'i. This was fortuitous for me, because in the early '70s, when we returned, the islands were in the middle of the Hawaiian Renaissance period in which many Hawaiians finally had had enough of being assimilated into American culture and losing their identity.

This awakening began for many, including me, who once was starving for any information on Hawai'i and its Indigenous culture. I was now in a brain overload about our language, our own Pacific Island knowledge, and our culture—why it was almost lost to early colonization and how this assimilation and loss of identity continues. Like the resistance against the Borg's imperialistic goals of *Star Trek* fictional lore and the American Revolution from Britain, the Hawaiian Renaissance was also an awakening, a resistance and a revolt. I should explain that, as independent thinkers, many Hawaiians have varied opinions, perceptions and understandings about life. Some Islanders love America and its modern ways and welcomed the assimilation; thus, there was no consensus, no unified perspectives and definitely no newsworthy Native uprisings. Nevertheless, I now understood the erroneous representation on our TV screen years earlier and why it was so important to my mother. Sometime later in graduate school, perusing Pacific Islands Studies, I came to learn much more.

Meanwhile, in the years in between, I was involved in the South Seas Cinema Society as lead researcher and archivist of informational data. I now serve as the Society's president. The Society's mission is to promote the fact that there is a legitimate motion picture genre set in Oceania (Pacific Islands) with all of their inhabitants, whether Indigenous, migrant, or visitor. To establish this genre, we needed to document histories and establish large numbers of titles of this unrecognized film category. What started as a club of movie fans viewing South Seas films and sharing collector ephemera about these films ended up as a serious film society documenting everything to do with each South Seas film. As such, these researched records are historical records that can be used by anyone from serious students writing about decolonization, film fans collecting trivia, or family members of past cast or crew of these films, who want to know more about the films that their relatives worked on. Whatever the case, these films are now history, and the Society is simply documenting this history. Many of our findings are at: http://southseascinema.org (the home page of South Seas Cinema).

I also worked, as my main career, in the Hollywood film industry itself in production management. I purposely was based out of my home island of O'ahu and did not like to travel to work in other places in the world (thus being away from my family), but I did enjoy filming on the outer islands of the Hawaiian chain, at times in very remote and culturally significant places. To keep busy, I learned to work in many types of filmmaking, including network TV series, major movies, national commercials and music videos. Hawaii will always be in demand as a backdrop. I have been involved in the production of many contemporary South Seas titles firsthand.

After retiring from film production and while in graduate school,

I contemplated my focus of study. How can I devote time with my background of being part-Hawaiian, a film researcher, a filmmaker, and a budding Pacific Islands scholar? Debunking Hollywood stereotypes of my Polynesian ancestry in American film is a good start. With this pursuit I can combine my knowledge, resources and experiences. Of course, I have other goals in regard to my background and aptitudes.

But in regard to this tome, when I first started to explore the copious Polynesian generalizations in film and in mass media in general, I realized I had better narrow down the stereotypes. In the vast majority of American and foreign film posters and other forms of advertising South Seas titles, it was not hard to notice a glaring constant in Polynesian imagery—that of the sexualized Polynesian. With the fact that my mother had passed and she, like my many Hawaiian relatives, were all pretty good hula dancers (some devoted to the art), I saw a direction. After examining many sensual film poster images and witnessing many terrible appropriated or faux hulas on film, I finalized my focus very quickly. My graduate school (The Center for Pacific Islands Studies) was part of the University of Hawai'i at Mānoa's system. UH was definitely the epicenter for Pacific Studies of any kind for the U.S. and arguably for the world. The library collections, knowledgeable and noteworthy professors, special guest lecturers, and fellow graduate students (some from throughout the Pacific) all aided my research efforts tremendously. Of course, the Internet with free access (for students) to other papers and electronic academic books from different universities and scholarly websites were also a modern benefit. After all, this is a major reason why the Internet was invented—to share academic knowledge. Being a faculty member or a university student can make a huge difference towards accessing all this data, and I took full advantage of it.

In early research, I noted that there was some, but not a lot, of scholarship on my subject and nothing in the commercial literature or in general debate. There is gratefulness when coming to the realization that this is an original subject, not in the sense that it has not been around but in the sense that it has almost never been discussed in the general public sphere. I hope this book will change that. In academia, there are some pertinent writings on this subject, but only as part of a bigger study and the few devoted books or papers would only analyze one, two or three titles at a time. With my background in film research and the South Seas Cinema Society database, I could examine hundreds of titles. This methodology was not done before. Not only did I want to study the sexualization of the Polynesian in American film, but also, I wanted to expose how rampant this sexualization is in American cinematic history.

Lastly, there is one important experience I need to share in regard to this sexualization topic. I was competent in film clip editing, and so in my early research, I was eager to share some of my research on film with my fellow graduate students. I did it twice, but both times there was an unease in the room. I was the only one in the classroom to be excited about my discoveries. Later I had a one-on-one discussion and critique on my thesis proposal (the same subject of this book) by a female fellow student whose scholarly focus was on Tahitian dance; surprisingly, she didn't like my subject and thought I should pursue another course. She could not explain why, but she was uncomfortable with the subject that I wanted to write about. I was confused. I thought there was a need to expose this subject. Finally, in my dissertation committee introduction to my paper, where I used a slide presentation, a female Hawaiian History Professor explained that I had to be careful revealing this subject matter without being like the filmmakers I was exposing— who expose Polynesian bodies.

At that moment I realized both Hollywood filmmakers and I had something to gain in exposing Polynesian nudity. I did not consider that the people that were exploited by Hollywood could be exploited again even in an anthropological perspective or academic review. I realized that this was the problem and a discomfort to my fellow students, especially the female ones. The solution was easy, and it saved all my work: never *exhibit* examples of the sexualization of the Polynesian, just argue about it in vocalized and printed words. In this book, I purposely show posters of South Seas films that are rated "G" but still represent or complement the written word well without bodily exposure. I am not trying to be a religious prude—I just don't want to be a hypocrite. There are ways to learn and educate others about sexualization without exhibiting nakedness and running the risk of becoming what you are criticizing.

Case in point, later in the book you'll learn the differences between the 1935 *Mutiny on the Bounty* and 1984's *The Bounty*. One had gratuitous nudity, and one did not, but they both expounded the story message well to their audiences—that the Polynesian females are so beautiful and devoted that men will sacrifice their careers, reputations, and lives for them. One received the Academy Award for Best Picture—the one that did not exhibit sexualization but deep love and commitment.

Introduction

A Brief History of Polynesian Representation by the Other

Since the earliest contact accounts between Polynesians and Europeans, it has been evident that Westerners have been fascinated by the peoples of Oceania as sensual and sexual beings. In Europe, early publications on the Pacific, as well as works of art, lectures, and stage plays, became popular almost immediately, often with exotic and erotic components. With the Pacific Islands halfway around the world and accurate sources limited, the content of these various types of 18th-century media frequently included a fusion of facts, fantasies and imaginations. By the late 1800s, this amalgamation of truth and fiction in Pacific Island representation had evolved into South Seas tropes found in various forms of mass communications and commercial entertainment of the period, including early American cinema. Today, even after 100 years of Hollywood-produced films, the Polynesian depictions on the American silver screen are still filled with clichés, stereotypes, and misappropriations. Among these many enduring representations, the trope of Polynesian sexuality has been one of the most popular for the American audience but simultaneously one of the most damaging to the dignity and cultural sovereignty of the Indigenous Polynesians. In a time of decolonization in the Pacific, this book illustrates and analyzes these degrading cinematic sexualized tropes of the Pacific Islander and documents their prevalence in the history of popular American cinema.

In researching this book, four significant tropes were identified to illustrate and illuminate the sexualization of the Polynesian in American film. They are the "Canoe Greeting" scene, the "Lagoon Swim" scene, the "Sensual Dance" scene, and the "Native First Kiss" scene. These four cinematic tropes will be established, examined, and critiqued in Chapters 3 through 6 of this book. Later chapters will explore other Pacific Island tropes in American film that contain sexual overtones.

All chapters will encompass a large sampling of romantic or sexual film clichés found not only with Polynesian sexualization but also with the Pacific Islands themselves as sexual locations—all with the purpose of enticing audiences to the theaters. Significantly, also found in this book is an exhaustive, annotated filmography of over 150 predominantly American film titles, all illustrating sexual relationships and the sexualization of the Pacific Isles that are prevalent in American and in global commercial cinema in general. This filmography is not only an interesting read and valuable resource for Pacific Film studies, but also this reference guide serves as evidence of the rampant and enduring colonial sexualized gaze, via Hollywood, of the peoples of the Pacific.

It is important to note at this time that films and other visual mass media that supposedly represent the Native peoples of the Pacific are not the only sexualized genre that is produced out of Hollywood. A simple visual search of publicity photo stills, movie posters and preview

Son of Fury (1942, 20th Century–Fox). British merchant marine Tyrone Power abandons ship in the South Seas and falls for a Native vahine played by American actress Gene Tierney in brownface. A typical American South Seas film in which a male foreigner seduces an innocent Native young woman. The sexual appeal of a young Polynesian woman displayed on this American lobby card (11" × 14") is typical of this genre.

clips from major and minor film studios will show evidence of many sexualized images from various other genres of film. For example, posters in film categories of crime dramas or comedies will exhibit sensual poses of the female form with much-exposed legs or breasts, but these images are usually used as sexist attention getters and are not integral to almost all (except for Romance) genres in general.

The issue here is that the frequency of sex and sexuality in the Polynesian film genre is so commonplace it seems almost a prerequisite or an inherent and indispensable part of any American South Seas plot. Unfortunately, this repeated use of the "sex sells" tool of Hollywood and other industries forms harmful stereotypes, especially for Polynesian women. Another danger of this overused sexual Pacific paradigm is that it becomes, at times, subliminal or out of the public consciousness. Worst, it becomes so stereotypical that the sexualization becomes expected and normalized. This book will explore, record, and discuss this prevalency and hope to awaken the public consciousness on these issues. Hopefully, new, quality Polynesian films and stories will emerge.

PART I

Race, Romance, and Representation

1

South Seas Cinema

Definition and Facts

Instead of an analysis of a whole field of film theory, which would be a more comprehensive and significant study, a closer examination of a specific genre with theoretical explorations, comparisons of data, and analytic critique is presented here. This book will utilize these explicit methodologies focusing on the esoteric film genre of South Seas cinema.[1] South Seas cinema is defined as the film category of commercial narrative motion picture types set on a Pacific Island and generally produced by modern, globally economic countries, such as the United States. More specifically, this book will scrutinize, in American feature film, the sexualized tropes of the Polynesian, examine the interracial romantic relationships between Polynesians and Euro-Americans or Europeans, and deliberate on the sexualization of Pacific Islands as romanticized set locations.

Even though the genre of South Seas cinema is little known, it encompasses a large number of films within the category, rivaling other more popular American movie classifications, such as the Western or Organized Crime genres. Another important note to consider is that feature films are just one "motion" picture media type within this genre. For example, animation, TV, cable or streaming shows, commercials, and music videos are some of the other media types within this motion picture category. This book will only examine feature films or theatrically released movies principally produced out of Hollywood. However, one must recognize that the same racial stereotypes, non-factual clichés and other incorrect representations of the people of Polynesia are found in all South Seas motion picture film types (excluding Indigenous Film), as well as other Pacific Island-themed popular mass media such as literature, art, stage, music, and even theme parks. These tropes of the Pacific, in general, have been perpetuated since the first contact period between Europe and Oceana and continue today in American mass media, including popular movies.

With regard to the South Seas genre of feature films, here is some numerical data of interest. For example, there are currently researched over 776 different movies produced and distributed by Hollywood that are set or partially set in the Pacific.[2] Interestingly, 176 of these films are from the silent era alone (1911–1929), and many of these features do not exist today. Two films found within the South Seas genre are Academy Award-winning features for Best Picture, 1935's *Mutiny on the Bounty* and 1953's *From Here to Eternity*. As of the printing of this book, in total, these films yielded 36 Oscar winners and 167 total nominations,[3] all from diverse award categories. While this genre is not commonly recognized by film audiences, when it is acknowledged, it is generally viewed as an entertaining and escapist film type. But judging by its cinematic awards, it is a serious genre as well. Major Hollywood studios invested heavily in this film category, utilizing major producers and directors and notable stars, as well as elaborate, expensive special effects. Many of these films were lensed on location, and a few titles have multiple settings. For example, some scenes in the 2001 film *Pearl Harbor* took place in the Midwest and Europe, but it was principally set

From Here to Eternity (1953, Columbia Pictures). **Winner of eight Academy Awards, including "Best Picture,"** *Eternity* **stars Burt Lancaster and Deborah Kerr, shown here in their famous kiss on a secluded Hawaiian beach. These actors received Oscar nominations for "Best Actor" and "Best Actress" in this film classic. British (30" × 40") quad poster.**

in and around Pearl Harbor on the Hawaiian island of O'ahu. Needless to say, it seems that Pacific Island settings are the memorable ones, even with a film that contains varied set locations.

No Hollywood audience can forget the clear skies, blue lagoons, swaying palm trees, grass shacks, mysterious tikis, outrigger canoes and exploding volcanoes, all distinct characteristics or icons of this genre. But most of all, one cannot forget the scantily clad, attractive Native people of Polynesia also established in these films. The Indigenous Islanders all seem to be handsome and beautiful, bronze-skinned, perfectly fit, semi-nude young adults, but in reality, their representations are as false as some of the faux palm trees and manufactured lagoons that inhabit this genre. Even most of the natural disasters that appear in many of these films are created by man. The film *The Hurricane*, from 1937, has a torrent of heavy winds and rough seas almost completely obliterating a Polynesian atoll, incredibly all lensed on a Southern California soundstage. The Oscar-winning storm effects of *The Hurricane* still hold up comparatively well with today's realistic, computer-generated effects. The point is that these same onscreen illusions of manufactured paradise apparently hold true for the manufactured sexualized Native people of paradise, the Polynesians. The documentation of this representation—the sexualized stereotype of the peoples of Polynesia—as well as an analysis of their interracial sexual relationships found in American film and the consequences of these representations are the scope and significance of this book.

Observed in the American cinematic records (see included Annotated Filmography) are at least 150 South Seas film titles that exhibit the sexualization of the Indigenous people of Polynesia or the sexually commodified Oceanic representation—and the discriminatory treatment of interracial relationships between a Euro-American or European and a Polynesian. Not surprisingly in terms of these interracial relationships, only .93 percent of these South Seas titles contain a plot with a sexual relationship between a male Polynesian character and a Euro-American female. Logically, in movie stories that are set during early contact periods with European ships full of only men, one can understand this gender relationship imbalance, but in features that are set in later historical periods this continued disparity of Polynesian males having relationships with Euro-American females can be accounted for by the Euro-American male-dominated lens of the Hollywood film trade.[4] The supremacy of European and Euro-American men over Polynesian women in Hollywood film reflects the Euro-American male-dominated entertainment industry and its male-centered imaginations.

There are other films in this genre with romantic relationships, especially in the silent period of filmmaking, between two Americans stranded on an exotic, yet deserted Pacific Isle. Some involve a three-person castaway group, with usually one female, all entangled in a dramatic plot full of sexual tension. But these films, with locations on beautiful, remote Pacific Islands, will be discussed but not focused upon in this study because our concentration is on the treatment of Polynesians in American cinema. Likewise, the more contemporary and popular films of simple romantic interludes between two visitors to the exotic Pacific Isles will be emphasized only in Chapter 8 for the same reason. In general, South Seas films in the context of this book should contain at least one Polynesian character of note. Later chapters do cover the sexualized islands themselves, which includes sex and romance by anyone on the isles.

Analyzing a broader body of works instead of the customary one or handful of titles found in this Hollywood genre will not only be a significant difference from other literary works, but this method of study will, all the more, validate this volume's arguments and demonstrate the prevalence of the subject matter. As mentioned, the subject of this tome is not in the consciousness of America. The flawed depictions of Polynesian people in much of American popular film are at times direct and sometimes subliminal and speculative, but nonetheless, these representations are still erroneous and reinforce the American stereotypical mindset.

The purpose of this book is three-fold: first, to demonstrate the general popularity of Polynesians and their cultures in American popular feature film, which is distributed worldwide. Second, to bring these discriminatory attitudes and incorrect sexual representations of the Polynesian to the forefront with numerical data, historical facts, and analytical theories. Lastly, to create a new awareness, leading to corrections of centuries-old tropes of the people of Oceania, an awareness which is paramount in the decolonization process in the Pacific. The demeaning psychological wounds caused by "Outside" political, religious and commercial forces were used to dominate the Indigenous Pacific Islanders historically. This book will expose the causes of these wounds, specifically in film. Then, hopefully we can begin to mend with the realization of facts and the contemplations of theory presented in this manuscript.

Some of the framework of this work will be shaped within the four aforementioned major sexualized tropes as in chapters 2–5: the Canoe Greeting, Lagoon Swim, Sensual Dance, and Native First Kiss scenes. This book will demonstrate the extensiveness of these tropes as well as analyze their deeper connotations within these chapters. For instance, the Canoe Greeting scenes in these American films unrealistically denote happy giving and eager acceptance from the Polynesians towards their visitors from Europe and America, but most significantly for this book, the images in these scenes introduce a stereotype of the scantily clad and seemingly promiscuous Pacific Island women found throughout this genre. This imagined free-sex environment symbolizes the free giving and taking of paradise or the islands themselves. In direct relationship to this concept, the male-dominated Hollywood lens will also be discussed in this same chapter. Correspondingly, numerous cinematic examples of these tropes and analytic detail will be discussed in each chapter of this work. The Lagoon Swim chapter will have a discussion on the American film industry lens (point of view) as well as the American audience lens and the ethnopornographic debate. In the Sensual Dance chapter, the selection and use of particular dances in American South Seas cinema—and the seemingly exclusive and ubiquitous choice of only the young and fit Indigenes that are used in all sexualized tropes of Pacific film—will be discussed, as well as the problematic "sex sells" marketing concept. The last trope chapter of this reading, Native First Kiss, is an exhaustive section covering interracial relationships in these American-produced films. Different racist cinematic relationships will be theorized, and the concept of miscegenation in South Seas movies will also be analyzed. Other chapters in this book will discuss the appropriation of the sexy grass skirt or sarong, prostitution on the islands, and subliminal sex in the tourist industry. The conclusion of this volume will examine possible solutions to reset the course of these misrepresentations, as well as a comparative argument between Hollywood and Pacific Indigenous filmmaking, recent Hollywood non-sexualized recognition of the Polynesian, the recognition of "whitewashing" in film, and finally the general support of Pacific Indigenous Film production.

2

Arriving in Eden

The Canoe Greeting Trope

Perhaps there is no better way to explain the essence of this chapter about the Canoe Greeting scene in American South Seas cinema than with a comparison of this clichéd scene from the surviving *Bounty* films. Only four of the five versions of this famous story, produced by American, British, New Zealand and Australian film companies, exist today.[1] Because the earliest version of the *Bounty* story, the 1916 Australian silent film entitled *Mutiny of the Bounty*, is a lost film, we will start with the background and analytical criticism of the 1933 Australian feature titled *In the Wake of the Bounty* produced by Charles Chauvel. There are three facts of significance about this film: one, it stars in his first role the then-untrained popular actor Errol Flynn; two, it is partially shot in Tahiti with its beautiful, expansive beaches, exotic mountains and erotic *kanaka* (people) of Tahiti; and three, it remains the only screen version of the *Bounty* saga to include scenes shot on location at the remote Pitcairn Island, where the mutineers eventually settled. Incredibly, Chauvel's film includes underwater shots of the keel or hull backbone remains of the actual *H.M.S. Bounty*.

In *Wake*, one of the ship's crew announces that the island of Tahiti has been sighted; at the same time the scantily clad, athletic Native male coconut tree climber spots the distant sails and signals to the rest of the village that a European ship is approaching. This common cinematic announcement causes the customary film routine of general havoc below, with islanders scurrying about in joyous anticipation of meeting the Europeans. In one nonsensical shot, during this flurry of activity, director Charles Chauvel stages a pretty, young, and topless Native woman in front of reeds, knee deep in water. She irrationally also poses with both her arms in the air. Was this a brazen attempt to accentuate even further the Tahitian's youthful ample breasts? For the other female greeters, Chauvel manages to stage these young and fit island maidens with clichéd fresh leis, conveniently positioned to (more or less) conceal their toplessness. There are also shots of young and fit Tahitian men carrying heavy wooden canoes across a shallow lagoon. All of the men have their defined and wet pectoral muscles awash in salt water and sunlight, and all wear short wraps around their waists, exposing their muscular thighs.

Then, as is customary with the Canoe Greeting trope, the Native canoes hit the water, frequently with the omnipresent double hulled canoe for the chief and plenty of bare-breasted vahines along for the ride. Such Polynesian greeting scenes usually depict European crew members, who have traveled for months with few rations, painful illnesses, and no female companionship, behaving with foolish abandon—but not in this film. Because of time and budget, Chauvel could not anchor a period foreign ship and crew at the real location (Tahiti); hence no customary Canoe Greeting scene with the interaction of atmospheric, sexualized role players (the Tahitians). Just point-of-view shots of the ship's crew or the fervent male gaze. Instead of first-time human interaction between two distant cultures, Chauvel uses the excitement of an older British sailor drunkenly and joyfully reminiscing about the experience of landing on the enchanted islands of French Polynesia in a saloon studio set. The old sailor rousingly recalls the viewing for the first time of the semi-nude and beautiful Tahitian maidens, with intercuts of separate island footage of the aforementioned scantily clad Polynesians.

Chauvel may have also been in a hurry to complete his film because of the Motion Picture Production Code of 1930, which, among other issues, prohibited the exhibiting of indecency. Director/producer Charles Chauvel had two loopholes to "the Code" in his favor. One, Chauvel could get away with this nudity in a major motion picture by virtue of the fact that it was an Australian-produced film, and the Code was an American construct[2]; two, the Code would not be enforced until 1934. Because of this late enforcement, other Hollywood producers competed to release racy films before the Code was truly compulsory. Due to the year in which it was produced, *In the Wake of the Bounty* fell into this non-enforcement window. Nevertheless, despite the American film Code, Chauvel still had problems with the Australian authorities over the topless Tahitian dancing scene found in this film (Sturma 2002, Douglas 1982).

For the future versions of the *Bounty* story, especially regarding the Canoe Greeting trope, the stakes and budgets got bigger, and the Canoe Greeting scenes became more and more grandiose. Just three years later, after the limited American distribution of *Wake*, it was now the turn of an American filmmaking behemoth, MGM, to lens the story of the *Bounty* in its film *Mutiny on the Bounty*. According to historian Greg Dening, MGM bought Chauvel's *In the Wake of the Bounty* to clear the way of competition, and also, with this acquisition, the giant Hollywood studio used clips from *Wake* as travelogues to promote their big movie version of the *Bounty* (Dening 1996). MGM was serious in its intent, contrasting as far as one could go in terms of budget and production quality from the Chauvel film. This 1935-released MGM *Bounty* won the "Best Picture" Oscar award, using a combination of a big budget, high production values and high-profile actors, including Clark Gable, who was the most popular actor in the world at the time, as Fletcher Christian. In fact, three of the male leads (Gable, Charles Laughton, and Franchot Tone) were nominated for the "Best Actor" Academy Award (SSCS)—all from the same picture, which is a record number for this category.

In contrast, the lead women in the film were two relatively unknown actresses playing the Tahitian love interests, but neither of them was actually Tahitian. One was Movita,[3] a Mexican-American who changed her name to a single Polynesian surname because she wanted to be, and was, typecast in popular South Seas movies as a Native Island female. The other lead female Islander was a new discovery, a Hawaiian student from L.A.'s nearby USC campus, named Mamo Clark.[4] Surprisingly, Miss Clark, as a first-time actress, could hold her own with the proficient male personalities onscreen. Unfortunately, the practice of using real Polynesian actors to represent themselves in film was a rarity in Hollywood, even after Mamo Clark's success. Latinas routinely replaced authentic Polynesians as Pacific Island women in South Seas Cinema (Barsam, Hershfield 2000). I theorize that the Hollywood routine of using Latinas as Polynesian women occurred for two reasons; one, the availability of somewhat trained actresses with an "exotic" appearance living in Southern California, where the major studios were filming many South Seas movies; two, racial misappropriation or racial ignorance by Hollywood filmmakers—a brown person is a brown person. Unfortunately, the power of popular media, like American film, inadvertently indoctrinates and magnifies these same racial attitudes and misrepresentations, injecting them into the mass audience. In general, because of this indirect indoctrination, to many within the massive American (mostly white) movie audience, a brown person is also just a brown person. Regrettably, this inference became established and consequentially validated by the commercial success of this *Bounty* film and other South Seas cinema titles.

As far as the Canoe Greeting scene for this 1935 *Bounty* feature goes, the first thing one observes is the large number of Native extras and outrigger canoes, by far the biggest Canoe Greeting scene in film by 1935. But most importantly, and probably due to the now enforced Production Code, one can observe that all the female vahines are covered in simple white one-piece or two-piece wraps made of foreign material. The Native men as well as the European males in some scenes were less covered in this same material. Not much sexuality here in this the most mature *Bounty* film, except for the English crewmembers who gawk at the vahines as they board the ship. The Natives climb and enter the *Bounty* in hordes, but there is no taking or trading of goods, as had been written in many historical accounts; instead, the islanders leave a lot of fruits. In fact, in one incident Franchot Tone (as Midshipman Roger Byam) is giving away nice trinkets to youthful Natives, but the *Ari'i Nui* (big chief or king) has his subjects give the items back. Later, the chief also freely gives 1,000 breadfruit saplings without barter. The chief did receive a hat "from King George," but not a genuine one. One fake hat for 1,000 tree saplings, room and board, and unlimited hospitality for a few months was not realistic, especially when considering writings in the historical record that show the Polynesians were savvy and intelligent traders (Barrow, Chappell 1992). This 1935 film version does demonstrate the stereotype of the freely giving Polynesian and the important plot element for the objectives of mutiny, which includes the sexual liaisons between beautiful Polynesian young women and sex-starved European men. This critically and financially successful *Bounty* film does (unlike other *Bounty* films) pointedly make it evident that it is not necessary to expose Indigenous private body parts to show this desire.

The next cinematic rendition of the Canoe Greeting trope of a *Bounty* film was another big-budget MGM release some 27 years later. This production took advantage of Ultra Panavision 70mm color technology and utilized the mix of three-time Academy Award-winning cinematographer Robert Surtees and Tahiti's colorful natural scenic beauty. All Hollywood knew this picture would be a visual delight, and it still is today, some 58 years later, on ultra-high definition 4K discs. Despite the many legendary stories of costly rewrites, weather, and the alleged irrational behavior of this film's renowned star, Marlon Brando, the production values of this 1962 version of *Mutiny on the Bounty* are spectacular. The cinematography and the Canoe Greeting and Sensual Dance scenes, both with thousands of seductively dressed indigenes of Tahiti, are embodiments of cinematic history. One of the largest scenes in a Hollywood-produced film, and definitely the largest in South Seas cinema, is the 100-canoe and 6,055-person Tahitian Canoe Greeting scene (Hudgins). Besides its magnitude, this scene also stands out from the other stereotypical Canoe Greeting examples in that the score changed the tone of the scene from a cheerful nonthreatening moment to a contrarily dramatic threatening scene as hordes of Natives and their canoes surround the *Bounty*. The tenseness of this scene may approximate the feeling of the British Captain Samuel Wallis and his crew on the actual first and violent contact with Tahitians when their ship was surrounded by hundreds of canoes, but by the time of the real *Bounty's* landing, it was the 11th ship arrival by Europeans and the second by the now-promoted Captain Bligh in Tahiti. So, by this historical period of the *Bounty* landing, the Natives would only be restless for trade and the anticipation to host more foreigners from distant lands and not have an appearance of threat.

Unfortunately, Hollywood avoids historical accuracy, and all the films in this genre ignore that in the all-too-human interaction between two cultures that have never previously encountered each another: misunderstandings are bound to arise. In real-life first-contact scenarios, due to unfamiliar languages and customs, and unknown intentions of each party, it is quite understandable but avoidable that what takes place is usually not positive. As stated, the first Wallis landing in Tahiti resulted in much bloodshed inflicted upon the ill-equipped and surprised Pacific Islanders, as in other first landings by Europeans and Americans throughout the Pacific. In the Hollywood Canoe Greeting scene, there is not only the absence of any violence but also the absence of any results of the devastating sexually transmitted diseases brought by European sailors found in historical accounts (Moorehead, Stannard, Jolly 1996, Hunt and Lipo) or as found in the writings of official ship's logs and personal diaries of these early European sailors and officers. There are no background island politics, societal customs, religious beliefs and personal intentions from the Indigenous perspective to help understand the Native motivations in these scenes (Kennedy), just the American and European film perception of euphoric greetings of the Islanders and their licentious women eager to throw themselves at any man in European-style pants. An "our island is your island" and "our women are your women" Native attitude is seemingly always portrayed in this American constructed Canoe Greeting scene. Political intentions and propaganda aside and more pertinent for this book, all "greeting" scenes also reflect the American male fantasy of arriving in a hedonistic, edenic paradise with perfect tropical year-round weather, majestic and lush island mountains, spectacular blue lagoons and most importantly, inhabited by beautiful, lascivious women wearing minimal attire and exhibiting no Christian moral limitations.

Referring back to this Canoe Greeting scene of the 1962 *Bounty*, even though the Native women were more covered because of the Hollywood Production Code, the women of Tahiti already had a licentious reputation among the ship's sailors. In this Brando version of the film, as mentioned, the tension was high until the Ari'i Nui giggles at his reflection in a mirror, supposedly gifted personally by King George, but one can spot sexualized glances at the island woman as the British landing party comes ashore. This preconceived notion of lustful Polynesian women is reinforced by this excerpt from a speech by the actor Trevor Howard who, as Captain Bligh, callously warns the crew before arriving:

> "In the event we find ourselves welcomed; you will discover that these savages have absolutely no conception of ordinary morality and you will no doubt take full advantage of their ignorance. It is a matter of supernatural indifference to me whether you contaminate the Natives or that the Natives contaminate you. (Raising voice in anger) I have but one concern—our mission—any one of you provoke an incident which endangers it, and I shall cause that man (pause) to curse his mother for giving him birth."

The men are attentive, but there is eagerness and excitement brewing within them despite the warning. Incidentally, the "contamination" Bligh's character refers to, as mentioned above, is the historically overwhelming outbreak of diseases brought by European and American sailors of the early contact period, which killed hundreds of thousands of Pacific Islanders who did not have immunities in their bodies to fight even common illnesses, let alone the more horrendous venereal diseases. This horrific devastation and depopulation of historic proportions[5] not only aided in the colonization of many of the islands of the Pacific by Europe and America but is never mentioned in more than a hundred years of American South Seas film, except for this snide comment by Captain Bligh in this 1962 *Bounty* and more specifically in James Michener's 1966 epic feature *Hawaii*.

Good case in point: when captain Bligh arrived in Tahiti, most of the Society Islands were controlled by *Ari'i nui* or King Tu. King Tu, like King Kamehameha of the Hawaiian Islands, united most of his archipelago through brains, brawn, and the use of modern Western weapons.

King Tu later changed his name and the name of his 102-year dynasty to Pōmare. The irony here is that there were obviously Western alliances made in some form, but Western diseases devastated these kingdoms and their heirs to the thrones. Pō mare means "night cougher." It is a strange name for a historically significant and powerful kingdom, but sadly the King renamed himself after his beloved daughter Teriinavahoroa, who died in 1792 of tuberculosis, one of the many Western-introduced lethal diseases in Polynesia.

On a more positive note, for this version of *Mutiny on the Bounty*, the canoes and royal costumes of the Ari'i were impressive and well-represented. This was no "savage" race in regard to the position of the Ari'i in Tahitian society. The royal respect was much the same for the English in their relationship towards their own crown. Other parallels between the production of the film and the Ari'i are also of some interest. For instance, at the end of this canoe scene, the Indigenous Tahitians show high reverence for the Ari'i Nui while in real life, behind the scenes, it was an actual Tahitian Ari'i who gathered the 6,000+ Tahitians with their canoes for this scene and told the film's executives to "take them all or none." Also, in recreating the *Bounty*'s arrival scene, not only were the European characters in the story sexually agitated but also the visiting cast and crew of the film production were sexually excited. One film crew member took a Tahitian wife all the way home to Canada (Hudgins), and it is well known that Marlon Brando married his Tahitian lover character and co-star Tarita.

More telling is this anecdote from the sexually charged set of the movie *The Bounty* (1984). Then-young actor Liam Neeson, on a beach scene with his shipmates and beautiful topless Tahitian vahines all around, laid an Easter egg[6] that shows the sexual environment on the set. In the opening wide shot of this scene—and with a pause button one can see this—near Neeson's feet there are two symmetrically formed women's breasts sculpted in the sand. One can almost see the mischievousness in all the actors' eyes, hoping they can get away with it. They did, the breasts made the final cut. As though the real thing, all around, wasn't enough.

Looking at the data of relationships within this South Seas film genre, Euro-American women who arrived in the Pacific in a later period almost always carried on a love relationship with men of their own race and rarely with Polynesian men (those rare exceptions will be discussed later). One has to take into consideration that these film plots were written and approved by the male-dominated Hollywood moviemaking industry, which did not want to see an American female character have the freedom to take the lead in having sexual relationships with anyone she chose, especially someone outside of her race. Hypocritically, not only was it permissible for a male European or Euro-American to have a sexual affair with a Polynesian female, but such relationships were also a dominant plot feature in many South Seas cinema titles.

That said, going back in "early contact" history between Europe and the Pacific, there was a French woman named Jeanne Baret,[7] who with her supervisor Dr. Philibert Commerçon, conspired to hide her gender identity aboard French explorer Bougainville's store ship, the *Étoile*, by being disguised as a male. The aged and physically limited naturalist Dr. Commerçon truly needed Baret's assistance to make the voyage of his dreams. Their deception worked for many months until a visiting Tahitian chief spotted her onboard the French ship. The chief knew right away that she was a woman, surprising Bougainville and the rest of his crewmen and officers. Already halfway around the world, it was too late for Bougainville to take her back home. The next day as Commerçon and Baret went ashore to collect plants and insects, they found themselves surrounded by hundreds of Native men, all shouting "Vahine!" or "woman" (Salmond). Understandably one can imagine that among these Indigenous men, with the Polynesian general notion that sex was simply a part of life, without the restrictions of Christian morality, and having peacefully shared many of their women with their European guests, along with adding the common human value of reciprocity, Miss Baret was in a huge predicament. The Native men promptly stripped her naked, not with the intention of raping her, but to ascertain simple proof of her gender. Remember, the concept of nakedness for sexual arousal is a concept for supposedly "enlightened" but sexually repressed Christians and other modest, faith-based societies—not for sexually open and minimally clothed societies like Tahiti. Those who were truly amused by Baret's nakedness were the French crew members who observed the incident from aboard their ship. Because Christian societies allegedly tend to shelter and protect their women, needless to say, Jeanne Baret, the first woman known to circle the globe, was from then on confined below deck whenever the ship was at a strange port.

Apparently, this Christian protection of women did not apply to the protection of women of other races. There was a hypocritical disregard by the so-called civilized "Western" world's "gentlemen's code of valor" or the sexual protection of the female sex. When it came to the Polynesian woman, European chivalry was dead. The sexually blatant lack of protection for women of Polynesian ancestry is manifest throughout both historical and American filmic records. Sadly, this gentlemen's code did not hold for Miss Baret, either, for she was later repeatedly raped by crew members, below deck, on her way home.

Like the 1935 *Bounty* and again, partly because of the constraints of the Production Code, some of the sexuality of the 1962 *Bounty* film was also conveyed by the Native males in its Canoe Greeting scene, since the exhibition of the male body was more permissible by the Code. Barely clad and muscular, their bodies glistened at every photographic opportunity, like competitors in a muscle competition. Although it's uncertain if this is from a common film practice called spritzing (spraying artificial sweat) or natural sweat from running in the sand, while dragging a heavy canoe to the water and furiously paddling to a foreign ship with also the addition of sea spray. In any case, with this exhibition of the glimmering masculine body, the female audience gaze is also apparent in this movie as well as throughout all Canoe Greeting scenes in other South Seas films. Because of the aforementioned non-stereotypical tension portrayed in this 1962 version of a *Bounty* Canoe Greeting scene, most of the sexualization of Polynesian females in this film takes place later during the Sensual Dance and Native First Kiss scenes. While the 1935 version of the Canoe Greeting scene was relatively tame sexually, the opposite holds true for the last version of this saga, titled *The Bounty*. This 1984 version of this famous mutiny story was shot 20 years after the Production Code began to crumble (Doherty) so the sexual tension in this latest film ran thick.

As the British ship enters Tahitian waters, the first things one notices while viewing *The Bounty* are the beauty of the island, exotic

The Bounty (1984, Orion Pictures). Shown here is the American lobby card (11" × 14") of the Canoe Greeting scene with a specially built replica of the *H.M.S. Bounty* and many Tahitian outrigger canoes. This "G"-rated poster image is for viewing by a general public audience, so only the bare backs of the island Natives can be seen, in contrast to the many bare frontal images in the movie itself. Also not viewed in the poster are the film's five Academy Award-winning actors: Mel Gibson (Christian), Anthony Hopkins (Bligh), Daniel Day-Lewis, Liam Neeson and Laurence Olivier.

flora, pristine ocean, and the many topless young Tahitian women. As in most South Seas films, drumbeats add to the sexual tension, and in this 1984 Canoe Greeting scene, the drumbeats are truly effective. Throughout history, the European imagination of this scene was a male fantasy of nearly naked and beautiful, wanton Polynesian women throwing themselves at any fair-skinned visitors to their islands. Director Roger Donaldson managed to recreate this trope to the fullest. Critics say besides the 1935 version of the film, this is one of the most historically correct versions of the *Bounty* story. Historian Greg Dening says this about film critics: "Each of the later versions (of *Bounty* movies) have been declared unhistorical by the critics for omitting all the 1935 version invented" (Dening 1992). Film critics are not historians.

Even if the producer and director of the film uses the "ethnographic reality excuse"[8] of realism for having semi-nudity run rampant throughout this 1984 Canoe Greeting scene, the question arises: why are only fit young women portrayed topless? Where is the toplessness of women who are overweight or elderly, pre-teen females or women who are handicapped or those disfigured by birth or by disease? They are not seen, or they are positioned in the far background—covered up. Yes, there are American restrictions on teen and preteen nudity, and this will be covered in another section of this book, but is this supposedly pre-contact or newly contacted reality? Where is the realistic balance of the varied female form? Realism does not really exist in these films—just sexism.

This same observation is shared by writer Judith Van Trigt in her article titled: "Reflecting on the Pacific: Representations of the Pacific and Pacific Island Women in Five Dominant Cinematic Texts." She writes:

> Pacific Island Women in these texts are primarily characterized in terms of their sexual availability. The motif that codes for this is the bare-breasted women. For the west bare breasts signify female sexuality on display.... However, not all are relevant: only young pert, full breasts.[9]

The young topless Tahitian maidens throughout *The Bounty* are examples of this principle. Van Trigt continues on this subject with an observation from author bell hooks[10] who calls this issue the "mammy" role—"they are not sexually desirable or available and so they get to keep their tops on" (hooks).

This semi-nudity is prominent in pre–Code or in other post–Code Hollywood Polynesian films. An example of the post–Code era is the film *Hawaii* (1966), which was one of the films of that year to defy the film industry's self-policing Code and force the film industry to restructure it. Another matter of interest in the film *Hawaii*, in regard to its Canoe Greeting scene, is that even though there were Indigenous topless females, family units with both spouses and children were featured with minimal attire and elderly and overweight semi-nude women were also represented. The female exposure was more balanced and tempered by a more realistic portrayal of Pacific Islanders and not just for the sexually stimulated male gaze.

Rapa Nui (1994) was also another post–Code major film production featuring not only Polynesians and the widely known giant mo'ai stone statues, but also the outdated theory of environmental self-destruction (Hunt, Lipo), and a multitude of bare breasted female indigenes. The big budget film was a huge flop with no solid theories for the reason of its box-office failure. Significantly, *Rapa Nui* was also a rare contemporary American produced film that featured a predominantly Polynesian cast (except for a Latin-American male and a part-Chinese English/Canadian female) in this pre-contact story. More stories like this (not centered on American or European characters) would be of significance, but unfortunately, because of *Rapa Nui's* financial failure, Americans will not see a similar Hollywood-produced picture for quite some time. Theories for its failure abound: mo'ai were fake looking; fuzzy and prejudiced science; non–Euro-American hero[11]; and finally, the "British" accents of the Polynesians. The last one must be from an American film critic because, through Hollywood's movie and TV indoctrination of the American masses, Americans assume everyone speaks U.S. English, and most Americans cannot recognize the differences between the British Commonwealth accents, in this case a New Zealand accent by Māori actors who were well-represented in this film as Rapa Nui Natives.

There are many other Canoe Greeting scenes in this South Seas genre, and a few should be mentioned. For example, *Tabu: A Story of the South Seas* (1931), contains the first large-scale "Greeting" scene. *Tabu* was co-directed by the famous German silent screen director F.W. Murnau and is considered a classic. *Tabu*, an American-produced film, is also unusually centered on Polynesians, not Euro-Americans. Another interesting fact for this section of the book is that the handsome and energetic star of *Tabu* is a young Tahitian man billed as Matahi, but his full name is Matahiari'i Tama—31 years later he played the Ari'i Nui or the grand Chief character Hitihiti of the aforementioned *Mutiny on the Bounty* (1962) (Hudgins). Matahiari'i is the only recognizable actor who played in two Canoe Greeting scenes over 30 years apart. The addition of "ari'i" at the end of his real surname signifies he may be of real chiefly rank of some kind and not just a humble fisherman, as written in the official movie promo book of the 1962 film describing Matahiari'i's real life.

Another silent classic, *White Shadows in the South Seas* (1928) is significantly important to this study because it is uncommonly themed as an "anti–European and/or anti–American presence in the Pacific" picture. Loosely based on a popular American novel written by Fredrick O'Brien, this film depicts a "sympathetic to Natives" medical doctor on a South Seas isle who is also a drunkard. This sympathy to Natives and drunkenness are common features related to the cinematic character of the "beachcomber" found throughout South Seas films. Note the subliminal content here: two characteristics (sympathy towards Natives and drunkenness) equate to a person with unrealistic or meaningless principles, too drunk to come to one's senses; hence, it is unrealistic or meaningless to sympathize with the Natives and their causes.

This beachcomber doctor in *White Shadows* is played by silent film star Monte Blue. Blue's character is very opinionated about the devastation by outsiders of the once lovely Polynesian island, its people, and their equally beautiful culture. Blue's sentiments anger his fellow American and European cohorts, who now reside on the island and who are most likely responsible for the island's devastation. The doctor then gets Shanghaied by these expatriates, and they tie Blue aboard a quarantined ship which they set adrift. Blue's character miraculously survives storms, starvation, and the deadly disease aboard the ship, and then lands on a far Polynesian island whose population is still untouched by the influences of Europe and America. But for Hollywood sensibilities, or lack of, all the Indigenes on this new island, ostensibly undiscovered by the West, speak English. The local tribe adopts Blue, and he loves his new, sober life living among the untainted Indigenous Polynesian Islanders. But one morning a European ship appears offshore of his newly adopted paradise, and a local frenzy occurs and the Canoe Greeting trope begins anew. According to the American cinematic record, this is the only time an American protagonist is frantically trying to stop the Natives from launching their canoes and greeting the "evil" ship. The doctor's efforts are in vain. Soon onshore, the antagonistic German captain of the European ship and our hero meet and fight, with this violence culminating in the death of our hero. The innocent island, now with the accepted Euro and American influences, then turns into the same diluted paradise as the first island in the story, with drunkenness and Natives being exploited by Europeans and Americans once again. *White Shadows* was a popular movie, but apparently the message didn't sink into the Euro-American consciousness because colonization and the devastation of Pacific Islanders and their cultures continued, as it did in the storyline of this film.

Regarding the trope that Polynesian women are eagerly sexually accommodating, one must consider the other half of this sexual relationship, the European or American male. As historian Noelani Arista so eloquently stated, "If God could not see what sailors did once their ships had sailed around Cape Horn, the illusion that English and American men could go to the islands and do as they pleased in a place where the laws of God and King and country were unknown—or at the very least unpublished and unenforced by any colonial administration—added to the heady pleasures of which paradise allowed them to partake" (Arista). Although rarely to blame for their sexual indiscretions in American discourse, and more specifically on Hollywood's big screen, the lay European and American crew are still routinely displayed as wild beasts, dying to be free to devour the scantily clad Polynesian women. Blame is usually credited to the "temptresses" of the Islands: W. S. Van Dyke's *Never the Twain Shall Meet* (1931), starring beachcomber Leslie Howard and South Seas seductress Conchita Montenegro as Tamea, epitomizes this trend. Even with the threat of the lash to curb the spread of deadly venereal diseases, many of the visiting crew disobeyed the rules (Jolly 1996). Who was the real lascivious partner, the one who broke the rules of the ship, his society and his Christian religion or the innocent Polynesian women who didn't have these rules in the first place? In American literature, the South Seas is commonly portrayed as an Edenic paradise, and the Indigenous females are referred to as innocent Eves—if so, what part do the European and Euro-American men play in this Canoe Greeting scenario? Are they the wolves or the snake in the garden?

Of the many instances of the Canoe Greeting scene found throughout this American South Seas film genre, almost all symbolize two dangerous misconceptions, both of which deal with fallacies of primitivism, of so-called uncivilized and uneducated people. The first misconception is the instant excitement and eagerness of the Polynesians to welcome and open themselves and their islands for the needs of their guests, and the second is the sexualized Euro-American male lens with the visual imaginations of wanton, minimally clad, beautiful Polynesian women who toss themselves into the arms of visiting Caucasian men.

The first misconception, as shown in early forms of popular media or political propaganda aired for the American masses, is that the Pacific Islander needs our assistance in becoming "civilized" and that they welcome Europeans or Americans to settle, colonize, Christianize and educate them to become such. While the sexualized Euro-American

lens of Hollywood is the main focus point of this book—not the political construct or historical intentions of Europeans and Americans—
perhaps a brief and simple explanation about the hospitality of Pacific
Islanders may show the Islanders' social intentions, especially in the
context of this arrival or Canoe Greeting scene. I will always remember what my Hawaiian grandmother, Agnes Kanahele, taught me that
was a serious breach of Hawaiian etiquette, which can be surmised in
her broken-English term "no *maha 'oe*." For years I thought she meant
"no *maha'oi*," which was another lesson from grandma on seriously
improper Hawaiian decorum: "Do not act boldly or impertinently"
(Pukui & Elbert). But she told me "no *maha 'oe*" was one of the most
inappropriate things a Hawaiian could do—and it simply means not to
"overstay" one's visit. I never quite understood why she was so adamant
about that little lesson until, as an adult studying colonization, I realized
the appropriateness of this Hawaiian idiom. It is one thing to be hospitable (the Aloha Spirit) but quite another issue for a friend, kin or visitor to
overstay a visit and take advantage of the host's hospitality. Even worse
is to permanently move in, settle and dominate the culture, laws and the
land of the hosts. The most egregious form of "no *maha 'oe*" is for an outsider to take away and claim one's land, replace one's sovereignty and
diminish one's identity, then claim to be Native or Indigenous.

The second misconception of the Canoe Greeting trope is the
unjustified portrayal of Polynesians in American cinema, especially of
Polynesian women as lustful sex objects. Many Pacific social academ-
ics have demonstrated that there are many reasons and different attitudes that explain why Polynesian women behaved as they did during
early contact. For example, Pacific scholar Katerina Teaiwa expands on
the concept of "mana," or simply put, inherent divine power, authority
or privilege, such as being born into a royal lineage. Many, but not all,
Pacific Islanders began to think during first contact that these European
visitors were godlike or beings possessing much mana. Consequently,
Teaiwa deduced that "having a child with a powerful person or an individual full of mana would ensure your progeny would have this mana"
(Graham). Thus, indemnifying the mothers of these special children
would move them up in the social hierarchy of Island society.

Historians Anne Salmond and Marshall Sahlins also expand on
this precept. Native Hawaiian scholar Samuel Kamakau writes that
in the early encounters with the European, some Hawaiians used sex
with their visitors as a test to see if these new arrivals were truly gods,
for gods would not need to copulate (Kamakau). Pacific social scientist
Margaret Jolly theorizes that some Native women would use their early
relationships with the seemingly powerful European explorers as an

opportunity to break taboos or be defiant of their established chiefs by ignoring local laws and customs of a caste society. Jolly also points out an opposite instance of a Tahitian woman disrobing in front of a European crew, not for sexual advances but as a simple matter of displaying her tattoos or symbols of rank (Jolly 1976). Again, nudity by Polynesians was a natural part of life and its common presence was not for sexual arousal—there were other ways to accomplish that for a Pacific Islander. Nicolas Thomas stated that at times when island food resources and precious chiefdom family heirlooms were depleted, trading for sex was a desperate last resort (Thomas p. 71, 188). Historian Serge Tcherkezoff relates stories of protesting and crying early teen Native girls being offered by elder tribesmen and women to European naval officers for the purpose of lovemaking (Tcherkezoff). This defiance clearly shows unwillingness by the Polynesian female, an attitude far different from the concepts of American cinema.

There are other reasons and theories explaining the sexual behavior of the Polynesians towards their European and American visitors, and I would like to suggest one more. There are a few historical accounts of Indigenous Pacific Island women wailing and gashing their heads to demonstrate *auē* or *auwē* (a deep weeping from sadness and pain) as European and American ships departed from their isles. These cries of "auwē," found throughout Polynesia and in some South Seas films, are a clear indication that relationships were deeply and emotionally invested (enduring committed love) and not enacted by women who blithely engaged in wanton spur of the moment sexual behavior. While it would be incorrect to suppose that this wanton behavior was *never* the case (from a non–Christian society), nonetheless it is important to demonstrate that Pacific Island females had other intentions, thus invalidating the promiscuous stereotype of Polynesian women, especially as it is portrayed in American film.

Historian David Chappell may sum up this relationship between Islander and Continental in the Canoe Greeting encounter, as he states in his article entitled "Shipboard Relations between Pacific Island Women and Euroamerican Men 1767–1887" in *The Journal of Pacific History*:

> [Q]uestions arise from these lines of reasoning. First, to what extent were the Indigenous women in control of their early relationships with foreign sexual partners? Were they really enhancing their own status, or acting as pawns for ambitious male Islanders? Thus sex-as-intercultural exchange would seem to have transmuted into sex-as-barter and finally into sex-as-prostitution—i.e., colonial dehumanization.... Eurocentric male biases pervade the written records [Chappell-1992].

Also, a brief example in Hawaiian epistemology or knowledge in regard to the concepts of male/female relationships would help recognize a Polynesian point of view on these associations. Throughout Hawai'i, one can find legends of deeply felt, devoted love relationships.[12] Interestingly, in a particular story involving the travels of the beautiful young goddess Hi'iakaikapoliopele, one can find a moral or ethical lesson of the proper way to treat women. The story tells of Hi'iaka and two female traveling companions in the southeast of Kaua'i entering an area known as Mahā'ulepū. There, Hi'iaka and her companions asked a local fisherman named Pakamoi for a piece of fish to eat. After summarizing the situation and noticing the beauty of the stranger Hi'iaka, Pakamoi responded that he would give them all fish if she would sleep with him. Hi'iaka then loosened her garment as to concede to Pakamoi's desires. This action, of course, excited the fisherman so as to eagerly acquiesce to her small request to meet her on a hilltop nearby. There on the hilltop, Pakamoi arrived and had the unexpected realization that Hi'iaka was a powerful goddess showing her true feelings of anger and disgust. As they confronted each other Hi'iaka mesmerized the fisherman by continuing to open her garment wide, whereupon Pakamoi's gaze turned him into stone. A large, protruding rock called Pakamoi can be found today in Mahā'ulepū. Hawaiian Pacific scholar Carlos Andrade comments about this legend that "he (Pakamoi) remains there, a cautionary memorial to the consequences of rude and lascivious behavior toward defenseless and seemingly helpless women, a reminder to succeeding generations to be respectful, even to strangers, as they could very well be especially powerful" (Andrade). This and other Hawaiian legends establish attributes of Hawaiian behavior of deep devoted love and respecting the other sex by not acting rudely and lasciviously. They were and still are taught to generations of the Natives of Hawai'i. These precepts of behavior, of course, run contrary to the popular European and American perceptions of Polynesian behavior as is told in many of their media types.

Of course, I would be remiss not to catalogue a few more South Seas film titles that include this Canoe greeting trope: *Bird of Paradise* (1932) and the 1951 version, *Last of the Pagans* (1935), *Robinson Crusoe of Clipper Island* (1936), *Paradise Isle* (1937), *South of Pago Pago* (1940), *Son of Fury* (1942), *Isle of Tabu* (1945), *Wake of the Red Witch* (1948), *Pagan Love Song* (1950), *Mister Roberts* (1955), *South Pacific* (1958), *Twilight for the Gods* (1958), *Donovan's Reef* (1963), *Devil's Mountain* (1976), and *Hurricane* (1979). Troubling as it is, this scene (as well as other tropes of the South Seas), is also found in cartoon form, indoctrinating the minds of very young Americans: *The Simpsons: The Wettest Stories Ever Told*, Fox TV, Sea 17, Episode 18, first aired in 2002.

The Canoe Greeting has evolved through the years. As visitors arrive on the islands today, it is neither for scientific exploration nor for acquisition by an imperialistic country, but for individual aspirations of discovery or relaxation—in other words, for commercial tourism. At first, a mixture of personal Polynesian greetings of friends and family on docks throughout Polynesia was soon adapted by the tourist industry for their greetings of large masses of paying visitors brought to the islands, through advertising, for the economic benefit of large American or multinational lodging and transportation corporations. More on this sensualized contemporary from of "greeting" can be found in Chapter 9. This continuous exposure of the modern Pacific Island tourist industry's greeting behavior, as well as the classical Canoe Greetings scenes of an earlier Pacific period in popular film, solidifies the erroneous trope as something to be expected or common behavior by Pacific Islanders with its dangerous connotations of wanton love, sacrifice and servitude to their guests, who do not truly understand Polynesian culture and intent.

Perhaps the antithesis or opposition of the welcoming Canoe Greeting trope is the Polynesian Farewell scene. Unlike the numerous greeting scenes in South Seas cinema, the farewell scene is uncommon in this film genre. When this scarce event is viewed, one will note the general tone of this scene, which is one of sincere and deep emotions. It depicts "auwē" or cries of sadness and of loss due to deep relationships with their visitors. These emotions can be seen in all members of a tribe, old and young, big and small, male and female. There are no overtones of sexualized behavior or undertones of political intent as in the Canoe Greeting scene, just simple and equal brotherly/sisterly love exhibited by both island host and visitor towards each other. A couple of these rare Polynesian Farewell scenes can be found in *Return to Paradise* (1953) and *The Other Side of Heaven* (2002).

Lastly, in this chapter, a correct definition of the Hawaiian word *aloha* is necessary for the understanding of Polynesian intent in regard to general concepts. Aloha is one of the most popular Polynesian words worldwide. Its layered meaning, to most people, is a Hawaiian word of greeting, goodbye, and love. A more authentic and less complex definition of aloha is an empathic compassion, love. For Hawaiians and other Polynesians, there is much love and emotion in greetings, in hosting one's visit, as well as in farewells. The culture clash or misinterpretation between the West in history, and as can be seen in film, is never more apparent than in the scenes discussed in this chapter. Granted, sexual morality was very different between the West and Polynesia in the 1600s and 1700s. But the expressions of aloha by the Indigenous Islanders to their early outside visitors were largely misinterpreted by their guests (and eventual colonizers) as sexual invitation and indications of promiscuous or lustful behavior. The same occurred with the Westerner settler: aloha or compassion was misinterpreted or taken advantage of by seizing land and precious heirlooms without providing equal-value exchange. 'A'ole (no) *maha*, or overstaying, or its extreme definition "settling" by guests and by their fellow countrymen, otherwise known as colonization, later took place. The Farewell scene expresses this aloha without any misinterpretation.

Finally, through the years and decades, the aloha spirit (which is proselytized by the visitor industry to Western tourists) prevails today, which truly is a spirit of love and forgiveness. The quagmire or dilemma of "Aloha" or in this case—when you ask, I lovingly give—adds to the loss of Polynesian culture, land, sovereignty, and self-worth. The misunderstanding here by the Native is not the giving but the receiving by the other. This is no in-kind reciprocity, only taking and taking advantage of. This selfishness by foreigners or the "Other" is still a hard concept for Islanders to comprehend.

3

Peeking Through the Ferns

The Lagoon Swim Scene

"Just as the 1927 film *Hula* opens with shots of Clara Bow swimming nude, *Blue Hawaii*—a film that one might think would focus on Elvis' body—offers its cinematic South Seas obligatory nude swimming scene by pointing the camera towards Joan Blackman, the actress playing Elvis' faithful *hapa haole* (half-foreign/half–Hawaiian or biracial) girlfriend." Three words in this quote from Houston Wood's book *Displacing Natives* (p. 108) are relevant to this section on the Lagoon Swim trope: "<u>obligatory</u> <u>nude</u> <u>swimming</u>." Obviously, it's being obligatory is to overemphasize the point, but in reality, there is an abundance of sexualized scenes of Polynesians swimming, naked or nearly naked, in this genre, and it appears as if it is almost compulsory for Hollywood to include this reoccurring trope in many of its South Seas films.

In these paradisiacal sites of blue lagoons, tropical waterfalls and idyllic ocean shores, our Pacific subjects are established as carefree, primitive beings with no concept of the word "naked." But in reality, this scene arguably represents the voyeuristic gaze of male Hollywood filmmakers and the paying audiences of America and elsewhere. These images represent the true escapist imagination of America with regard to the Pacific. "The association between women and waterfalls or the lushness of local vegetation is a constant trope in her purple pose...." "It is down the waterfalls, sliding on slippery, mossy rocks that we witness Polynesian beauties—women and men—cavorting in the water and swimming sinuously, as they have done in most movies about Polynesia since the silent films of the 1920s" (Jolly 1997).

Perhaps there is no better way to introduce the subject of this chapter than from a movie itself. The film *Irma la Douce* (French for Irma the sweet) was a popular 1963 movie directed by Billy Wilder. *Irma* was produced by the Mirisch Corporation and distributed by United Artists.

Irma is a French prostitute played by Shirley MacLaine, who was nominated for an Oscar for the Best Leading Actress for her performance in
this romance/comedy. To make a long story short, MacLaine is courted
by Jack Lemmon as an honest Paris policeman who loses his job trying
to bust local prostitutes, who are politically connected. MacLaine take
him in, and they fall for each other. Being a moral and guilty man, Lemmon plots to play an older wealthy British lord who pays MacLaine so
well that he's her exclusive client. He only pays to play double solitaire
with her on every visit. Jack's moral dilemma is solved until one session
in which Irma gets to know the lord better. She probes deeper as he lies
himself deeper into a corner—to the point at which he confesses that he
has an impotence problem and was on his way to see a Swiss specialist.
She has none of that because a local psychiatrist has sent her many difficult patients with the same disability, and she has cured them all. In the
following dialogue, in script format, MacLaine will cure her faux British
lord. She lays him down on the bed to relax him as she sits on a nearby
chair like a shrink and says:

IRMA

(demandingly) Now concentrate.

Now Hawaiian STEEL GUITAR MUSIC plays in the background.
The Brit closes his eyes. After a few beats Irma continues in a soft tone.

IRMA (continuing)

Palm trees swaying in the breeze. A smell of ripe papayas.
A blue lagoon, white sand, golden skin girls.
(to the British Lord) You got that?

BRITISH LORD

Blue lagoon, white sand, golden skin....
The image is sinking into the faux Brit's imagination.

IRMA

They're beautiful, aren't they?

BRITISH LORD

Oh ... ever. Oh....

IRMA

How many do you see?
The Lord counts with his pointing finger in the air.

BRITISH LORD

Fourteen, to be exact.
They are wearing grass skirts and coconut shells.

IRMA

No, they're not.

BRITISH LORD

No?

IRMA

They are wearing sarongs and hibiscus blossoms in their hair.

BRITISH LORD

Oh. (concentrating more) By George you're right!

IRMA

Now they take off their sarongs
and they start washing them in the blue lagoon.

Concentrating, the Lord's eyes still closed,
he points into the air in front of him.

BRITISH LORD

(devilishly) Indeed.

Our faux British Lord suddenly opens
his eyes wide and sits up shocked. He is cured.

This film illustrates the sensual Lagoon Swim scene in Polynesia with total imagination. Many films have done so with direct imagery throughout South Seas film history. Barring the discovery of a previously lost film, the first sexualized nude swim scene in a Pacific film happened early in American film with the 1916 feature *The Pearl of Paradise* from Mutual Studios. This early silent film featured the daughter of a Spanish ruler of an island who was, like Clara Bow in *Hula*, an outsider raised by the South Seas Natives. She falls for the only Euro-American on the island and tempts him to join her in a nude swim. Thus, this cinematic trope begins. There are a number of film examples of women of European descent on a Pacific Isle who behave like their Native counterparts in this romanticized and sexualized world of the Pacific Islands; however, this section of this manuscript will cover this trope with the more predominant celluloid stereotype of barely clad Polynesians cavorting within the clichéd lagoons and under their omnipresent waterfalls. This book chapter will discuss some of these specific Lagoon Swim scenes, as well as the American gaze and the theory of ethnopornography in South Seas cinema.

According to Catherine Lutz and Jane Collins, there are a number of different gazes in still photography, and I would argue the same holds true for motion picture[1] cinematography. The predominant gaze that will be presented in this Lagoon Swim trope chapter will be the American male gaze. This gaze is not just from the male audience but the gaze from all the male participants of the cinematic production of the story, as well as the gaze of the American male characters within that story. What are they gazing at? Mostly the young female form of Polynesians as they frolic carefree and mostly clothes-free among idyllic waterfalls and blue lagoons. Even if a South Seas film was produced in the middle of the Production Code era and South Seas maidens had to wear clothes, the clothes they wore were tight-fitting, scant sarongs—and the waters of the lagoons or reefs made the sarongs cling to their bodies even more tightly. Interestingly, there were a handful of films where the gazes in the story were from male Natives, either ready to have fun and scare their fellow tribeswomen (*Tabu*, 1931), or a rival tribe of men hunting for wives, as in 1935's *Last of the Pagans*. In either scenario, the peeking at Native women frolicking in the water only partially clothed or naked is not for the Native male character gaze (theoretically they are acclimated to nudity) but primarily for the peering of male audiences, gathered *en masse* in theaters throughout America.

The seemingly quintessential film for the American gaze of South Seas maidens swimming in an island lagoon is *White Shadows in the South Seas* (1928). In the previous section we observed that *White Shadows* had the distinction of trying to prevent the inevitable result of the Canoe Greeting trope or symbolically the arrival of colonization, but here the main character, Dr. Matthew Lloyd (Monte Blue), is shipwrecked on an island where the Polynesian inhabitants have never seen a man of European descent. Blue, like other Euro-American characters in the same situation, first stumbles onto this Lagoon Swim scene, which is described by American Studies professor Jeffery Geiger: "Peeking through dense foliage at women bathing and tossing flowers, the camera mimics the forward movement of Lloyd's voyeuristic gaze.... The power of the cinema screen to construct the masculine imaginary is communicated through the delicate gaze of De Vinna's [the cinematographer] filtered lens, through which Lloyd and the viewer glimpse nude and seminude women, framed by leaves, tossing their hair back and diving from rocks." I wholeheartedly agree with Geiger's statement. In fact, the title of this book directly alludes to De Vinna's filtered lens (and the lenses of other Westerners) and the "viewers glimpse" or gaze, but after observing this voyeuristic scene (seemingly similar to Irma's description above), I may differ about the intent of Blue's character.

It should be noted that Blue does not know that these Natives have never seen a Euro-American before, and he seemingly does not stare at the women lustfully: he is realizing that there are other people on the island—not staring. Given his character's sympathetic experience with Polynesians, he would not have them run in fear, as happens shortly in the scene; his intention was not to scare. Blue's character is also a medical doctor, so theoretically he sees the female form from a different perspective than the typical man. Blue simply seeks aid because he has just been shipwrecked and is weak. The women were not horrified because they spotted a peeping Tom; voyeurs don't announce themselves and wave for attention, as did Blue—voyeurs stay quiet and hidden. The women ran in horror because they have never seen a white man before. What they never saw, figuratively, was the lens of the camera, the lens of the director and the lens of an American audience. They are the real voyeurs in this case, not the innocent character played by Blue.

Before the doctor ever arrived on this scene, there were shots after shots of naked and semi-naked Polynesian young women frolicking in the lagoon. The camera seemingly lingers on these Pacific bodies. This is a different lens than Blue's who, again, has not even arrived on the scene yet.

Incidentally, the next two words coming out of Blue's mouth are the first words to be heard by an audience in MGM studio's attempt to render synchronized voice on screen. The words Blue shyly utters are: "Hello.... Hello." Then our heroine turns to see her first Euro-American man, screams in terror, and then all of the mostly nude Native women swim for their lives.

One has to ponder whether, during the silent or early period of narrative talkies, these Indigenous actresses and background players at distant Polynesian Isles really understood the breadth and scope of being exposed in a Hollywood picture? Would they really understand that millions of fully clothed strangers could be watching in a dark theater, not just the handful of film crew members? What is the true meaning of a camera lens—not just the physical aspects of it but what it represents in a social context? I argue that most Islanders today understand how commercial cinema works, but I would think anyone in the far-away Pacific, who had never seen a movie theater of any kind, especially in the early 20th century, would not truly understand the power and range of popular American cinema. Empirical review of an exhaustive record of Hollywood's films of the South Seas shows that during the early silent and pre-Production Code era of filmmaking, all nude or semi-nude scenes of Indigenous islanders were shot on the very distant Pacific Isles inhabited by, undoubtedly, very ill-informed and naïve Christian Islanders of the South Pacific.

By the 1920s of the silent film era, Christianity had been on most

Polynesian islands for four generations. By then, there would not have been island women running around freely with no or few clothes, free to be filmed, except possibly in far-reaching valleys or distant and remote outer islands where it would be cost prohibitive to take a camera crew. By the time the first motion picture cameras had arrived on the islands, Native nudity of some level had to be staged. Coercion or persuasion and also permission of some kind must have taken place. From the book *The Innocent Eye: The Life of Robert J. Flaherty* by Arthur Calder-Marshall, we know this is the case. *Moana : A Romance of the Golden Age* (1926), *White Shadows in the South Seas* (1928), *Tabu: A Story of the South Seas* (1931), *Mr. Robinson Crusoe* (1932), *In the Wake of the Bounty* (1933), and *Last of the Pagans* (1935) are all good instances. One will note, even in these film classics, the semi-nudity is specific to a handful of characters. Most islanders were not persuaded to expose themselves. Those who were are only the young and fit adult females.

There is also a current debate on the issue of the term *ethnopornography* or *ethnoporn*. Peter Sigal and the late Neil L. Whitehead have argued that there is no difference between ethnographers and pornographers. On the other hand, pioneering media studies veteran Bill Nichols and co-authors Christian Hansen and Catherine Needham posit the two are very similar in many regards, but not the same. I am sure most anthropologists would not agree with Whitehead and Sigal's assessment.[2] Standard definitions of ethnographic film are centered on authorship, purpose and audience. According to David MacDougall, this purpose must be stated as captions on photographs or by narration in film. MacDougall also points out that these explanations should be authored by a trained anthropologist, so that there are no misunderstandings in purpose. MacDougall goes on to explain that a photograph could speak volumes to an anthropologist, but: "An uncaptioned photograph was full of unidirectional potential.... There is a moral imperative against allowing viewers to jump to the wrong conclusions." In cinema also, it is imperative to recognize authorship and the intended market of a film. But in popular commercial narrative film, a medium that could lie somewhere in between pornography and educational ethnography, the questions still should be asked: Who is the author, what is the intent, and what are the target markets, when displaying sexualized Pacific Island Natives?

Whitehead and Sigal summarized the whole picture well with the following:

The kind of materials involved are thus highly heterogeneous including both written travel accounts and academic treatises, but also early woodcuts, copperplates and later photographic and cinematic items. What is important is the manner of the circulation of such materials, what the contemporary ideas of "intention" and "reception" for such materials may have been, and how usage and commodification interrelate in their circulation. Therefore, critical to the identification of this paradigm of "ethnopornography" is also the relation between observer and observed and the degree of consent present in such a relationship. The implication here is that Native codes of bodily presentation were distorted in the process of external representation to produce sexualized meanings that made such bodies desirable to colonial consumers [p. 2].

To add to the overall complications of this subject, in the pornography industry the term *ethnoporn* incorrectly means sex between people of different racial backgrounds. However, I argue an alternative definition of *ethnopornography* or *ethnoporn* is that it is not some kind of amalgamation of pornography and ethnographic film types—instead, the terminology would be more effective in describing the evolved colonial effect of exploiting and commodifying Indigenous bodies for Euro-American male sexual desires for profit *under the guise of ethnographic correctness.* The exhibition of graphic bodily content of commercial narrative film to the mass audience for commercial gain as a pretense for ethnographic presentation is not only a better definition of the term *ethnopornography* but also weighs agreeably with what this book is conveying. If directors Roger Donaldson (*The Bounty*), Charles Chauvel (*In the Wake of the Bounty*) or Kevin Reynolds (*Rapa Nui*) used purported ethnographic realities as a reason for portraying naked or semi-naked Polynesian bodies onscreen, then I label that as "the ethnographic excuse" without unassailability or sensibilities; thus, the results are ethnopornography. In Donaldson's case, it is conjecture, but Chauvel vehemently used this excuse so that the Australian censors would not cut up his film *In the Wake of the Bounty* (1933). For Kevin Reynolds of *Rapa Nui* (1994), there was painstaking research and approval from the Chilean officials and most importantly from the local Rapa Nui council, but the following research and analysis might prove other intent.

The first mention of females in the script of *Rapa Nui* is located in this early scene description: "Long Ear girls shout and giggle from a tide pool. They have tattoos and are bare-breasted...." Following the criteria of the Lagoon Swim trope—which should contain basic elements of young fit Native girls or women, a water element, an attitude of frolic or play, and nudity or semi-nudity—all are contained in this short scene description. The author does not explain the background, intent or motivation of the scene, he just indicates four important details: "girls," "giggle," "tattoos," and "bare breasts." Approximately 640 extras and actors were cast for the film, and they all were topless.[3] This could be the most in film history. In the film's companion book *Rapa Nui: The Easter Island Legend on Film*, the costume designer of the movie, John Bloomfield, noted an aspect about part-Hawaiian star Jason Scott Lee, "I don't know why they are paying me, when he is almost naked anyway. He's in such great shape that you want to cover as little of him as possible" (p. 137). The book says 2,000 costumes were made, mostly from tapa cloth imported from Tonga. Bloomfield also commented that, in the beginning, in regard to the many Rapa Nui extras used, "they were shy about getting out of their normal clothes and going half-naked." The book's editor continues, "But they soon grew into seasoned veterans, arriving on the set with clothes already off and their make up on" (p. 136).

In a private conversation with a couple of Māori actors, male and female, who had substantial parts in the film but will remain anonymous, the male actor told me that, like the local Rapa Nui extras, he would get used to going mostly naked after a while; however, the female actress obviously felt uncomfortable about the subject and refused to talk about it. But she did tell me she was very enthusiastic during filming, although the aftermath wasn't pleasant for her. Yes, there is the question of realism and authenticity, but as mentioned, the American masses failed to turn out to watch the film. Maybe, as the cast and extras would take days to get used to the near nakedness, the intended mass general audience could not get used to their near nakedness in just two hours of viewing the finished product. In this case, the uneasiness of the audience could be a good lesson for Hollywood to learn. They, the unaware audience or an audience of a different intended reception, wanted to see the spectacular moʻai; instead, they saw an epic ethnoporn and, in some instances, uncomfortably saw it with their children. The gaze from outsiders was a possible intent, even though it seemingly backfired.[4]

The film *Lure of the Islands* (1942) has a couple of FBI agents covertly swim onto a South Seas island to find out about the enemy during World War II. The bigger of the two men, named Jinx (played by Guinn "Big Boy" Williams), barely survives the swim ashore. After the two agents land on the isle, they then head into the jungle, and the first thing they run into in this elaborate jungle set is the trope of young Native women frolicking in a lagoon. Dialogue follows in script format:

<u>JINX</u>

Wally, look! (they both look) Suffering catfish-babes!

<u>WALLY</u>
(to Jinx seriously) I thought you were dying?

<u>JINX</u>
Not anymore brother, this is just what the doctor ordered.

It is as if an eyeful of Polynesian beauties swimming in a lagoon can cure anything; this imagined elixir seems to work for heterosexual American men. Although this Los Angeles soundstage jungle set was large, the water feature, the lagoon, was small and barely accommodated the four women involved. Of the four females, two were L.A.-based Polynesians. One was a Euro-American starlet in brownface named Maui (depicted by Gale Storm), and the final actress, the female protagonist, was a half–Irish, half–Polynesian named Tana O'Shaughnessy (in the story) and played by former Euro-American stripper (in real life) Margie Hart, which is an indication that a lot of her skin was going to be shown in this "B" picture.

This is a good example of the ethnopornographic phenomenon in Hollywood. The gazes of Wally (Robert Lowery) and Jinx on the women are intense, forgetting for the moment the reason they are there. The gazes of the writer, cameramen, lighting technicians, costumer, and director are intent on making the women look sexually appealing. Unfortunately, because of budget limitations, the water feature did not look realistic, and there is no omnipresent waterfall. The Hollywood illusion of an ethnographic look was gone and replaced by the ambiance of a faux soundstage interior. Part of the definition of a "B" movie in film production and film critique terms is a film of lower budgets and lower production values. Some of the South Seas lagoon sets built by the bigger studios were elaborate, e.g., *Honolulu* (1939), *Aloma of the South Seas* (1941), *Song of the Islands* (1942), and *Lt. Robin Crusoe, U.S.N.* (1966).

Other South Seas Lagoon Swim scenes should be noted. The first three are films involving a Native male and Native female: *South of Pago Pago* (1940), *Aloma of the Seas* (1941), and *Tahitian Nights* (1944). Many movie titles have Euro-American and American men swimming with or gazing at Polynesian women bathing: *Bird of Paradise* (1932), *Mutiny on the Bounty* (1935), *She-Devil Island* (1936), *Typhoon* (1940), *Son of Fury* (1942), *Devil Monster* (1946), *Bird of Paradise* (1951), *Land of Fury* (1954), *She Gods of Shark Reef* (1958), *Tiara Tahiti* (1962), *Lt. Robin Cruso, U.S.N.* (1966), *South Seas Massacre* (1974), and *The Ride* (2003). In the above sixteen example titles, nine films expose nude or topless Native women. Of course, in the few American movies released while the Hollywood Production Code was in force (Chapter 2), the naked Natives are implied, not actual; nevertheless, they are still all eye

Bird of Paradise (1951, 20th Century–Fox). A Lagoon Swim trope is clearly illustrated here with a brownface Debra Paget (top center) playing the female lead as the part-Caucasian granddaughter of the chief and lover of a French foreigner played by Louis Jourdan. At the top right is Hawaiian actress and hula dancer Mary Ann "Queenie" Ventura. Queenie was the Native girlfriend of lead Jeff Chandler, who also played Paget's older brother in brownface. American lobby card (11" × 14").

candy for "Western" imagining male audiences. This assertion should be applied throughout this book: in films that, for various reasons, don't explicitly display Polynesian nudity, it is usually inferred.

According to Hollywood, only young fit *wahines* (women) bathe in Polynesia, and when they do, there is much frolic, play and stealing of sarongs from each other. It is a wonder that anyone gets clean, but that would not matter to the American male gaze that gawks at them. Realism in this lagoon/bathing scenario can be found in the film category of Indigenous Pacific Film. As historian Huston Wood states, Indigenous Pacific films "offer non–Eurocentric tropes and narratives rather than attempt to revise or reverse those established in Hollywood films." Simply put, the intended realism of Indigenous Films offers an alternative to the European and American imaginations and narratives of Hollywood filmmaking. The Indigenous filmmaker is well acquainted with the realities of Polynesia, with its customs, beliefs, knowledge, and social structure, usually from an education of a lifetime of experiences and not by a formal "Western" education—or by a lifetime of inaccurate Polynesian exposure in popular "Western" media.

I will discuss Indigenous filmmaking more thoroughly at the conclusion of this work, but a good case in point, for this section on the Lagoon Swim, comes from an Indigenous Samoan film entitled *O Le Tulafale*, aka *The Orator* (2011). *The Orator* is set in contemporary Samoa and is shot with an all-Samoan cast and in the Samoan language. The plot is original, yet people worldwide could identify with and enjoy the story. I will not go into plot details, but interestingly, the film has a Native Lagoon Swim scene with only female Indigenes. It may be a familiar setting but as Wood alluded to, it is not a Hollywood trope. The scene consists of half a dozen women, fully dressed (as the custom is today in a Polynesian/Christian world) but submerged, except for their heads, in clear and refreshing water. The women are from about 40 to 75 years old, and most are overweight, except for one, our heroine. There is no frolic, just the women keeping cool at midday. The Native women also engage in subdued idle gossip. Our heroine, the youngest one in the scene, sits alone, downstream, and in pain. She is dying with a possible undiagnosed illness. She doesn't talk about it, presumably so the women do not gossip about her personal health. We find out early in the film that she is from another village, but even being from a chiefly family, she was still cast out because she became pregnant out of wedlock. Being from another village, she bathes alone as she probably does every day. There is no sexualized lagoon trope in this film. There are no young, beautiful, fit, and naked or near-naked Polynesian women frolicking under the waterfalls here—only island reality.

4

Climax of the Feast
The Sensual Dance Cliché

Beyond the exoticism of the places, people, and cultures of the Canoe Greeting and Lagoon Swim scenes that we discuss in Chapters 2 and 3, the Seductive or Sensual Dance scene is the pinnacle of sexuality in these films. The sexualized Indigenous Islander now takes the audience to a new level, that of open eroticism. It is not the innocent edenic play of earlier story scenes: there is purposeful intent, now, to seduce the visiting Westerner. Of all the many and varied dances of Polynesian cultures, American and other outside filmmakers almost always choose to exhibit a dance of procreation or at least dances featuring feminine hips swaying in a thin grass skirt or in a tight-fitting sarong. Using the quasi-intended license of ethnography or the acceptance of nude or semi-nude Polynesians, Hollywood can capitalize on this marketing of sex with a lower rating bestowed by the Motion Picture Association of America (such as a "PG-13" instead of a more restrictive "R" rating), which potentially translates to bigger audiences and bigger box office. Meanwhile these films objectify Polynesian men and women and perpetuate a dangerous sexual stereotype. This is not the old colonial tool of representing the Indigenous as savage primitives that need reform but simply a voyeuristic gaze with the intent of profit through titillation at the expense of Polynesian dignity.

This chapter on the Sensual Dance scene will produce evidence of this trope from the early silent era of cinema that illustrates, from a male-dominated Hollywood, that their actual intention was to sell sex to fill theater seats, and the popular genre of the then-fledgling South Seas films was a way to do it. The use of exotic and beautiful Polynesians, a rare popular non–European race that is deemed acceptable by America for romantic fraternizing with Euro-American masculine leads, is the first main ingredient of this cinematic formula for profit. Along with the combining of the idyllic South Pacific and Hawai'i set locations, the shedding by the young and beautiful Polynesians of most of their clothes, along with the use of the "ethnographic excuse" was—and still is—a paradigm for success in Hollywood. Unfortunately, the insensitivity of displaying the erotic objectification and sexualization of the Polynesian on film is ignored by American filmmakers but justified in their minds by inaccurate ethnographic realities or supposedly authentic representation and/or simply for the filling of theater seats for profits.

One of the main plot points for this genre is the music and dance of Pacific Islanders. In historical terms the "hula hula,"[1] the popular American name for the Hawaiian dance craze around the turn of the 19th to 20th centuries, held connotations or the lure of a sensual and forbidden dance (Imada, Hopkins). Also, evidence of this sexualized representation can be deduced by the exhibit locations of this now-altered Hawaiian dance. During this period, the exhibition of hula was relegated to the fairgrounds or circus midways where barkers would recruit or tempt adult males in the crowd to buy a ticket and go into the back tent to basically see the feminine hips swaying and some leg appearing between the long grasses of a hula skirt. An authentic hula performance was not necessary for this audience; nor was an authentic Polynesian dancer: just the shaking of the female hips would do. The hula hula soon graduated to the stages of vaudeville, another racy adult and popular form of American entertainment. Also included in this era was an early form of both American narrative and pornographic motion picture—the peep show or Mutoscope wheel. Some of the Mutoscope titles that were listed under the "Adult" category of this media type are: *Native Hawaiian Hula Dance*, *The Native Hula Hula*, and *South Sea Jazz*, all produced in the early 20th century.[2]

This was a dark period for the history of hula on the North American continent, with its well-received, marketable, and invented sexual connotations. Ironically, during this same era in the Hawaiian Islands, the practice of dancing authentic hula was suppressed and legally banned by the hegemonic or rich and politically powerful Euro-American ultra-conservative white Christians who settled in Hawai'i. These religious zealots perceived the hula as a form of an uncivilized and sexually perverted act. In other words, while the hula was forbidden to be displayed or practiced in Hawai'i by the extreme and powerful Christian right, its derivative, the hula hula, was welcomed openly on the continent by the powerful American entertainment industry for its sexuality and profit. The irony here is that both powerful entities, on the islands and on the mainland, used the same perceived or augmented sexualization of the hula as the main impetus to push their very conflicting agendas. Interestingly, this Hawaiian Indigenous dance was changed, sexualized and commodified by Americans on the continent for their own gain much the same way as the belly dance from the Middle East was. The exotic and erotic hula hula dancers and belly dancers of this period usually performed next to each other onstage or on the midway, and reportedly they would spend time together after work (Imada), probably because of the commonality of being sexualized and exploited by the male-dominated American entertainment industry.

This sexualized representation and reputation of the hula hula dance easily transferred over to film, along with other common South Seas tropes from early European authors, artists and playwrights. Possibly the earliest scene of the Polynesian Sensual Dance trope can be witnessed in the 1914 silent film *Brute Island*, later retitled *McVeagh of the South Seas.* Perhaps "brute" was too strong a word for an audience that just wanted escapist entertainment, but the character McVeagh, an American sea captain, is truly brutish to those around him, especially to the ethnic Pacific Islanders of the isle he rules. The captain even had a relationship with a local Native woman that he bosses around. Despite McVeagh's behavior, his island woman stereotypically worships him. More to the point of this section on Sensual Dance is the following description of a Native dancing scene in *Brute Island.* The scene in question is about McVeagh bargaining with the local chief for an Island woman. The process of selecting from among the now-objectified Native women is not going well until one of McVeagh's American henchmen suggests that all the young women, who seemed to be forced to be exhibited in front of McVeagh, should get up and dance. The men agree. The women, who look even more uncomfortable with the idea but are also forced to dance, are now turned into even more of a sensualized commodity to be handpicked by the evil island Euro-American male ruler.

This picture has many issues; despite the fact it does symbolize the brutality of the colonizer well, the film also presents another South Seas cinema first. This time, Hollywood had economized and shot a South Seas setting in Southern California. This money-saving practice resulted in a disastrous case of Pacific misrepresentation. The people, costumes, music, dance, and scenery were horribly incorrect. The Native dance in this film was one of the worst cases of misrepresentation, especially from a Polynesian perspective. But despite its gross cinematic fabrications, this film, with its new economical concept of shooting the "South Seas" on a Southern Californian backlot, proved to be a financial success.

In the following years other South Seas features were shot in the

Los Angeles area or Florida, most notably Thomas Ince's *Aloha 'Oe* (1915) and *The Idol Dancer* (1920), which was directed by Hollywood great D. W. Griffith (whose *The Birth of a Nation* [1915] is arguably Hollywood's most racist-centered movie ever). These Polynesian films were shot on the continental U.S. with similarly calamitous results of representation but successful results of profits. As the title suggests, *The Idol Dancer* (partially shot at the Bahamas), is about a "half-caste" Native (played by a Euro-American) who worships a Native idol by dancing in front of it. She also woos a couple of American men with her faux sensual hula. Both dances are Hollywood fabrications. Similarly, the infamous "It Girl" Clara Bow and her seemingly ad-libbed sensual hula drove two Euro-American males mad with jealousy in the Hawai'i-set feature film *Hula* (1927), which was also shot in California. These very successful early films demonstrated that a mass American audience didn't know the difference between a real Pacific Island and a Southern Californian (or Florida/Caribbean) locale; thus the many Pacific misrepresentations began with this location concept in South Seas cinema, including the Sensual Dance trope.

The danger here is that millions of Americans who were not educated about the geography and anthropology of the South Seas were then being incorrectly inundated by Hollywood with improper representations, interpretations, illusions, and imaginations of the Pacific. Starting with early childhood visual memories, a mindset is formed, and future generations of Hollywood directors and other creatives used these inaccurate notions and tropes of the Pacific in their future works. Thus, a recycling occurs. Samoan model Rosanna Raymond experienced this mindset working with international photographers. She states in Marata Tamaira's article "From Full Dusk to Full Tusk: Reimagining the 'Dusky Maiden' through the Visual Arts," "that *Papalagi* (foreigners) have pretty fixed ideas of Polynesian women—they have an image that they can picture in their mind's eye that seems to overshadow everything they see...." Similarly, the seminal works of Edward W. Said expounded on the recycled repertory of the same tropes of the Orientalist West that can be found in their literature and film.[3]

There are many sexualized dance scenes in South Seas cinema, and many are intentional, even from the initial silent era of American filmmaking. In an early film history book penned by Arthur Calder-Marshall on American director Robert Flaherty, the author recounts the early pre-production days of *White Shadows* when a new producer by the name of Hunt Stromberg was assigned to the film. One of the first things he did was gather his "yes men" into a private screening room to view a cut of Flaherty's earlier film *Moana: A Romance of the Golden Age.* "When it was over, the yes-men who filled the theatre waited for Stromberg's reaction. 'Boys, I've got a great idea!' he is supposed to have exclaimed. 'Let's fill the screen with tits.'" It seems that was the only thing on Stromberg's mind after viewing what was supposed to be the first South Seas documentary. Additionally, regarding the silent film *Moana,* in Brawley and Dixon's book, *Hollywood's South Seas and the Pacific War: Searching for Dorothy Lamour,* the Paramount publicity department for the film complained that there were "not enough tits" in the film. The department went on to run a campaign with the slogan "The Love Life of a South Seas Siren." In point of fact, there is not much of a love life in *Moana,* and secondly, Moana is not a "Siren," but a very masculine young man. Polynesian names are unisex.

In the same book, Brawley and Dixon have a similar narrative regarding the producer Stromberg. That story involves the future legendary Hollywood producer, David O. Selznick, who was a young and inexperienced producer at the time. Selznick was hired by MGM to help in producing *White Shadows.* He loved the book *White Shadows* by O'Brien and the supposedly innocent Flaherty film *Moana,* so his intention was to make a film sympathetic to the Polynesians. But Stromberg was then hired to be young Selznick's superior, and he had a different mindset, that "Tits and sand sell tickets." Soon both Flaherty and Selznick left the project with an indifference of selling tits (sexualization) with sand (South Seas islands). From both the publicity department of Paramount and an executive of MGM we can witness the early prevailing attitudes of Hollywood vis-à-vis the profiteering by means of Polynesian sexuality on film. Author Ed Rampell reflects: "It was just natural for Hollywood, that always peddled sex, would peddle (sex in) paradise."[4]

Brian Manley, the author of the article, "Moving Pictures: The History of Early Cinema," simply states that in early commercial films "filmmakers quickly realized that comedy, action, sports and provocative images would sell tickets" (p. 6). The dances, as well as other aspects of Polynesian films, became sexualized for commercial gain, and it continues today. Just some examples of this sexualized trope of Sensual Dance throughout the film record are: *Aloma of the South Seas* (1926), *The Delightful Rogue* (1929), *Bride of Samoa* (c. 1930), *Tabu* (1931), *Bird of Paradise* (1932 and 1951), *South of Pago Pago* (1940), *Lure of the Islands* (1942), *Son of Fury* (1942), *Rainbow Island* (1944), *Song of the Sarong* (1946), *G. I. Jane* (1951), *Down Among the Sheltering Palms* (1953), *Land of Fury* (1954), *The Revolt of Mamie Stover* (1956), and *Hurricane* (1979).

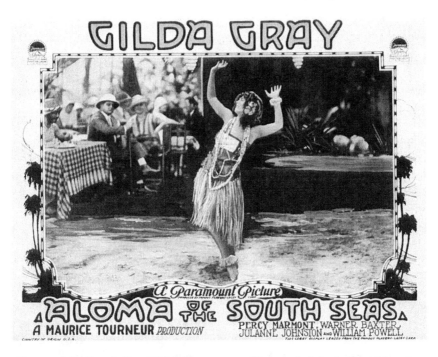

Aloma of the South Seas (1926, Paramount Pictures). A lost silent film starring Gilda Gray, the famous shimmy dancer of the Ziegfeld Follies. This #1 box office film has Gilda (above) dancing a provocative Hollywood shimmy/hula while sexually enticing the visiting men in the background. Wearing a bikini top and baring full leg in a grass skirt was very sensual, especially in 1926. Gilda, born in Poland, plays a brownface Native who falls for one of the visitors. American lobby card (11" × 14").

Intriguingly, as in the Canoe Greeting trope, three of the most paramount examples of sexualized Polynesian dances can be found in three of the *Bounty* films (1933, 1962 and 1984). This fact is quite significant considering that in 1988 the U.S. Secretary of Education William Bennett stated the story of the *Mutiny on the Bounty* is a story every "American child ... should know." This statement concerned noted historian Greg Dening, and it is of equal concern to the points of this book and one that must be reiterated. From Dening's book *Mr. Bligh's Bad Language*:

> "I cannot really say why Mr. Bennett thought every American boy and girl should know why there was a mutiny on the *Bounty*. My prejudices suggested to me that Mr. Bennett would not have been the first in President Reagan's administration to confuse history with some product of the film industry" [p 343].

In context, Greg Dening's comment was based on his exhaustive research between the "story" of the *Bounty* and the fact-based history of the *Bounty*. More specifically, my concern is that it is acknowledged that the *Bounty* saga is an intriguing and important story but one that has the most potential to have American imaginations run uninhibited in regard to the sexualization of the Polynesian.

In the pre–Production Code film *In the Wake of the Bounty*, director Chauvel took every opportunity to show young Polynesian female breasts. In the dance scene, which he was forced to cut down by Australian censors, the female Islanders wore leis but because of the rhythm of the dance and the swaying of the bodies, the leis swayed also, exposing many breasts. The fact is the supposedly Tahitian female dancing was intentionally augmented with more raising of the hands above the head and footwork to sway the upper torso than was normal, all to expose more breast. The women in three of these cinematic *Bounty* versions were tantalizing to the European men, with their sexualized dancing creating a sexual frenzy, especially among the *Bounty* crew members. Towards the end of the Production Code, the 1962 *Mutiny on the Bounty* had what seemed like hundreds of topless dancers, all covered with thick leis held by double-stick tape, dancing the now-synonymous-with-Polynesian-sexuality Tahitian tāmūrē dance. In actuality, the tāmūrē, which is recognized by its simple fast and sensual hip swings, and usually associated with a grass skirt, is a post–World War II invention for the tourist trade. This *Bounty* film contains the famous solo and sexual dance scene of Maimiti (played by Tarita) inviting Fletcher Christian (Brando) to be intimate with her. Brando, as an officer and a gentleman, keeps his cool, barely, and he soon succumbs to her charms.

The final, post–Production Code, "no leis" version of the infamous mutiny story is *The Bounty* (1984), which has one of the most sexually intense dance scenes in Hollywood history. A couple of dozen mostly nude Tahitian dancers, all young, fit and covered with body oil, perform a procreation dance with copulation undertones and overtones along with a tense drumbeat. Intercut into the final film is a setup of this scene, by means of a flashback, depicting Captain Bligh's trial in England where a military solicitor questions Bligh about his reason for exposing his crew to such sexual rituals. This fictional court scene foreshadows the sexuality of the upcoming dance scene, even though it was probably not necessary. Either way, this trial scene emphasizes the sexuality found throughout this film. Another more noticeable sexual Easter egg ad-libbed in this film is when, during the sexually intense dance scene, the Native King Tynah, played by noted Māori actor Wi Kuki

Kaa, tries to covertly hand Captain Bligh, played by noted British actor Sir Anthony Hopkins, a banana. Of all the foods in front of them, he chose a banana, a well-known metaphorical phallic symbol. The reaction to the offering by Captain Bligh was one of repugnance. One tends to wonder if these few frames were improvised or scripted and whether Anthony Hopkins' reaction was scripted or a real reaction by the serious actor to an ad-lib. Either way, the banana as a sexual symbol was apropos for the erotic atmosphere of the scene.

As in the movie *Hawaii*—made in 1966, the year the Production Code was broken by defiant films such as *Blow Up*[5]—explicit Hawaiian procreation dances and nudity were used. Of the many different types of dances available about various aspects of life in Hawaiian society, why were these "coupling" or procreation dance types exhibited? One can understand a few story-point reasons, such as for intimidating an extremist missionary, as in this film and in *Miss Sadie Thompson* (1953), or for embarrassing the colonial representative, as in *Hurricane* (1979), or for inciting mutiny. Hollywood's reason to exhibit such lewdness is simply to sell tickets. Polynesian societies have a deep and rich variety of customs, and the subject of sex is well-represented, but sex is only one aspect of their lives and culture. It is no surprise that Hollywood would focus on sexualized procreation dances and ignore many of the other beautiful and fascinating—nonsexual—dances of Pacific Island cultures.

Eighty years after 1914's *Brute Island*, the already discussed *Rapa Nui* (1994) was released. In *Rapa Nui's* script are simple words describing a tribal dance in the Short Ears village: "And these people singing and dancing around one particularly big fire in their equivalent of The Blues. Young women writhe to the sensuous beat." The intent of this part of the script was fully translated visually onscreen. Two points here: one, the participation of the writer in perpetuating tropes, and two, no one knows how the Short Ears people of Rapa Nui danced centuries ago. I understand the reference to the Blues because this was, in the film's story, a disadvantaged people, but why "sensuous" when things are not going well? And frankly, who are the topless dancers being sensual to in an all-village event with fathers, mothers, grandparents, neighbors, and children present? Sensuality does not seem appropriate in this depressed community setting, but for male Hollywood, it is obligatory in the making of a Polynesian story and in making profits.

Another important issue with regard to the Polynesian Sensual Dance is its proliferation in America's 48 contiguous states and onto foreign soils. This enigma of the Polynesian dance is widespread in lands outside of Oceania, and its propagation is also reflected in American film. In a genre I call Polynesian Pop Pictures (see footnote 1 of Chapter 2), in which one can witness the Polynesian influence in American Pop Culture, the tactless trope of the sexualized Polynesian dance also exists. Unfortunately, and not unlike South Seas cinema, many of the dance performers are not Indigenous to the dance culture they represent, and authenticity is very questionable. In this Poly Pop film genre, we find invented and incorrect Polynesian dance routines that are offensive to Pacific Islanders and extremely sexualized. Examples of this in film are in scenes of pre-wedding parties: *Runaway Bride* (1999); bachelor parties: *A Guy Thing* (2003); crime syndicate adult Polynesian clubs: *Blood Money* (1933), *Dance, Girl, Dance* (1940), *The Frightened City* (1961), *Dime with a Halo* (1963); Tiki bars and Polynesian restaurants: *Wild Women* (1918), *A Shot in the Dark* (1964), *The Animal* (2001), *Bring It On: In It to Win It* (2007); carnival midways: *The Barker* (1928), *Hoop-La* (1933), *Love in Bloom* (1935), *Hello Frisco Hello* (1943), *The Egg and I* (1947), *Are You with It?* (1948), *Young Man with a Horn* (1950), *Carnival Story* (1954), *The Women Eater* (1958); company parties: *Bedtime Stories* (2008); stage shows: *Love and Hisses* (1937), *St. Louis Blues* (1939), *Tin Pan Alley* (1940), *Ship Ahoy* (1942), *My Blue Heaven* (1950), *Holiday Rhythm* (1950), *Primitive Love* (1964); male lodge conventions: *Sons of the Desert* (1933); and burlesque shows: *Sarong Girl* (1943) and *Show Business* (1944).

There are also, in film, a few Polynesian themed frat parties: *Real Genius* (1985), *A Sure Thing* (1985) *Van Wilder* (2002), *American Pie: Book of Love* (2009), *The Newest Pledge* (2012), and strip joints: *Backdoor Follies* (1948), *Happy Girl* (1965), and *Nothing to Lose* (1998). These films have sexualized quasi-Polynesian dancing in a sexualized quasi-Polynesian environment. The association of Polynesian culture and sex is well ingrained not only in the American imagination, but also, literally and more injuriously, in the American social environment and pop culture. These films, set outside of Pacific Islands, represent and demonstrate this Polynesian sexual pervasiveness throughout many aspects of American life.

Lastly, in terms of the Sensual Dance trope, a good case in point of this embedded sexualized ideology can be found in that popular icon of American Poly Pop culture, the dancing hula girl car bobblehead. Much like hula lamps and chalk hula maiden figurines, these miniature bobbing dolls are symbols of sexual Polynesian dance, complete with grass shirts, sexy poses, swaying hips, coconut or bikini tops; some are topless. Many of these commonly sexualized hula bobbers are found in American film, advertising, music videos and television. Some hula bobber examples in popular American media are *Space Cowboys* (2000),

American Wedding (2003), *He was a Quiet Man* (2007), *Deadpool* (2016), *Alien Covenant* (2017), *Deadpool 2* (2018), *The Predator* (2018), *John Wick: Chapter 3—Parabellum* (2019), *Greenland* (2020), and *The Addams Family 2* (2021). They are also found in many TV commercials, e.g., AIWA Electronics (2000), VISA (2000), Target (2001), Trivial Pursuit (2001), Captain Morgan (2006), Carl's Jr. (2007), Sunny-D (2008), Verizon Wireless (2009), Dunkin' Donuts (2015), and ARCO (1917–19).[6]

5

Solidifying the Conquest
Native First Kiss and Beyond

The final trope chapter of this book encompasses the South Seas cinema cliché of the "Native First Kiss." This sexualized Polynesian trope follows the basic Hollywood formulaic plot structure of first arriving on an island with a Canoe Greeting scene of barely clad Native men and women, then a voyeuristic scene of discovering nude or semi-nude Polynesian beauties frolicking in a paradisiacal lagoon, followed by an invitation to a Native feast that almost always includes a very sensualized dance performed by alluring Island performers. Now, after mutual sensual stares between our visiting European or Euro-American male and a beautiful Island Maiden during the arousing dance, the clichéd coupling begins. Once the watching and admiring of the island women from a distance is over, physical contact commences. Now our Euro-American hero and our enticing wahine hold hands and run off to the jungle together, they find a secluded spot, usually under some tree ferns, and then the strong and handsome foreign protagonist begins to teach the innocent island woman to kiss European and American style, lip to lip. There is some resistance at first, but always in American film, the outsider European or American subdues her for his wants and desires.

In South Seas films this subjugation takes place in various forms. Scenes vary from a so-called American hero controlling the Indigenous heroine with dramatic, rape-like masculine force to simple scenes that still illustrate this same domination but in a modest manner. After the initial kiss with our now subdued Island Maiden, a basic cinematic technique occurs: the couple slowly drops in unison below the frame. The question is, just who is this visitor from Europe or America kissing? The classic metaphor is the dominant foreign male kissing or conquering the Island female, with the male representing the conquest by dominant imperialistic Western countries and the

Native innocent young women representing the beautiful islands—ripe for the picking.[1]

Onscreen these men are supposedly kissing an innocent and vivacious Pacific Island woman, but offscreen there are written and social rules as to whom an American may kiss. These social racial norms of 20th-century America are transferred to 20th-century American film, especially in the South Seas genre. This first kiss also establishes the beginnings of a sexual relationship, which, for most American adult audiences, is assumed—especially when sharing a hut or, on a few occasions, bearing children together. In addition to the literal trope of the Native First Kiss and its consequential sexual coupling, this section will explore the racist and sexist social norms of America regarding the interracial relationship between the Polynesian subject of the kiss and her or his foreign lover, particularly during most of the twentieth century.

As mentioned in the introduction, in the male-chauvinistic 20th century and the associated male-dominated Hollywood, 0.93 percent[2] of South Seas films featured a relationship between a female Euro-American and a Pacific Island male. South Seas cinema is predominantly a male-imagined fantasy. Throughout the history of Pacific Pictures, the American feminine fantasy is usually denied. Despite the numerous shots of scantily clad and fit Polynesian males during the Canoe Greeting and some Sensual Dance tropes, there is almost never any development of a relationship with a female visitor and one of these Indigenous males in American South Seas films. In the actual history of early contact between Polynesians and Europeans, except for the Jeanne Baret incident, Polynesian males did not have contact with European females until the early 19th century, and the encounter with Miss Baret was minimal because she was confined below decks by her French male peers, while her male shipmates were free to enjoy the womanly island inhabitants in any way that their hearts and bodies would desire. The paradigm or pattern of female film characters of European descent denied sexual imaginings onscreen parallels the female movie audience and the denial of any fantasies of their own. Ostensibly, this feminine denial was a strong racist and sexist notion that signified the times of the early decades of American cinema in general.

The following quote from the biography of the noted silent film director Rex Ingram illustrates this attitude in America during the lensing of *Where the Pavement Ends* (1923), which was set in Samoa:

> "Even Rex had to admit that the public would not tolerate a story with a love affair between a man of color and a white woman. Hollywood shared with

its audiences a fascination with exotic (Native) female types ... but a relationship between a member of the 'fairer sex' and a Native man would have been out of the question."[3]

The exceptions are few but worth mentioning. The most noted example of interracial relationships between a Euro-American female and Pacific Island male can be found in the 1979 Dino De Laurentiis-produced film *Hurricane*. Interestingly, in this film there is a Sexualized Native Dance scene in which the scantily clad Native male Dayton Ka'ne seduces the visiting Mia Farrow while he makes eye contact with her. She is extremely embarrassed, and her naval commander father, sitting next to her, seems visibly upset. Nevertheless, Farrow cannot take her eyes off of handsome Ka'ne and his largely exposed body—a total reversal of most South Seas films. While this affair later in the film between the pale Farrow and brown and fit Ka'ne was socially progressive, it was almost overshadowed by the many incorrect Polynesian representations in the film.

For Hollywood and its mass American audience, the various cultures and societies of the Pacific are all one and the same, but to Pacific Islanders this ignorance and/or arrogance is objectionable. For example, the actor Ka'ne is, in reality, a Hawaiian playing a Samoan in a Tahitian location. Some Samoans protested this film because they were not correctly represented. Similar to misrepresentation within South Seas films that were lensed in Southern California, *Hurricane* was shot in the Society Islands of French Polynesia; hence, the supposed people and culture of the film's setting, Samoa, were replaced by Tahitians and their Tahitian culture.

There were other reverse sex interracial relationships in South Seas cinema. Note that the majority of these occurrences are spread throughout the 20th century: *Where the Pavement Ends* (1923), *The Love Trader* (1930), *South of Pago Pago* (1940), *Pearl of the South Pacific* (1955), *Diamond Head* (1962), *Bora Bora* (1968), *Sons for the Return Home* (1979), *Other Halves* (1984), *Aloha Summer* (1988), *Broken English* (1996), and the *River Queen* (2005). Pitifully, five of the twelve films mentioned are not American titles. One is an Italian/French collaboration, and the other four are from New Zealand. The American film *Aloha Summer* has only one scene in which Hawaiian male Blaine Kia is suddenly, in the background, coupled with a blonde Euro-American female at a wedding, but there was no established relationship of this twosome in the plot.

While the imbalance of the genders in interracial relationships is a sexist issue, so is the following concept. In some Pacific Island movies a few American male survivors land on an island inhabited by only

Hurricane (1979, Paramount Pictures). Hawaiian Dayton Ka'ne, playing a young Samoan chief, carries his fair American lover, played by Mia Farrow, in this Dino De Laurentiis-produced feature filmed in Bora Bora. This movie plot reverses the sexes from the usual pattern in South Seas cinema, but also contains the common Sensual Dance and Native First Kiss tropes. The Sensual Dance scene has Native male dancer Ka'ne seducing Caucasian Farrow in the audience—also a sex trope reversed from the norm. American lobby card (11" × 14").

young fit beautiful Native women, as in *She-Devil Island* (1936), *Nothing but Women* (1951), *Untamed Women* (1952), *She Gods of Shark Reef* (1958), and *Pagan Island* (1961). Also, in part of the film *Lt. Robin Crusoe, U.S.N.* (1966), star Dick Van Dyke is pursued by dozens of young sarong clad island beauties while he is the only male on the island. There is not one South Seas film in which a female of European descent shipwrecks on an island of only young, fit, handsome Polynesian men. This concept of an island of all young and beautiful wahines is a total masculine 20th-century sexist fantasy. Many questions have to be asked in this scenario: Where are the parents or grandparents of these single women? Do they all eventually die off since there is no chance to procreate? What if Euro-American heroes are shipwrecked on such an island 45 years later and find only overweight, saggy-breasted (not pert-breasted), 70-year-old women with teeth missing? For shallow men and sexist Hollywood that would be a nightmare, not a fantasy. Unfortunately, that would not be a marketable film unless it was a comedy or, in other words, women's issues would not be taken seriously. While the preceding concepts encompass a sexist tone, the following observations and arguments are racial in nature.

Found in the exhaustive South Seas filmic record are a surprising number of plots that involve the improbable circumstance of a Euro-American female infant surviving, alone, from a shipwreck and landing on a Polynesian island. Usually out of compassion, the local chief and his family raise the infant as the future princess of the island—or under the false pretense that the fair-skinned baby is a goddess sent by other gods and to be treated as such. For example: *The Woman Untamed* (1920), *Shark Master* (1921), *Her Jungle Love* (1938), *Call of the Jungle* (1945), *Song of the Sarong* (1946); or many other variations of the theme: *Isle of Content* (1915), *The Quest* (1915), *Island of Regeneration* (1915), *The Pearl of Paradise* (1916), *A Virgin Paradise* (1921), *Isle of Lost Men* (1928), *South Seas Rose* (1929), *Typhoon* (1940), *Tahiti Honey* (1943), and *Weird Woman* (1944). There is also the plot of Euro-American women who were born on Pacific Islands and raised in the culture of the islands by friendly Native subordinates. *Hula* (1927) and *Song of the Islands* (1942) are examples. More on these films in the next chapter. There is also an outlandish plot of Euro-American shipwrecked survivors on a deserted Pacific Island, who after generations of isolation somehow adopted Polynesian customs and the sensual sarongs found in the feature *By the World Forgot* (1918).

All of the above films incorporate a female protagonist of European descent portrayed as an Island female, complete with sarongs, flower in hair, leis, and minimal clothing, whose attitude is carefree, promiscuous, and free of responsibilities—the stereotypical South Seas island female. So, I surmise, when the European or American hero does eventually arrive on the island, the feminine "island" protagonist is racially pure for him, and they are permitted to fall in love with each other. The adopted island female carries that sexually free and innocent appeal of the Polynesian beauty stereotype, except the hero or film studio does not have to worry about the American social taboos of interracial love. In every one of these titles this happens. There is no South Seas American film plot that exists wherein a Caucasoid raised as an Islander did not fall in love with a visitor of European descent or vice versa. The adopted faux Polynesian princess never chooses, at the end, a Native lover; nor does the faraway male visitor pick a darker skin Native as a love interest. He will always choose the only "white" Islander. As one can observe, most of the film titles above are from the early silent era with some others being produced during and just after World War II. My proposed position is that, even though disguised, the importance of a racially pure sexual relationship was a bigger social concern during these time periods.

Sample evidence of this veiled racist position of Hollywood comes from Andre Soares' 2002 book, *Beyond Paradise: The Life of Ramon Novarro*, in which he describes this incident in Novarro's acting career:

> In the picture, initially called *The Passion Vine* but released as *Where the Pavement Ends*, Novarro plays Motauri, a carefree Pacific Islander in love with a white missionary's daughter, portrayed by Alice Terry—the two stars' first romantic pairing ... used images to depict the freedom and innocence of the natural world being destroyed by the zeal and prejudices of European culture.
>
> Before the national release of *Where the Pavement Ends*, the studio demanded that Ingram (the director) film an alternative happy ending (exhibitors could then select the one they preferred). In the original ending, Motauri throws himself off a waterfall because his love for the white woman cannot be consummated (in deference to the Bible, miscegenation was a film taboo). In the alternate ending, there is a prologue explaining that Motauri is in reality a nicely tanned white boy who grew up on the island unaware of his ethnicity. All is revealed at the end so the lovers can return to New England together for a life of blissful racial purity [p. 45].

Originally, this Hollywood production was a story meant to reveal the "prejudices of European culture," but hypocritically this film ends up being an example of American racism instead.

Another bias issue is this: In the Euro-American male-dominated film industry, South Seas films set in earlier time periods seem to eliminate, almost entirely, all reactions of the male Polynesians when their Island daughters, sisters, girlfriends or wives throw themselves at foreign visitors. Actually, there are a small handful of Indigenous males who do react after their women are whisked away, generally voluntarily, by the visiting or shipwrecked European or American protagonists. In two early silent features, *The Altar Stairs* (1922) and *Through the Breakers* (1928), Native Island males react very violently—killing their Native female companions, as in the case of *Breakers*. But in *Altar Stairs*, the Native male mate kills a Euro-American outsider for having an affair with his wife—the only example of this behavior in South Seas cinema. In *Altar Stairs* the murdered white male was a brutal person and after all, he was cheating on his new American bride with the married Native woman. His character was so bad the wife left him at the altar, thus the title.

In general, however, Indigenous boyfriends or husbands in Hollywood South Seas stories are conveniently nonexistent, or their characters are written in a bad light, such as a dominant male in an arranged
marriage so that the Native women could justify (in the American
perspective) an annulment in the first place. Examples include *Bird
of Paradise* (1932), *Mr. Robinson Crusoe* (1932) and *Lt. Robin Crusoe,
U.S.N.* (1966). Significantly, in the current existing film record, *Paradise Isle* (1937) and *Land of Fury* (1954) show fierce Polynesian warriors
who inexplicably do not react when stealthily witnessing their Native
women in the arms of a European or American visitor, passionately
kissing for the first time with their lips. These normally strong and
able Indigenous warriors are suddenly and uncharacteristically submissive and retreat without being noticed, metaphorically giving in to
an alleged "superior race" or giving in to all their demands, including
those for land. This is another example of the American male sexual
fantasy of being caught but left alone by a strong, but now subjugated,
male Islander without any physical or violent encounters. Commonly
an American protagonist can pick and choose any Native women on
the Island without any worries about the women's current relationship
or its consequences.

One has to seriously ponder such illusions in regard to this concept, especially in the film *Take a Chance* (1933), in which co-star
Cliff Edwards (AKA Ukulele Ike) cheers up his friend, played by James
Dunn, by telling him he should be more sensitive to women and needs
to play an ukulele to woo them. Edwards then relates a long story, by
song, about when the ukulele saved his life in the South Seas. In flashback, Edwards shipwrecks on an island where the fierce Native men
were about to eat him, but his ukulele playing saved his life. He also
became king of the island and had many Island Maidens as wives, and
they gave him children. Imagine, going from the "main course" of a feast
to king of the island just by being a good ukulele player. At the end of
his story, Edwards left the island because he missed his wife and kids
back home. Edwards sings to tell his story, and, in the lyrics, he relates
that to acquire his large harem he had to "burn a husband daily, with a
passion Polynesian." "Every South Seas mama came (to me) to shake a
mean Pajama." In other words, with little interpretation and the accompanying visuals from the flashback, Edwards became king of the island,
took many wives from single wahines to women from previously established families, women whose husbands who were fierce warriors but
didn't put up resistance. Then suddenly Edwards became homesick and
abandoned his Native wives and young children to go home because he
didn't tell anyone he was already married. Only in male-run Hollywood

can this story be remotely possible or even plausible. How unbelievable this story is! What does it convey to America about Polynesian men and women?

Another racist and emblematic attribute of a South Seas movie is that the vast majority of female heroines in this genre are played by either a light brown-skinned, dark-haired Latina woman or a young Euro-American starlet out of Hollywood who is covered in brownface make-up. In his book *The Vision of Robert Flaherty*, Richard Barsam calls these types of misrepresentations of Polynesians on film "Hollynesian" (p. 51).[4] The first known instance of Latinos and Latinas playing Polynesians occurred with the casting of Beatrice Dominguez in the role of Lehua in the 1919 silent film *Light of Victory*. The first male example is the already discussed Ramon Novarro in *Where the*

Take a Chance (1933, Paramount Pictures). Above is an American lobby card (11" × 14") of the film featuring James Dunn and Cliff Edwards (aka Ukulele Ike). In a large song and flashback scene, Edwards shipwrecks on a Polynesian Isle and after exhibiting his ukulele talents is appointed king of the island with the bonus of having many Native wives. The above poster displays King Edwards with only some of his Polynesian brides. What one doesn't see are the many island children he fathers. *Chance* was originally a Broadway musical comedy starring Ethel Merman, but without the polygamous Polynesian backstory and accompanying song.

Pavement Ends (1923). The use of a Latino playing the lead Polynesian character is uncommon, but then again, any male Polynesian heroes in South Seas island movies were infrequent. Novarro also played the Native protagonist in one other South Seas film, *The Pagan* (1929). In 1937 the Mexico-born Anthony Quinn was cast as Kimo in *Waikiki Wedding.*

One year earlier than *The Pagan* was the 1928 release, *White Shadows in the South Seas.* Latina Raquel Torres was cast as the Polynesian tabu Princess Fayaway (a name derived from Herman Melville's first novel *Typee,* which was set in the Marquesas Islands and is, for the purposes of this book, rather interestingly subtitled *A Peep at Polynesian Life*). Besides Dominguez, there may have been earlier Latinas playing Polynesian maidens, but because many silent films are lost, there is currently no verification of other earlier Hispanic actors playing the roles of Pacific Islanders at this time. But for Hollywood, Miss Torres' being half–German made her a safer bet to cast in any South Seas film. The experiment was successful; the American audience seemed to accept Torres' role as a Polynesian, judging by the overall success of the film. But in actuality, anyone with an observant eye can attest to the fact that she seems out of place onscreen among actual Tahitian Maidens playing Marquesans.

Even so, Raquel Torres' role opened the floodgates for more Latinas to play in the popular South Seas features. In her short career, Torres managed to play two other Polynesian roles, in *The Sea Bat* (1930) and *Aloha* (1931).

This practice of using Hollywood Latina starlets was so popular that one Latina actress, as mentioned, changed her name from Maria Castaneda to the Polynesian sounding name Movita, to help her land Pacific Island roles. (See footnote 7 in Chapter 3 relating to her relationship with Marlon Brando.) Movita not only shared the female Polynesian lead with Mamo Clark (one of the few Polynesian actresses to get enduring attention in Hollywood during most of the 20th century) in *Mutiny on the Bounty* (1935), but Movita also starred in *Captain Calamity* (1936) and *Paradise Isle* (1937). Prominent Latina film star Dolores del Rio also jumped onto the South Seas bandwagon when she starred as the Polynesian Luana in the first *Bird of Paradise* (1932) onscreen. Joanna Hershfield, who wrote a scholarly biography on del Rio entitled *The Invention of Delores del Rio,* quotes from a *New York Herald Tribune* review of the movie that comments that del Rio "is perhaps no more skillful or experienced than usual, but her dusky, alien beauty fits in so effectively with her role" (p 18).

Supposedly educated and cultured film critics of major

American newspapers of the time could never be so wrong. She was too fair-skinned, her hair was too full and too short, and she spoke too rapidly—and with a Mexican accent, at that. Del Rio did not look at all like the real Polynesian extras and bit-part actors surrounding her. I can imagine what Hollywood producers and studios were thinking: "We got away with it, so we can do it again." Consequently, the general American public was ingrained and inundated with South Seas films featuring another misrepresentation, the Latina passed off as a Polynesian. Here are some other Latina actresses of note playing Polynesians: Conchita Montenegro in *Never the Twain Shall Meet* (1931); Lupe Valez in *Honolulu Lu* (1941); Maria Montez in *South of Tahiti* (1941), *White Savage* (1943), and *Cobra Women* (1944); Rita Moreno in *Pagan Love Song* (1950); Yvonne De Carlo in *Rainbow Island* (1944) and *Hurricane Smith* (1952); and Barbara Carrera in *When Time Ran Out...* (1980) and *Emma: Queen of the South Seas* (1988), a miniseries. Also wearing sarongs by the legendary costume designer Edith Head in *Rainbow Island* were Olga San Juan and Elena Verdugo, along with the legendary Louisiana-born Euro-American Dorothy Lamour playing the female Polynesian lead. Besides *Rainbow Island,* there are some films, lensed in L.A., that have whole Pacific Island villages filled with Hispanics, like the films *Island Captives* (1937) and *Devil Monster* (1946).

Of the first American narrative films that came out of Universal distribution, two 1913 films entitled *The Shark God* and *Hawaiian Love* were Pacific Island-themed films. Both were filmed in Hawai'i and starred Virginia Brissac, as well as other mainland actors who were performing in a play along with Brissac at Honolulu's Hawai'i Theatre at the time. During the run of this play, the director, John Griffith Wray, also directed these two short films. All involved with the play and films were Californian Euro-Americans. The first film, *Hawaiian Love*, had two Hawaiian characters, one "a pretty Hawaiian" played by Brissac, the other a Hawaiian Native named Kalike played by fellow Euro-American James Dillon. There was even a Chinese character played by Euro-American Ray Hanford. The second film, *The Shark God,* had a pre–European contact plot, so all of the characters were Hawaiians played by the same actors from the Californian theatrical company. (Brissac's final screen role was as James Dean's grandmother in 1955's *Rebel Without a Cause.*).

Not only were these the first American commercial narrative features of the Pacific but also the first South Seas films to use Euro-Americans in brownface make-up to represent Polynesians. Perhaps it was a theater tradition for Caucasian theatrical actors to play all races, such as they did in minstrel shows. Maybe they, as trained thespians, were above using or even trying to audition (presumably) untrained Islanders for roles playing Islanders. Even so, there should have been some thought or sensitivity to the real people they were trying to represent and to the consequences of misinforming the American mass audience. Subsequently, these two films with their incorrect racial representation set the tone and were Tinseltown's templates for continued erroneous and damaging representations in large quantities.

In the same year, 1913, renowned French pioneering filmmaker Georges Méliès sent his brother Gaston Méliès to the actual South Seas to film a few early short travelogues promoting distant locales for the travel industry plus short dramatic narrative films. Gaston's half a dozen film short stories were set and filmed in Tahiti and New Zealand and used real Pacific Islanders to play Pacific Islanders. After all, he was on real locations and on a budget; consequently, he successfully used Indigenous stories and Indigenous actors within these films.

Wray and company were also on a real location, Hawai'i; however, they perpetrated the ill-conceived notion for future American filmmakers that realistic representation is not necessary or required. Like blackface, brownface was also accepted for most of the first half of the 20th century. In his 2003 article "Exotics, Erotics and Coconuts: Stereotypes of Pacific Islanders," Tom Brislin is also concerned with this overuse of makeup, writing: "Long after the deplorable practice of Anglo actors minstrel-like in blackface, Hollywood has continued to cast Anglos in yellowface playing Asians, or brownface playing islanders" (p. 105).

Here are many instances of this racist practice of brownface in South Seas cinema: *McVeagh of the South Seas* (1914), *The Hidden Pearls* (1918), *Idol Dancer* (1920), *White Flower* (1923), *Isle of Forgotten Women* (1927), *Never the Twain Shall Meet* (1931), *Birds of Paradise* (1932), *Pardon My Sarong* (1941), *Son of Fury* (1942), *The Tuttles of Tahiti* (1942), *Rhythm of the Islands* (1943), *Isle of Tabu* (1945), *On an Island with You* (1948), *On the Isle of Samoa* (1950), *Pagan Love Song* (1950), *Birds of Paradise* (1951), *All the Brothers Were Valiant* (1953), *Down Among the Sheltering Palms* (1953), *His Majesty O'Keefe* (1954), *Return to Paradise* (1953), *The Women of Pitcairn Island* (1956), *Don't Go Near the Water* (1957), *Enchanted Island* (1958), *Blue Hawaii* (1961), *Diamond Head* (1962), *Ride the Wild Surf* (1964), *Lt. Robin Crusoe, U.S.N.* (1966), and *Pippi in the South Seas* (1974), to name a few. So, in actuality, the vast majority of South Seas Euro-American heroes were not kissing authentic Polynesian women but Latinas and brownface women of European descent. On a positive note, for the *Bounty* films, all the versions of this film used actual Polynesian women as the female leads with the exception of Movita in 1935, but again, her female co-star, Mamo Clark, was of Polynesian ancestry.

Blackface was abolished during the late '60s in America due to the Civils Rights movement,[5] and as one can see, brownface had also disappeared by then, not because of Pacific Islander protest but by the larger consensus of a more enlightened nation. Even Japanese-produced South Seas cinema used much brownface on their Japanese extras playing Pacific Island inhabitants during the '60s—e.g., *Son of Godzilla* (1967) and *Mothra* (1961)—and has also ceased its use since then. Yellowface—with the ridiculously fake slanted eyes, buckteeth and thick, round framed glasses of Asian characters played by white actors—was also eliminated, more specifically by a group of Asian-Americans named the Visual Communications (V.C.) organization.

The V.C. has tirelessly complained to the studios and to the press, especially when a film premieres with a false representation of an Asian. Their efforts have paid off. Today, if a young American viewer watched an old film with a blackface Fred Astaire or bucktoothed, slant-eyed Mickey Rooney, they would be confused and wonder how studios had gotten away with these racist and offensive depictions. I argue that if each race was represented truthfully in all media and within the larger context of history, and not centered on one race as the protagonist all the time, a lot of prejudices would never have been formed because of the power of mass media. Unfortunately, this same power can be made to misinform the masses, as in tropes of South Sea Cinema. If mass media would represent peoples and cultures realistically, a better understanding and respect for each other would prevail. Personally, I have followed V.C. throughout the years and have admired their efforts along with the Media Action Network for Asian Americans (MANAA), which took over the watchdog and protest duties of the V.C. in the early '90s. But unfortunately, they do not lambaste the film studios or TV networks in the press when Asian-American actors misrepresent themselves by playing Polynesians, as in the newer *Hawaii Five-0* TV series and other productions. (V.C. also annually presents the Los Angeles Asian Pacific Film Festival, which includes productions from Oceania.)

From the books *The First Strange Place: Race and Sex in World War II Hawaii* (Bailey and Farber) and *Hollywood's South Seas and the Pacific War: Searching for Dorothy Lamour* (Brawley and Dixon), it is well documented that this ingrained mindset of a nonexistent fair Polynesian beauty, created from the imagination of Hollywood, actually caused psychological damage to thousands of incoming soldiers entering the Pacific Theater during World War II. Looking for and never finding their dream Hollywood-Polynesian beauty caused a serious morale problem that the U.S. military recognized and had to solve though reverse indoctrination, the educating of the troops about the realities of the Pacific and its peoples. Ironically, beautiful Polynesian women do exist, but why these soldiers could not find them is a subject for another text. Nevertheless, this is a prominent case of serious psychological effects produced by Hollywood's imagination and fabrications that can influence the masses.

Another racist practice of Hollywood, in respect to the production of the South Seas film genre, is the audacity that a Euro-American of any class of society, even homeless drunken beachcombers, usually has a sexual relationship with a Pacific Islander of the highest class, usually an island Queen, Princess or Chief's daughter. It is very infrequent to find plots in which the Euro-American protagonist falls for a Native woman with a low-class station or a class of unidentified origins in her society, as in the film *The Beachcomber* (1915). The high social status of a Polynesian woman is always well announced in film stories. In other words, if there is an interracial coupling in a Pacific Island film, it is almost always with a regular Euro-American or European male and a stereotypical Islander with a royal pedigree—a scenario that signals that average white males are on an equal status only with high-ranking Polynesian females and only on a temporary basis. A permanent relationship or marriage is, as earlier stated, very uncommon in South Seas film. In contrast, a common American romantic film set in the milieu of European aristocracy will almost always have a royal coupling between a prince and a princess or a commoner who discovers he is a prince later, and there is almost always a royal wedding at the end. Not so in South Seas cinema. There is almost always an unbalanced social status and almost never a wedding. This is a very egregious, racist concept that never enters the American audience's consciousness.

Also, at times, our Euro-American hero falls for what he thinks is a commoner Native, only to be reminded at spearpoint that the young island woman he's about to touch is taboo and the virgin princess, who must remain as such.[6] Or it's the luck of the draw that when a Euro-American male outsider shipwrecks and washes ashore, it seems to always be the beautiful princess of the island who discovers, aids, cures, and protects him from the other Islanders who want to banish, kill, or even eat him. No matter how serious the taboo, the island customs do not matter to a Euro-American centric mindset. In general, our protagonist is always in the right, his country is always more powerful, and so is his God, and, in these films, he usually gets away with stealing a taboo island princess after selfishly ignoring or disrespecting island customs and protocol. To pour salt on the injury, the sexual relationship that follows is almost always intended only to be a temporary bond by the Euro-American or European visitor.

Listed are some examples of Polynesian queens and princesses in film: *The Shark God* (1913), *Aloha Oe* (1915), *A Fallen Idol* (1919), *A Woman There Was* (1919), *Never the Twain Shall Meet* (1925), *White Shadows in the South Seas* (1928), *Tabu* (1931), *Bird of Paradise* (1932), *Flower of Hawaii* (1933) (German), *Down to Their Last Yacht* (1934), *Mutiny on the Bounty* (1935 and 1962), *King of the Islands* (1936), *South of Tahiti* (1941), *Call of the South Seas* (1944), *Devil Monster* (1946), *Tahiti Nights* (1944), *Nothing but Women* (1951) (Philippines), *What the Butler Saw* (1950) (UK), *Hula-La-La* (1951), *Down Among the Sheltering Palms* (1953), *Hell Ship Mutiny* (1957), *Enchanted Island* (1958), *Pagan Island* (1961), and *The Bounty* (1984). For the female audience there are three and only three Polynesian princes who have affairs with American women. Those films are *Where the Pavement Ends* (1923), *South of Pago Pago* (1940), and *Hurricane* (1979).

Many of these princesses in South Seas cinema are also of European descent for two reasons: one, to explain why brownface daughters and granddaughters of the chief have blue eyes and Caucasoid facial features and two, owing to the racist ideology against miscegenation or marrying and having offspring between different races. The rationale that the Euro-American hero has a sexual relationship with a part-Caucasian makes it more palatable to an American audience, but it is still a racist concept.

Hershfield explains the difference between interracial romance and miscegenation: "Interracial romance is about desire and sex, whereas miscegenation is about bloodlines and procreation" (p. 24). There are two racist issues here. The first one is hypocritical; that is, would it be permissible for a Euro-American male to have an interracial romance or a physical love affair with a Polynesian young woman? Back home in Europe or North America, until up to the early 1970s, it would be socially distressing if a Euro-American man "shacked up with" or cohabitated with a female of his same race without the bonds of matrimony, breaking conventions and community norms. This practice would have been a devastating societal circumstance, breaking the hearts of his close family and his Christian preacher, and, in many cases, it would have been illegal. The second racist issue is that apparently in a Hollywood Pacific Island setting, an interracial romance can be forgiven by Euro-American audiences, but miscegenation or a relationship to have children seems to be a greater prohibition and was not as tolerated in America, apparently even on a fictional South Seas island found on the silver screen. It is another addition to the American male imagination of exotic lovemaking without any responsibilities, commitments or social pressures.

Of the over 750 American South Seas feature films, there is only one that produced a simple and unmuddled example of interracial offspring presented though a committed relationship and without repercussions. That biracial child was produced from the least sexualized film of the *Bounty* movies, the 1935 *Mutiny on the Bounty*. There is a Christmas scene were Clark Gable, as Fletcher Christian, proudly holds up the biracial baby he conceived with his Tahitian wife, played by Hawaiian Mamo Clark. Hernán and Gordon also state that "*Mutiny on the Bounty* combines the fascination with mutiny with the fascination with miscegenation; both involve the breaking of powerful social taboos.... To twentieth century white America, interracial marriage still poses the threat of the breakdown of boundaries, the confusion of strict racial categories and the eventual dissolution of white identity" (p. 69). This is the only scene within the South Seas film genre in which miscegenation is freely exhibited on screen with both parents and biracial child positioned in the same frame as in a family portrait. An obvious and clear biracial family poses for the American and worldwide audience. There is no unusual circumstance that has to explain this committed interracial relationship. There is no missing parent or blurring of a shot in which a biracial offspring and one or both parents are rushing to go somewhere, as in the other rare mixed-race relationships onscreen. Even after this film won the highest honor in worldwide cinema, the Academy Award for Best Picture, implying the admission of guilt and greater acceptance or tolerance of miscegenation by the Academy voters, this issue continued to be a serious exclusion or taboo (ironically, a word commonly used in English that's of Polynesian origins) in Hollywood.

In almost all South Seas films, if miscegenation is about to take place, a tremendous unforeseen event suddenly arises in the plot that thwarts the plans for a certain upcoming interracial marriage and/or the producing of biracial offspring. Jeffrey Geiger writes that there are "plots or subplots involving interracial romances ... but the interracial relationships were almost always hazardous to the health of one or both parties..." (Geiger 2002). Geiger is referring to hurricanes, earthquakes, many other natural disasters and the breaking of serious taboos and the ensuing consequences, which are all prevalent in South Seas cinema. With closer analysis, I concur that these thrills and eye-catching effects are not only a plot trait for capturing the audience's attention but used time after time as a script diversion to undermine the previously planned nuptials or the possibility of miscegenation between the Polynesian and European races.

There are other plot devices that thwart the plans of a serious biracial couple who intend to raise a family. The following are some examples: a Native lover is shot and killed—*As Man Desires* (1924), *Isle of Forgotten Women* (1927), *Diamond Head* (1962); husband dies of leprosy—*Moon and Sixpence* (1942); American fiancée arrives to take her engaged boyfriend back home and he obediently leaves his Island lover—*McVeagh of the South Seas* (1914), *Never the Twain Shall Meet* (1925, 1931); the island queen is actually an American raised by Natives—*Shark Master* (1921), *Typhoon* (1940); accidental death of island princess—*A Woman There Was* (1919); half–Polynesian fiancée's local religion is a higher priority than her Euro-American lover, so she sacrifices herself in a volcano—*Aloha* (1931), *Bird of Paradise* (1932, 1951); film usually ends before children—*The Beachcomber* (1915), *Paradise Isle* (1937), *Son of Fury* (1942), *On the Isle of Samoa* (1950), *Hell Ship Mutiny* (1957), *Blue Hawaii* (1961); pet leopard of betrothed American, who was forcing a marriage to a wild half–Irish South Seas Maiden, kills the evil owner—*The Leopardess* (1923); Island wife goes insane before offspring is produced—*The Hawaiians* (1970).

In addition to *Blue Hawaii*, only a handful of South Seas titles show a proper engagement or a marriage by the end of the film, but again, like most films with a happy ending between a Polynesian and a Caucasian, the plot ends before the bearing of children. The earliest film with this plot scenario is from a non–American film by Frenchman Gaston Méliès called *Loved by a Maori Chieftess* (1913). Then *South of Pago Pago* (1940), wherein a Polynesian hero gets married to an American woman, with Jon Hall (who was part-Tahitian in real life) as the Polynesian prince, and Francis Farmer as the Euro-American love interest. Also: *South of Tahiti* (1941); *Wings Over the Pacific* (1943); *Drums of Tabu* (1967), which was an Italian and Spanish co-production; and *Savage Play* (1995), a New Zealand production.

In some cases, in which young biracial offspring do exist, they are hidden AND at least one of the parents of a mixed-race coupling are nonexistent in the whole plot, as though Hollywood does not want to show that miscegenation took place. The pre-plot death of a Polynesian mother or European/Euro-American father erases their existence in the film, and this scenario takes place in many South Seas cinema titles. Two prominent features with this racist scenario include *Donovan's Reef* (1963) and *South Pacific* (1958). A death of an American husband of a Hawaiian woman before the story begins is found in *Diamond Head* (1962). In the early silent *The Idol Dancer* (1920), our heroine is established as a mixed-raced person of French and Samoan lineage who is currently being raised by an American beachcomber, not by her nonexistent interracial parents. In the 1951 *Bird of Paradise*, both brownface Native protagonists have an American grandfather, never to be seen, because he left the island and died. Likewise, the parents of these mixed-raced heroes are never seen or discussed. Also, in the film, there is a banished Englishman on a small outer island with six biracial children around him, but there is no Polynesian mother in existence. "She'll come crawling back. She always does." In *Blue Hawaii* (1961), it is well established that Elvis' mother is a Southern racist, but we also never see or even know that his half–French and half–Hawaiian girlfriend has a Hawaiian mother. We are introduced to the Hawaiian royal grandmother and French father, but the father is alone, with no mention of a wife. In *Enchanted Island* (a 1958 adaptation of *Typee*), brownface Jane Powell is the biracial granddaughter of the chief with nonexistent interracial parents. In *Return to Paradise* (1958) Gary Cooper's mixed-raced daughter has a nonexistent Samoan mother due to her death.

In the Sadie Thompson films *Rain* (1932) and *Miss Sadie Thompson* (1953), there is an expatriate innkeeper who is married to a Native woman and has many children, but their family life is in the background and incidental to the plot, with rarely a shot of at least one biracial child and both parents—or we get a quick partial glimpse of a whole miscegenetic family. In *Miss Tatlock's Millions* (1948), we witness a biracial marriage and clearly see the Hawaiian wife and two boys; oddly, however, we never see the dad's face. Fifty-two years after the 1935 *Bounty*, we finally see again a biracial child with both interracial parents together on a few frames of film, in the Hawai'i movie *North Shore* (1987). Here, we witness a common mixed couple, with children, which are realistically widely found today throughout the Pacific.

Within the just mentioned film *Miss Tatlock's Millions* lies another exception of note. The film shows fairly young offspring from the union of a Euro-American and a Hawaiian, but with a catch. It was a comedy in its time, but today it would be considered politically incorrect and deplorable since it deals with a mentally challenged heir of a millionaire who, with his sister, will stand to receive all the inheritance if he signs the right papers on the right date. The problem is he went missing, and as time passes, a horde of family members are standing by hoping to receive the missing son's share. Cutting to the end, the son shows up in the nick of time. We discover he was apparently hiding out in Hawai'i and married a Hawaiian woman (played by Hilo Hattie). He comes home with her and two young biracial boys. As appalling as the plot sounds, equally appalling is the thought that if an American is mentally challenged, does that make it permissible for him to marry into another race and be an exception to the miscegenation rule? In this case, the American father does exist—but in an abnormal mental state. In other words, to the previously discussed class imbalance between a commoner European or American with a Polynesian of chiefly ranking—and the not discussed physical imbalances, at times, between much older and unpleasant looking Euro-American or European males with beautiful, young and fit Polynesian females—we can add a mental imbalance between a healthy Islander and a mentally challenged Euro-American.

As mentioned, there is also the common relationship between a young and healthy Polynesian woman and her homeless and alcoholic beachcomber lover. In all these relationships, class, wealth, physical, and mental imbalances all principally have a very racist basis before the 1980s. After all of this, there is a huge irony in American cinema, which will be explained in the following paragraph.

There is an actual rule in the Production Code against miscegenation,[7] but while most producers at the time understood that this meant sexual relationships between "white" and any "non-white" races, most Hollywood filmmakers did not know about what I call the "Polynesian Exception," which is not written in the Production Code itself but in a companion handbook to the Code. Mentioned by Brawley and Dixon in their already cited book was a little 1937 handbook by Olga Martin entitled *Hollywood's Movie Commandments: Handbook for Motion Picture Writers and Reviewers.* Further research finds that Olga Martin was the personal secretary to Joseph Breen, the Chief Administrator for the Production Code.[8] Apparently, Olga Martin was tired of explaining to film producers, writers and new censors the ins and outs and details of unpublished intricacies that the Production Code administrators decided on behind closed doors. So, Olga Martin, with apparent approval of her boss, the powerful Mr. Breen, published a companion booklet for limited distribution. In her "official" handbook there are some interesting addendums to the Code:

> The Code specifically prohibits miscegenation in its regulation which reads, "Miscegenation (sex relationship between the white and black races) is forbidden." The dictionary defines miscegenation as, "A mixture of races, especially amalgamation of the black and white races."
>
> The Production Code Administration, in interpreting this regulation for application to film stories, has regarded miscegenetic unions to be any sex relationship between the white and black races, or in most cases sex union between the white and yellow races. The union of a member of the Polynesians and allied races of the Island groups with a member of the white race is not ordinarily considered a miscegenetic relationship, however. The union of a half-caste of white and Polynesian parentage with a white

member would also be exempt from the ruling applying to miscegenation [p. 178].

Seemingly, most of the producers of South Seas cinema were not informed of the Production Code's Polynesian Exception (a tantalizing loophole for a society in which Jim Crow and segregation were still widely enforced)—again, not found in the Code itself but in its supplemental handbook. To those few producers who did show marriages between Euro-Americans and Polynesians in their films, we now have evidence as to why they got away with it. Another scenario is that a few movie producers actually knew and took advantage of the exception, but knowing Hollywood producers (I worked in Hollywood management for over 25 years), they were not about to tell competing filmmakers about this unusual exception. The question here is not the exception but why Polynesians? Singling them out from other races, even in a positive manner, is still a racist construct.

Another term, which I label the big "Paradox in Paradise," is that in many of these Pacific films, there are two racial principles that have a self-contradictory paradigm or concept. On the one hand, there is the racist trope of using part-European and part-Polynesian romantic lead characters to soften the interracial relationship issue, but at the same time this means that in order for these multi-racial Island heroes and heroines to exist, the production of biracial offspring must have taken place in the past, breaking the other racist trope, that of miscegenation. This is found in many South Seas films without most people—filmmakers and audiences—noticing the quandary. My previously discussed theory of the practice of hiding the interracial parents or having them become non-existent is one reason for this undetected dilemma. Miscegenation was then forbidden and avoided, but miscegenation has to have taken place in order to produce a racially mixed Euro-Polynesian person to make tolerable an interracial relationship with our protagonist of pure European descent. You cannot get away with one racist concept (mixed-Euro/ Polynesian sexual relationships with Caucasians) without creating another one (miscegenation); hence, the paradox.

Another means to avoid a miscegenetic relationship is to have a romance set on an idyllic Pacific Isle with the hero and heroine both being visitors of European descent or, as discussed, having the Pacific Islander protagonist actually being of pure European descent but adopted and raised by Indigenous Islanders. In other words, same race coupling.

Lastly in this section on the Native First Kiss, one must realize there are other hypocritical contradictions in American South Seas movies besides being able to have a socially accepted affair with a Polynesian woman on the islands but not with a fellow Euro-American woman on the continent, especially during the first half of the last century. Another hypocrisy is the acceptance of exposure of Polynesian nudity, but for some reason Euro-American nakedness in these films intended for general audiences is not only intolerable but illegal. In pre–Code and post–Code Pacific Island movies, as we discussed earlier, we find a lot of nudity and semi-nudity of the Polynesian form, but theoretically if one places a Euro-American woman dancing alongside a Polynesian female in a sexual and semi-nude Indigenous performance, that film would not have even made it to the screen, especially for general audiences. Consequently, even a misrepresented Polynesian maiden played by a brownface Euro-American actress was never filmed nude or semi-nude, but two Latin actresses were: Delores del Rio in *Bird of Paradise* (1932) and Rosenda Monteros in *Tiara Tahiti* (1962).

Classic film director Robert Flaherty had to ask permission from chiefs and fathers to photograph certain young women of the islands topless for his early 20th-century South Seas movies (Calder-Marshall). At this time, missionaries had been on the islands for four generations, and the local adolescent Indigenous females had not run around the islands nearly naked for some time. In her Ph.D. thesis, Carolyn O'Dwyer also concluded this fact regarding the making of Flaherty's 1928 *White Shadows*:

> The film shows Samoan women bare-breasted, despite the fact that Western modes of dress and Christian ideas about modesty had been widely adopted. In choosing to display them thus, Flaherty was adhering to a widespread existent tradition in popular ethnography as well as to persistent notions about the erotic excess of Polynesia.

In his early films, Flaherty's wife came along to assist him with film production. Would Flaherty, at this time, dare or even consider asking permission of his father-in-law to photograph his wife topless for one of his films?

These double standards in the film depiction of the "Other" or non–Caucasoid bodies is summarized in Pulitzer Prize-winning film critic Roger Ebert's poignant review of the film *Rapa Nui:*

> *Rapa Nui* slips through the *National Geographic* Loophole. This is the Hollywood convention which teaches us that brown breasts are not as sinful as white ones, and so while it may be evil to gaze upon a blond *Playboy* centerfold and feel lust in our hearts, it is educational to watch Polynesian maidens frolicking topless in the surf. This isn't sex; it's geography.
> For years in my liberal youth, I thought this loophole was racist, an evil

double standard in which white women were protected from exposure while "Native" women were cruelly stripped of their bras....

Pacific Island scholar Alex Mawyer also documented this American moral contradiction in his early paper on Pacific Film in 1997's "From PŌ to AŌ: A Historical Analysis of Filmmaking in the Pacific" (p. 40).

Later in the 20th century two extreme national media instances illustrated this racist and hypocritical practice of exposing the female Polynesian body versus the exposure of the Euro-American female body. Case #1: The already discussed movie *The Bounty* (1984), with its highly sexual dance scene and toplessness throughout, was released in America with only a "PG" rating and in Canada with a "G" rating. Mothers and fathers are urged to give parental guidance at "PG" pictures, but anyone is admitted to an exhibition of a PG or G film without adult supervision. In America and apparently in Canada, it is okay for a child to see half-naked Polynesians preforming copulation movements in dance, but they would definitely not be allowed to view Euro-American or Euro-Canadian performers doing the same thing on the silver screen. Amazingly, 10 years later another South Seas movie with copious Native nudity, *Rapa Nui*, was assigned an "R" rating, stipulating that at least adults or parents now had to accompany children to see the film.

Case #2: In 1980, a primetime made-for-TV movie aired across America on CBS titled *Gauguin the Savage*, staring David Carradine (as Gauguin), Lynn Redgrave (as Gauguin's wife Mette) and Edwige Taie (as Teha'amana, Gauguin's young Tahitian mistress). In real life, the painter Gauguin lusted after young Tahitian girls around 13 to 14 years old. His main vahine, Teha'amana, was 13 when they first started living together. Teha'amana was the subject of many of Gauguin's nude paintings, which are now found in prestigious museums throughout the world. Edwige Taie, the Tahitian actress who played Teha'amana, appeared to be about the same age, an early teenager. In one scene in the TV movie, it was obvious Gauguin was painting Teha'amana. As I watched this as a young man, I thought to myself, "Good, the shots are on Carradine and not the supposedly nude young Taie posing for the painting." But to my shock, the editor cut to a full frontal shot of a nude young Tahitian teenager on national TV during primetime. If young Taie were an American 14-year-old blonde from, say, Minnesota, the country would have been in an uproar. I was shocked that the director, editor, and the CBS executives in charge would let this happen. How did the the National Association of Radio and Television Broadcasters' self-regulating, industry-guided censor board[9] (similar to the film industry's MPAA, Motion Pictures Association of America, censors) and the Federal Communications Commission let this happen? I waited for America's reaction the next day—there wasn't any. Apparently, all these entities permitted this national exposure of full-frontal early teen nudity to occur, and the American mass audience did not stir, including the Christian silent majority.

The following is an example of a typical news article with commentary and interviews by some of the moviemakers of this TV-movie version of the Gauguin story. Obviously, this information was gathered from a press junket after the writer of the article had viewed the film. Here are some excerpts from the *Pittsburg Press* news article:

> [From the writer J.P. Miller]: "Aboriginal (sic) nudity, with no sexual enticement." [From Executive producer Robert Wood]: "He (Gauguin) was a womanizer but he did seek the truth and he reflected that truth as he saw it in nudity. To do a film and deny that would have been to destroy the man." [From the author of the article Barbara Holsopple, TV/Radio Editor]: "The brief scenes of nudity are inherent to the drama and are done in good taste; in fact, one hardly notices them, so much a part of the story are they."

Even though American society will not admit it, for American audiences all nudity has a built-in sexual enticement, even aboriginal nudity. It is common knowledge that many young boys in America have their first desire for sex aroused when exposed to nude ethnographic photos of women of "other" races in *National Geographic* magazine. Even so, full frontal underage nudity of a person of any race needs no associated enticement to still be inappropriate for such unrestricted and unwarranted nationwide exposure, especially without any warning of such nudity beforehand. We can't destroy a man that destroyed himself— Gauguin arguably sought child nudity and sex, and this film exploits and condones this behavior. The editor of the article hardly notices a young teen's full-frontal nudity? It is hard to believe. Nevertheless, these are typical hypocritical attitudes from Hollywood and in America in general.

6

Sexual Appropriation
White Women in Grass Skirts

There is a very revealing image on a lobby card from the movie *Away All Boats* (1956) featuring George Nader and Julie Adams. This beautifully illustrated poster represents an early scene in the movie right before the Pearl Harbor attack and America's involvement in World War II. Nader's character is a very competent merchant marine, who has sailed the Pacific regions for years. Soon after the Pearl Harbor attack, many experienced men were called up to serve, including Nader's character. The image in question, displaying imported American popular culture icons of the Pacific in an American home (the embodiment of Tiki Culture), has an erroneous timeline. In America and in World Word II Axis and Allied countries where the modern Tiki popular culture has developed, the Tiki or Polynesian Pop (Popular) culture phenomenon was solidified by experiences in the World War II Pacific Theater after the Second World War,[1] not before, as the timeline suggests in this poster and in the movie.

Besides the chronology, *Away All Boats* illustrates this movement or appropriation of Pacific cultures into American pop culture perfectly: the ukulele playing, the Pacific Island trinkets, the symbolic ceramic tiki mugs, the leis and, more importantly for this chapter, Nader's pretty wife Julie Adams' "sexy" hula outfit. But again, this image more approximates an American home following the conclusion of World War II with war veterans returning home with their island souvenirs *after* their positive Pacific war ventures, psychologically leaving their dramatic, negative, violent war memories back on particular islands of battle. This mid-century film, *Away All Boats*, although set during World War II, was made in a period in American history (1956) after the war when the Polynesian pop culture was thriving in America. The incorrect time frame here is further illustrated with the aforementioned ceramic tiki mug, an invention in America[2] after World War II.

Away All Boats (1956, Universal International Pictures). The poster shown above, which features actor George Nadar and his lovely wife, played by Julie Adams, not only displays the early love of anything from the Pacific in a mid-century American home but also more specifically exhibits the appropriation of the sexy hula skirt by women who are not Polynesian. American lobby card (11" × 14").

Back to the focus of this chapter and book, sexualization. The hula skirt is very symbolic of this precept. The semi-revealing of bare legs, ascending up towards the female hips, has had the sexual imaginations of men racing for centuries. This lobby card or small movie poster also exemplifies another paradigm, a sexualized one—the "Other" in a grass skirt—or the appropriation of the Polynesian grass skirt, which generates sexual desire in men. An important insertion here is that the intent of a woman in donning the grass skirt is not identified in this definition of this sexualized concept, but rather the male arousal caused by this Polynesian attire is the significance of this tome. It is clear in this poster image that George Nader's character's gaze is on his wife's hula skirt with the hip-swaying hula dance—an incidence I'm sure that was duplicated in many American homes. Reviewing the actual scene in the film further discloses this supposition of yearning for sexual desire, since near the end of the scene Nader suddenly jumps off the couch and almost attacks his wife with hugs and a sensual kiss, while adult audience members can easily imagine what happens next.

This precept of the "Other" wearing a hula skirt did not dawn on me until I visited a special and limited exhibition of Hawaiian Art Deco artwork of the early 20th century in the prestigious Honolulu Museum of Art[3] (formerly the Honolulu Academy of Arts). After viewing many classic and gorgeous works of Hawaiian-centered art from the time period, I encountered, in the last room of this exhibit, two beautiful paintings of blonde American women sensually wearing hula skirts. It made me curious because neither painting was done in Art Deco style; although the dates of these paintings were in the correct time frame, they were rendered in a more realistic style. Both feminine figures posed in a sexualized manner, tempting the viewer. Again, after seeing many other Art Deco paintings and sculptures, some with sexualized images but all with Polynesian subjects, the images caused me to ponder. The two early 20th-century artworks in question, with blonde Euro-American women, signified what was happening throughout American and other parts of the world. This precept of the "Other" or foreigner in a grass skirt is perpetuated not only in homes but in other forms of popular art, e.g., chalk figurines and sheet music covers. Later in that century, popular artists flourished, like Alberto Vargas, Earl Moran, and Gil Elvgren, with the "pin-up girl" art style. Among the main subjects of these and many other amateur artists or imitators of this style (for example, World War II bomber nose art, tattoo art, or blue-collar calendar art) were sexy Caucasian women in grass skirts. There is even a retro movement of this art style today led by artist Garry Palm, whose claim to fame is the sexy Euro-American female in a sexy grass skirt.

How this recurring image of the outsider in a grass skirt connects to American film is clearly illustrated by America's pin-up girl herself, Betty Grable. The blonde actress slips on the grass hula skirt or the equally iconic and sexy South Seas sarong a few times on screen—first and most notably in *Tin Pan Alley* (1940). The title refers to West 28th Street between Fifth and Sixth Avenues in New York City (Wyeth). In the first half of the 20th century this section of New York City was known for its proliferation of music publishing, which at the time was a giant American mass media industry, not unlike the Hollywood film industry on the West Coast. Unfortunately, Tin Pan Alley is the origin of "Wiki Wacky Hula" music of the time. "Wiki Wacky Hula" is appropriately named because the clearly misappropriated Hawaiian language is used in vastly popular sheet music of the period. It was obvious, just by the use of correct or incorrect Hawaiian words in the title or in the lyrics of a song, where Hawaiian sheet music was published, either in Honolulu or New York City. This film perfectly chronicled this misappropriated language and dance because the main song of this movie is a wacky Hawaiian tune "Hawaii, [pronounced Ha•why•ya] Lovely Hawaii." The last lyrics of the song are: "I'm just wacky about the beach at Waikiki."

One of the most memorable scenes in the film depicts blonde stars Betty Grable and Alice Faye playing two vaudeville[4] sisters recruited to perform the future hit. They wear sexy cellophane hula skirts and perform hula and tap dance moves, singing and dancing the song on a New York City stage to a rousing applause. A shot of the two starlets in sexy hula skirts is the main image of the film on its posters and in publicity photos, with full leg exposure. This film, along with *Down Argentine Way* (1940), helped catapult Grable to stardom. Soon after becoming America's pin-up girl during World War II, the 20th Century–Fox studio made her don the cellophane hula skirt once again on film, but this time in a movie in living color with a huge production budget. While *Alley* was set on the East Coast of the U.S., Betty's new film, *Song of the Islands* (1942), was set in the Pacific itself, on the tiny fictitious Hawaiian Island, Ami Ami Oni Oni Isle. The name of the island could very well be referencing the 'ami and 'oni, which could be interpreted as a hula hip move with lots of wiggling or stirring. But this is neither a real Hawaiian phrase nor a real hula movement; rather, it is a made-up one, like the Hollywood hula move it represents.

As mentioned, Grable's character is born on the island. Somehow, her poor Irish father owns half of the isle. He also has loyal Native laborers who help raise the very fair and blonde Grable and teach her island ways, including music and dance. Of course, most of these songs and hulas are of Hollywood origin, with her famous "million dollars legs" showing through her hula skirt. To be fair, one could observe in the film many real Hawaiian hula dancers and many proper hula moves by Ms. Grable and her Native village companions. The final big Hollywood hula number, *O'Brian Has Gone Hawaiian*, is actually a clever fusion of Hawaiian and Irish cultures in its lyrics and dance styles.

In another hula dance number, Grable can be seen purposefully exposing as much leg as possible within the dance choreography and wearing thinly striped leaf or "grass skirts." Without today's technical advances of viewing film like "pause" and "rewind" for personal use, these calculating sensual dance moves would be missed but their sexual intentions will still be felt. Many other authentic young and fit Native hula dancers (who were living in Southern California at the time) join Grable wearing the same, much-leg-revealing grass skirt outfits. In

Hawai'i, hula dancers have multi-layer grass or whole ti leaf skirts to minimize the leg exposure. Striped leaves are more commonly used in the tourist trade, resulting in the same sexualized costuming. Beyond the leg-baring moves, the words of the theme song "Ami Ami Oni Oni Isle" set a romanticized (for adults meaning sexualized) environment. Here are some samples of the song's lyrics: "Mr. Cupid goes to town … down on Ami Ami Oni Oni Isle," "Everybody feels terrific and romantically prolific," "When you're underneath the banyan with a beautiful companion, close your eyes and dream it up for a little while," "When the breezes begins a blowing and the (grass) skirts to and froing there is a tricky little wicky in her smile, no Melani (a typical Island woman's name) turns a *kāne* (man) down, down on Ami Ami Oni Oni Isle." Despite the set up that main island of the film is sexualized, the huge success of this film elevated Grable to be Hollywood's highest paid film star (unusual for an actress) and a consistent box office draw (McGee).

A later Grable film is *My Blue Heaven* (1950), which is set in mainland America and is about traveling musical performers. In one major stage number, Grable plays an Islander and dons a two-piece tight sarong with a slit up from the bottom, and she lifts up the skirt to show her bare legs. The other faux or staged Polynesian maidens of her village also bare as much leg as possible and are each accompanied by U.S. sailors as lovers. Her husband in the story, Dan Dailey, sings as a Euro-American visitor surrounded by beautiful Island women. Then Grable pops out of a hut, now wearing an Art Deco style Pacific Island white feathered outfit, with the shortest possible feathered skirt. This musical stage scene is in high contrast to the actual main storyline of the film, about two parents who lost their first offspring and struggle to adopt a new child. Despite the tragic story, Hollywood still manages to sneak in a Polynesian sexualized sub-plot. Back to the staged South Seas scene, even more grass skirted Euro-American female dancers converge on the island stage. As a sub-note, Grable was not only a sex symbol but also a noted dancer, which many people seem to forget. As in *Song of the Islands,* she does do some authentic hula steps in her Hollywood hulas, which she integrates well with steps from other cultures.

Another huge female star known to don the cellophane grass skirt is tapdancing phenom Eleanor Powell. In *Ship Ahoy* (1942), the blonde actress is a featured hula dancer for a big band on a cruise ship. In *Honolulu* (1939), Miss Powell dances three big hula numbers, two with decent interpretations of the hula dance. The third was an obvious Hollywood-style hula number, because it included her tapdancing skills. Eleanor Powell also appeared in a hula skirt in *The Great Morgan*

(1946). These three films featured Powell and her long legs wearing the Hollywood hula skirt standard of thin white cellophane strips, with the associated back light to help accentuate feminine hips and legs. The first two, *Ship Ahoy* and *Honolulu*, featured Powell's legs within and out of her hula skirt in most of the films' official stills and posters—an obviously objectifying advertising ploy to attract audiences to the theaters.

But before 20th Century–Fox and MGM put Betty Grable and Eleanor Powell, respectively, in grass skirts, Paramount Pictures had Dorothy Lamour in a sarong.[5] The sarong is synonymous with the grass skirt, especially for the purposes of this writing. Both are symbolic of the sensualized Pacific Island female dress of a Hollywood starlet playing a brownface Native or a non–Native visiting or raised in the islands, to tantalize the screen audiences. Born in New Orleans, Louisiana, as Mary Leta Dorothy Slaton, Ms. Lamour was famously dubbed the "Sarong Girl" of Hollywood. In fact, later in her career she and Hollywood producers made fun of it. In *Star-Spangled Rhythm* (1942), intended as a USO film to boost the morale of real troops during World War II, Lamour, along with Paulette Goddard and Veronica Lake, sing a dejected song of unhappy ladies of the silver screen: "...we're sorry that we came, for our only claim to fame is a sweater [Goddard], a sarong [Lamour], and a peek-a-boo bang [Lake]." Three typecast sex symbols of Paramount Studios complain in song to hundreds of disappointed and silent naval shipmen ready to deploy overseas. Goddard was known for her tight little sweaters; Lake, for her sexy dresses and hair covering half her face (some say the sexy female animated character, Jessica Rabbit, was modeled after Veronica Lake. In this film it is easy to see why). Lastly, Lamour wears her ever-associated tight, short-fitting sarong, and she is feeling sad because of it. No wonder the silence.

In a later film, *On Our Merry Way* (1948), Dorothy sings a song satirizing her career as a Polynesian sarong-clad goddess, appropriately entitled "The Queen of the Hollywood Islands." The stage set features South Seas cinema icons, palm trees, sandy beach, muscular Native men, exotic drumbeats and, of course, a sexy sarong. Some of the lyrics were very representative of her faux Hollywood Polynesian maiden characters, e.g.: "She couldn't even sing aloha, they had to get a guy to show-ha."[6] Much later, in 1964, Lamour sang a tune in *Pajama Party*, criticizing the dress and dance of the new beach culture movement, singing about things back in her day, like dressing in sarongs and dancing the hula. She did not wear a sarong in this scene, nor in *Donovan's Reef* (1963). The older and less petite Lamour then donned a muʻumuʻu[7] in this South Seas movie. In *Donovan's Reef*, as in many of her Pacific pictures, in Lamour's ethnic background is not revealed.

The most significant film illustrating Dorothy Lamour's sexy, sarong-girl stereotyping is the film *St. Louis Blues* (1939). In a sense, this story's plot is surprising because it's as if Paramount Pictures confesses what they are doing to Dorothy Lamour's pigeonholed career. Miss Lamour is still young in this film but already typecast. She still has more "sarong" movies to do at this point. In *Blues* Dorothy plays a Broadway star stereotyped to play only a South Seas girl, believe it or not. She runs away from her publicity obligations and ends up aboard a Mississippi river showboat. There she eventually falls for the captain, who has no idea who she is. Sadly, the Captain (Lloyd Nolan) has always had a dream, to stage a South Seas musical, and thinks Lamour would be perfect for the lead. He imagines his new girl wearing a sarong in the role. Sadly, Lamour concedes to Nolan's dreams, and she even helps direct the onboard musical. The dialog near the opening of the film between Lamour and her producer is noteworthy for the purposes of this chapter. Some examples appear below in screenwriting format:

PRODUCER
Now you paint your legs and get into your sarong.

NORMA (defiantly)
Why don't you have that thing [the sarong] tattooed on me!

PRODUCER
Oh Norma, please don't be cross.

NORMA (angry)
I am not cross. I'm just tired of undressing to appear
in public and dressing to go to bed at night. I'm disgusted and sore.

PRODUCER
Oh, with me?

NORMA
Yes, with you! Nobody recognizes me with my clothes on.
Soon the Producer gets angry in this scene:

PRODUCER
Norma, this is a business proposition. I've created an illusion
about you that makes us plenty of money. At the moment
you're the world's most profitable peep-show.
Now stop this nonsense and get into that sarong!

Lamour is still defiant in the scene, but the producer reminds her of her signed contract. Perhaps Paramount thought they could get away with this plot by positioning Lamour as a Broadway star, not a Hollywood leading lady. The Producer here is clearly emblematic of Hollywood itself. As stated before, in chapter 5, "sex sells."

"Lamour is defined both in terms of the sarong and in terms of her alleged rejection of the sarong. This opposition would follow her for the rest of her career" (de Seife). In 1946, just prior to the shooting of Paramount Studio's comedy/mystery *My Favorite Brunette* (1947), in a publicity stunt obviously dreamed up by the studio's P.R. department, Dorothy Lamour staged a memorable exploit. She burned a sarong in front of fans and the press.

The popularity of Lamour and her sarongs can never be more represented as in the film *Gung Ho* (1943), a South Seas World War II yarn. In a cramped submarine, a sergeant of a group of Marines hands out a map of islands to his men. The men grumble—they were hoping instead for something like a picture of a pin-up girl. Angry at their attitude, the sarge huffs: "What did you expect, movin' pictures of Dorothy Lamour on those islands!" Self-reflective cinema: A South Seas picture referring to South Seas pictures. Of course, Dorothy Lamour did make a lot of South Seas sarong films, at times as a Native, at times as an outsider raised on an island with island culture, and at times her character's ethnic origins were purposefully left ambiguous. Some of her "sarong" films are *Jungle Princess* (1936), *The Hurricane* (1937), *Her Jungle Love* (1938), *Road to Singapore* (1940), *Typhoon* (1940), *Aloma of the South Seas* (1941), *Beyond the Blue Horizon* (1942), *Rainbow Island* (1944), and *Road to Bali* (1952). She even wears a sarong in the snow in *Road to Utopia* (1946), when Bob Hope naughtily imagines her wearing a sarong in the snows of Alaska as she approaches him. Lastly, Lamour dons not a sarong but the strangest spiky hula skirt in a South Seas circus number in the film classic *The Greatest Show on Earth* (1952).[8]

Another momentous film where the "Other" wears a grass skirt is the silent *Hula* (1927), starring one of Hollywood's first sex symbols, the famous flapper known as the "It Girl," Clara Bow. First mentioned in Chapter 4, Bow, like Grable in *Song of the Islands* (1942), is a plantation owner's daughter raised by the Native help. Bow would rather wear the grass skirt instead of "Western" clothes, which reflects her carefree island attitude. Her grass skirt and semi bare legs are all over the publicity photos and posters for *Hula,* a coup for the studio because in the 1920s the exhibition of so much leg was very unusual: using the "ethnographic excuse" for minimum dress, even for a non–Indigenous person, was an accomplishment for the sales department of Paramount Pictures. She dances an inauthentic hula at a family gathering of the "white" social elite of the islands. With her swaying hips, a few alluring winks, and exposed legs through the grass skirt, she manages to attract two men in the crowd with much sexual tension in the air.

The Hawaiian Islands were a popular subject for Americans in the early 1900s. It was a territory of the United States, and powerful forces in America wanted to make sure the country knew that fact, with hardly any information about how the annexation of Hawai'i came about. Political, military, educational (or the lack of), and private entities such as the tourism, commerce, sugarcane and pineapple industries—and indirectly entertainment businesses (i.e., music and film), along with the advertising and publicity trades—helped make this omission of information or nationwide ignorance possible. As mentioned, at this time, Hawaiian song sheets and music were the craze, whether authentic or not, and South Seas cinema was becoming more popular. Learning to play the ukulele for young American men and learning to dance the hula for American young females were national fads in the early 1900s. Even innocent, popular six-year-old Shirley Temple donned only the hula skirt and a lei in 1935's *Curly Top*. If you dance the hula you have to have a hula shirt. While one should not rely on one piece of film to know the true facts of historical events of a certain society, one can better ascertain historical social norms through a number of stills and moving images of that same time period. With the films mentioned throughout this chapter, one can surmise the prevalence of the ukulele and the hula skirt in America, especially in the first half of the 20th century.

A few films mentioned in Chapter 5 were about the inauthentic hula dances originating on the mainland U.S. But not mentioned was the intent of these films, not just to appropriate Hawaiian culture elsewhere but to sensualize these dances for general film audiences, even if the women wearing those alluring skirts were not of Polynesian ethnic backgrounds. *Dance, Girl, Dance* (1940), starring popular and beautiful young Hollywood starlets Maureen O'Hara and Lucille Ball, was a film on how the hula dance craze was more popular to learn, at that time, than more "proper" dances like ballet. This film also shows the darker side of the hula and its accompanying grass skirt, via profiteering by questionable men in the adult entertainment business. Apparently, while learning the dance and wearing a hula grass skirt was popular and cute for female youngsters, learning to dance as a young adult while wearing the same skirt was sensualized and profitable.

Others' films have shown this adult entertainment atmosphere with the grass skirt (and what is behind the grass) as the main attraction in their shady businesses. This adult faux hula and the inauthentic origins of its performers can be found in: *Blood Money* (1933), *Ever Since Eve* (1937), *Sarong Girl* (1943), *Mildred Pierce* (1945), *My Dream Is*

Yours (1949), *The Frightened City* (1961), and *Dime with a Halo* (1963). In *Mystery Streets* (1950) there is even an adult hula club called "The Grass Skirt." This appropriation of the female outsider in a grass skirt doing some kind of hula still happens relatively recently, such as in *Runaway Bride* (1999) or *A Guy Thing* (2003).

In the 1949 released film *My Dream Is Yours* we even find wholesome Doris Day dancing the hula in a two-piece sarong with a man flirting with her as she sways by his table in an adult drinking club. She politely smiles then ignores his continued inappropriate advances. His female dinner companion has had enough and jealously throws her drink in Doris' face. Doris then runs in disgrace. It was the man that deserved the splash in the face, but not in male Hollywood. Here, the hula entertainer is lower in status and dignity than an older, heavy-set, rude and publicly unfaithful husband. The connotations of an adult wearing a grass skirt in the first half of the American 20th century was not only that of sexuality in private, but in public it carried the stigma of a harlot, no matter what race wore the Polynesian skirt.

Later in the century, the sexualized grass skirt was appropriated into the tourist industry of the islands. This is illustrated in the contemporary film *Just Go with It* (2011), in which both female visiting stars (Jennifer Aniston and Nicole Kidman) have to wear the ubiquitous grass skirt and its equally ubiquitous accompanying coconut shell bikini top, so both are subject to what is in essence an objectified beauty contest with howling men in the audience.

Also, during this time, Caucasian hula dancers at frat parties were also common in American cinema. One film stands out because the female lead also wants to stand out and does so in an impromptu Hollywood hula dance in *Pumpkin* (2002). In a sorority scene, a blonde Christina Ricci and other freshmen pledges are in hula outfits sensuously dancing a faux hula. Ricci is especially risqué. There are lots of shots of Ricci bending over, showing her cleavage, and shaking her upper torso, and lots of shots of the senior jocks' gaze taking it all in. A famous frat party in which many participants don the grass skirt, including the two male leads John Cusack and Anthony Edwards, is in *A Sure Thing* (1985). Nicollette Sheridan (later a co-star in the *Desperate Housewives* TV series), who plays "The Sure Thing," wears a sexy sarong. Other Polynesian-themed frat parties in American cinema, as mentioned in Chapter 4, feature the grass hula skirt, which is almost obligatory as costumes in these scenes.

Euro-American Hollywood beauties or sex symbols are shown in films clad in grass skirts. In *Primitive Love* (1964), sex symbol Jayne Mansfield wears one, and so does Shirley Ross, opposite Bing Crosby, in

Waikiki Wedding (1937). Comedienne Martha Raye also wears a grass skirt in the latter, but somehow Shirley Ross shows much more leg. Not only does Ava Gardner don the skirt in *The Little Hut* (1957), but studio publicity releases emphasize that the grass skirt was designed by famed fashion designer Christian Dior. Along these lines, Dorothy Lamour's sarongs were designed by multi-Academy Award-winning designer Edith Head. Unlike the design simplicity of a grass skirt, apparently Lamour's simple wrap was more complicated. How? It was specifically designed in detail for Lamour to accentuate her body and sex appeal (McInnes). "Why don't you have that thing tattooed on me"!—as an earlier line of Lamour dialog notes in this chapter regarding Dot's trademark, the very feminine, form-fitting outfit.

Another interesting occurrence in Hollywood, especially from the

The Hurricane (1937, United Artists). This film made stars out of Jon Hall and Dorothy Lamour, whose Native characters kiss and embrace above while an angry Captain Jerome Cowan looks on. The captain is angry because Dorothy has just been caught as a stowaway. This popular film, produced by Samuel Goldwyn, unusually features two Polynesians in love while the whole outside world seems to scheme to break them up. The film might be better known for its special effects hurricane that breaks up the couple's whole island, but it is also known for Miss Lamour's minimalistic sarongs. American lobby card (11" × 14").

1930s till the 1960s, is that it seemed almost every aspiring actress who came to Tinseltown needed a portfolio photo of herself in a sexy grass skirt. There is much empirical evidence of this. Through the years, I observed many such photographs on the Internet or at collectors shows. Even established actresses who did not appear in a South Seas film as a Native will certainly have a publicity photo along these lines in her portfolio. I assume that this is to show the sexiness of an actress, without coming off as a soft porn model or trashy. For some reason, at this time, American society did not deem a Hollywood grass skirt or sarong clad photo to be tasteless as it did earlier in the century with adult club hula dancers. I also suspect that male-dominated agents and managers in Hollywood require this type of sexy attire in their clients' portfolios. The selling of sex by the studios and the selling of the sex appeal of their female clients by Hollywood agents go hand-in-hand.

Another observation is that the vast majority of the feminine "Others" who don the grass skirt onscreen wear them in a scene set on the continent. In film, only a few Euro-American females "go Native" at the islands for two reasons. The first is that most female visitors who end up visiting the islands are fiancées, wives (some married to preachers or missionaries) or simply stereotypical high society pompous ladies or prudes who wouldn't dare reveal too much to the public or to the audience, no matter how hot or humid a Pacific Island can be. This is intentional in scripts as a high contrast to the Islanders, because the baring of skin is usually left to the Native women. The second reason why few white women on the islands do put on the sarong or grass skirt is because, as established earlier, not too many Euro-American females have romantic lead roles in South Seas yarns, which tend to be male-dominated.

One of the few who do go Native in dress is Frances Farmer in *South of Pago Pago* (1940). In that story, Farmer is a hardened blonde American who was aligned with pearl thieves, but she falls for the Native prince of the island, Jon Hall. Later she not only sympathizes with the Natives, but also goes Native, donning a sexy sarong. *Pearl of the South Pacific* (1955) with Virginia Mayo has a similar plot, but in this story, Mayo confesses to the island prince that she was already married to one of the pearl thieves. Mayo and her husband both change their ways, support the Natives, and ask for forgiveness. Blonde Mayo also goes Native, putting on a two-piece sarong. In *Adventure Island* (1947), Rhonda Fleming borrows a sarong from an Islander and steals the screen and all the publicity print for the movie with her beauty and skimpy Native outfit. Also stealing the publicity print in her sexy sarong was Patricia Medina in 1954's *Drums of Tahiti*.

There were many "outsider" men on Pacific Islands who wore either a grass skirt or a lava lava—a simple short wrap, which complements a sarong, and which is both a modern invention used to cover Polynesian male Indigenes, especially in film, and is now adapted by Native Islanders in real life. It appears that there is a very distinct motivation behind the two types of male outfits. In the American perspective, in South Seas cinema, a man who wears a grass skirt does so in a mocking, comic, or drunken manner. This outfit usually is supplemented with the omnipresent coconut bra. Many drunken naval men involved in a Honolulu bar fight were caught wearing this attire as in *Operation Pacific* (1951). Luther Billis, the famous naval character in *South Pacific* (1958), not only traded grass skirts but also wears one as he dons a feminine Polynesian persona in a stage play to entertain the troops. As an example of simple comic relief, Rob Schneider dressed as a female Native, including a coconut bra, in *50 First Dates* (2004); Pauly Shore dons the grass skirt in the comedy *Bio-Dome* (1996); so does Ronald Shiner in the British World War II comedy *Up to His Neck* (1954). By considering the grass skirt to be "feminine," the above may be examples of homophobia by mocking males who don this grassy aboriginal garb.

A much more interesting subject is the image of the other male Native outfit, the lava lava. It seems frequently in American film, when a Euro-American or European male character wears a lava lava on a Pacific Isle, it signifies a "going Native" attitude or empathy towards the Native, much like Farmer or Mayo above. They are literally making a fashion statement. This is an atypical occurrence in a South Seas film. It denotes total disenfranchise from one's origins, true escapism, freedom and more importantly, acceptance of his new home and culture or a denial that his former society is the better life. It expresses understanding of true Native ways, as not inferior, not less intelligent, but a life that works for him, a life and society that he truly accepts. Most foreign characters like this in a film's storyline are found to be sincere and accepted by the Natives. These characters are infrequent in American film because of their anti–American attitudes. Note, of the following short list of these films, only two are American characters. Those uncommon male Euro-American or European leads who "go Native" are Robert Preston in *Typhoon* (1940), Tyrone Power in *Son of Fury* (1942), Louis Jourdan in *Bird of Paradise* (1951), James Mason in *Tiara Tahiti* (1962), Troy Donahue in *South Seas Massacre* (1974), and Mel Gibson, who plays Fletcher Christian in *The Bounty* (1984).

I previously observed that other Euro-American characters who are at first sympathetic to the Islanders' struggles either turn into drunken beachcombers or madmen. Remarkably, both of these character types always keep their "Western" attire. In later, more modern plots, sympathetic expatriates like John Wayne in *Donovan's Reef* (1963) don't dress Native because the storyline is set after World War II, when most Natives have gone "Western" in their attire. Finally, other understanding expats keep the attire of their origins because they are ship's captains and their boats, not the island, are their homes. George Houston in *Wallaby Jim of the Islands* (1937) and Gary Cooper in *Return to Paradise* (1953) are good examples of this concept.

7

Other World War II Conquests

Prostitution in the Pacific

While the evolution of the image of the Polynesian female, as discussed in Chapter 3, went from free sex to sex-as-trade to sex-as-prostitution, this chapter will analyze a different "Siren of the South Seas" or the cinematic stereotype of an imported laborer to the Pacific Islands, the woman with a "questionable past" or the prostitute. Different, because as with the previous chapter, this chapter will focus on Euro-American women, more specifically, Caucasian women in the Pacific Islands who are participating in the sex trade. Obviously, there were also some prostitutes of Polynesian and Asian descent, but for the focus of this chapter and the reality of Hollywood representation, the vast majority of characters of "ill repute" and a questionable past in South Seas pictures were fair-skinned Americans.

There is no individual and no profession more sexualized than that of the prostitute, for obvious reasons. The combination of a sex profession in the sensualized environment of a tropical Pacific Island is not only of huge sales value for Hollywood productions but also for the American publishing industry. In the print trade there were fewer limitations about prostitution and all of its facets, but in the film industry it was more forbidden to display this profession directly. This chapter will discuss how Hollywood disguised the sex trade while producing very popular movies centered on this vocation. Adding to this subject matter is the setting of the beautiful Pacific Isles, which was a profitable formula for the American film industry. It is often said that prostitution is the oldest profession. The validity of such a statement will not be discussed here, but what will be deliberated upon is this character type in South Seas cinema, along with some relevant historical background.

Although prostitution existed on the islands before World War II, it was not as widespread or open as during its heyday in said war. A smaller and more discreet industry existed in a few port cities in the

Pacific. Seemingly, wherever there were sailors (merchant or military, as well as whalers), there were also enterprising women. This was even more the case during World War II, especially in proximity to the docks of Pearl Harbor in Honolulu. Soon after an invasion (of another kind) of thousands of U.S. troops entering Honolulu, low morale occurred among many of these servicemen, as previously discussed in Chapter 6. The troops were searching for a sexy sarong-clad Dorothy Lamour–like woman and could not find her. This low morale, especially before combat in the Pacific Theater, is what Brawley and Dixon call "the sexual vacuum counternarrative" (p. 9).

During World War II the military controlled all aspects of Hawai'i's governance under martial law. Through this period, unofficially sanctioned illegal prostitution in Hawai'i was relegated only to the vicinity of Honolulu's Chinatown, where prostitution had been found before the war and is still somewhat found today. The local Honolulu Police vice squad was unofficially in charge of the trade and all major personnel involved with it, such as in-house madams and their call girls. A strict policy of where they could go, live, and privately date existed. The details of the trade are well documented in Chapter 3 of Bailey and Farber's *The First Strange Place: Race and Sex in World War II Hawai'i*, entitled, "Hotel Street Sex."[1] This trade was obviously sanctioned by the military and local police, given the fact that during the war the military controlled all transportation and who was transported. Thus, sex workers were labeled as "entertainers" on transport manifests and had to register as such with the Honolulu Police Department (Bailey and Farber p. 98).

This same anonymity of people in the sex trade was carried over into films of the Pacific. In most of the 20th-century's U.S. films, it was more of a taboo[2] to give a direct name to this profession in public. This is probably because of the conservative attitude and the simple reason that Americans would not have to explain prostitution to children. Also, although not mentioned in the Production Code, many notes from the Breen office to studios over scripts prohibited studios from using the term "prostitute." An article written by Russell Campbell of Victoria University of Wellington entitled "Prostitution and Film Censorship in the USA" mentions many of these notes or memos to the studios. Here are responses to some submitted South Seas movie scripts in these notes: "We feel that the girls could be characterised [sic] as B-girls, but it should be quite clearly and affirmatively established that they are not prostitutes" (*From Here to Eternity*, 1953); "The essence of the discussion consisted in our emphasis once more that Sadie should not be a prostitute" (*Miss Sadie Thompson*, 1953). The Code does state that the words "brothels" and "house of ill-fame," as well as depictions of them, cannot exist onscreen.

More examples from Campbell's article on this subject include *From Here to Eternity*: "As we explained the other day, we feel that this club has all the appearances of a house of prostitution"; *The Revolt of Mamie Stover*: "We think that the two or three scenes of servicemen cueing [sic] up to get into the 'Bungalow' will lend an unconvincing flavour [sic] to our protestations that this is not a brothel." In South Seas cinema "dates," "dance partners," "entertainers," and "women of questionable pasts" were a few euphemistic titles given to these women and simple names like "dance halls" and "clubs" substituted for brothels. Many of these feminine characters with a past were also found in popular books and plays, written by famous authors, before they appeared on the big screen. Literature did not have the strict prohibitions like those in American cinema's Production Code (perhaps because at the time the written word was considered to be more constitutionally protected by the First Amendment than movies were), so if there are doubts regarding many of these female characters' occupations, one just has to read the books where these roles originated: the word "prostitute" is clearly and literally spelled out.

One character was a very prominent figure in American popular media: Sadie Thompson. Sadie was a Honolulu prostitute trying to run away and change her life. She was first depicted in the successful short story *Rain* by Somerset Maugham, then a larger book and play augmented by John Colton and Clemence Randolph, which was based on Maugham's main character and story. Finally, there were three major films shot 26 years apart, all starring big-name actresses. The first, *Sadie Thompson* (1928), was a silent film starring Gloria Swanson. The studio, United Artists, was hesitant because of the nature of the main character but the books and stage play, at that time, did very well financially. The gamble paid off because just four years later the studio/distributor United Artists remade it as a talkie with Joan Crawford, a much better verbal actress than Swanson. This film, now titled *Rain* like the stage play and larger book, was also a success and it made Crawford's character, Sadie Thompson, a Hollywood icon with her then signature small, checkered outfit, wide white belt and white feathered boa. Later in mid-century Columbia Pictures released *Miss Sadie Thompson* (1953) with the so-called "Love Goddess" Rita Hayworth. Of all the Hollywood sex symbols during this period, Rita Hayworth had the most talent, and she needed it with her heavy character and co-stars Aldo Ray and the fine actor José Ferrer, who, in a four-year period, was nominated for a Best Actor Oscar three times, winning once.

Interestingly, that same year, 1953, the British released a sensualized South Seas film titled *Our Girl Friday* starring the UK's young sex symbol, Joan Collins. This typical South Seas story features four survivors of a sunken cruise ship—Collins is one of them, along with three single men. Collins manages to make an iconic hula grass skirt (see previous chapter) with lots of leg showing, a fresh flowery lei and wears a flower over her ear, all Polynesian style. One can imagine the male conflict and sexual tension on this island. Based on the book *The Cautious Amorist*, the film was released in the U.S. with a different title, *The Adventures of Sadie*. No doubt, the studio releasing this film had Sadie Thompson in mind for marketing purposes. Like many films about the "Other" in a grass skirt, Miss Collins' grass skirt and legs were splattered all over the film's posters and advertising.

I should mention, the original Sadie Thompson story was set way before World War II, with lots of aroused U.S. Marines, starving for Euro-American or European women at Pago Pago, a remote South Pacific outpost of America's empire. The writer of the original story, Somerset Maugham, infused the territorial capital of American Samoa with an abundance of rain, hence some of the ancillary titles for this narrative, as well as an additional story tool for tension. The same elements were in the 1953 version, but this mid-century film iteration was easily adapted to a World War II setting. Not much had changed in almost three decades in film regarding attitudes towards women, especially from the Hollywood perspective. In other words, there was not much difference, in Hollywood or in 150 years of real life, between the sex-starved enlisted men in the earlier era of ships of Pacific explorations and modern Marines in the 20th century stationed on Pacific Isles—both groups being ravenous wolves in a sheep's pen.

Another South Seas 1953 film featuring Honolulu prostitutes was the award-winning, critically acclaimed *From Here to Eternity*, Fred Zinnemann's silver screen adaptation of James Jones' U.S. National Book Award-winning 1951 novel. The film's entry in Wikipedia[3] states that it won eight Academy Awards out of 13 nominations and, "In 2002, *From Here to Eternity* was selected for preservation in the National Film Registry by the Library of Congress as being 'culturally, historically, or aesthetically significant.'" Set on O'ahu during World War II, the movie is also famous for probably the most passionate and romantic scene in film history, of Burt Lancaster and Deborah Kerr being washed over by a wave while kissing and embracing on a secluded Hawaiian beach (see poster image in chapter 1). What most people don't realize is the rest of the scene is full of internal rage and anger caused by Lancaster's accusations of Kerr based on hearsay that she has had various affairs in other military bases where she lived in the past. Not so romantic. Another huge issue in this storyline that most viewers don't realize is the large part Honolulu prostitutes play in this story.

Another star in *Eternity*, Montgomery Clift, falls for a "woman of the night," ironically played by future all-American wholesome TV mother Donna Reed.[4] As mentioned, in regard to anonymity or secrecy, in Hollywood film most of the career choices of these women were veiled or concealed by name. A child or pre-teen watching these South Seas siren films will probably not know the true nature of the employment of these ladies, but the adults will. For *Eternity*, Reed and many of her workmates have the appearance of being just dancers who will escort you onto a dance floor with a ticket. A very similar scene and circumstance appear in a rare South Seas cinema film noir titled *Hell's Half Acre* (1954). Although this dance floor and ticket setup was common in Honolulu's seedy Chinatown, there were also basic whorehouses with long lines running down the block of servicemen waiting for their eight minutes of sexual pleasure, especially when the fleet was in (Bailey and Farber). This common occurrence of our "greatest generation" was not only covered up by America in Hollywood plots but also in real life. An average American at the time would never see that experience in a newsreel or find it in a high school history textbook. Today, one could read about that assembly line sex only in obscure scholarly history texts in graduate or postgraduate university studies.

Another significant and powerful film regarding this veiled subject is *The Revolt of Mamie Stover* (1956). This 20th Century–Fox film stars another mid-century sex symbol, Jane Russell. The film starts off on the docks of San Francisco where police are escorting prostitute Russell out of town and into a freighter bound for Honolulu. Like fellow female thespians playing similar roles of this type onscreen, Russell also gives a powerful performance. The Raoul Walsh-helmed movie is loosely based on a self-published autobiography by former Honolulu call girl Jean O'Hara.[5] O'Hara's story not only exposes government corruption vis-à-vis regulating the sex-trade in Honolulu, but also entails her struggles as a woman entrepreneur. The same is true of Mamie Stover, except in the Hollywood version she is a skilled and fair businesswoman (not just in the sex trade but also in real estate). Stover becomes financially successful but loses it all at the end. Again, male-dominated Hollywood wants to keep men on top by not having successful female business role models in their films.

I will say that male locker room banter on this subject might not take on a serious tone, but all of the films discussed so far in this chapter were taken very seriously (except for the UK's *The Adventures of Sadie*) by Hollywood. These features had excellent writing, directing, and performances onscreen, and as previously noted, *Eternity* is one of only two movies in our genre to win the much-coveted Best Picture Oscar. More so, they should be must-see movies for most adults (who understand the underlying drama portrayed). Even John Wayne, the States' conservative all-American, has a serious and well-written scene with a prostitute in a seedy Honolulu setting during World War II. After a personal problem with his ex-wife and feeling sorry for himself, in the film *Sands of Iwo Jima* (1949) Wayne sits alone at a Honolulu bar. When a prostitute attempts to sit with him, he roughly snaps "Drift!" because he knows who she is and what she is trying to do. After calming Wayne down, she escorts him back to her apartment. There, Wayne catches her concealing a semi-neglected baby in another room. After a snide remark by Wayne, she retorts: "There are a lot of tougher ways to making a living than going to war." As a tough Marine, Wayne is taken aback by her comment. He then throws the money intended for her services into the crib and says, "So long." The down-and-out single mom is grateful and kisses him goodbye. Outside the apartment, Wayne is surprised by a Marine mate waiting for him to be done. Wayne says to him: "You can call off the dogs because I'm about five years smarter than I was five and a half hours ago." The scene wasn't a Christian morality lesson but a lesson that some women have it really tough out there and they should not be judged by the way they are trying to survive and provide for their families.

Amazingly, there are many other South Seas films with the subject matter of outsider women with questionable pasts on the islands. Most island prostitutes were former escorts elsewhere, some are running from the law but end up in the same or a worse predicament. With minimal education and no regular job experience, they usually end up working for a bad guy in a sleazy bar. The "prostitute in paradise" general theme of this chapter offers the high dramatic contrast between the outer beauty of the islands and the inner turmoil of the soul of near destitute and desperate female sex workers. For some, it's a different kind of escapism to an island far away, not escaping one's nine-to-five society, but trying to escape one's past and not really being able to ... no matter where one goes.

Sadly, there are unwanted sexual judgments throughout these storylines. No South Seas plot covers the story of how a woman becomes a prostitute in the first place. What was the true questionable past of these women, starting with their childhoods? These films cover the current struggles of these women, and one can be more sympathetic and less judgmental towards their characters and the women in real life they are portraying. No story covers the internal struggles of the life and judgment of a prostitute more than the Somerset Maugham's "Sadie" films. As discussed earlier, Sadie is on a faraway island with many sexually inflamed Marines and a zealous preacher unfairly telling her to repent after every friendly, not sexual, gesture she makes towards men. At the end, when the preacher converts Sadie to a truly repentant and emotional state, he rapes Sadie and commits suicide. We, as the audience, witness Sadie's struggles, when her soul is torn even more. No one can truly imagine how low she can feel.

Miss Sadie Thompson (1953, Columbia Pictures). **The third of three major motion pictures featuring famed novelist/playwright W. Somerset Maugham's infamous title character, a prostitute traveling through Samoa. This 1953 version stars the talented singer, dancer, and actress Rita Hayworth as Sadie. Miss Hayworth is pictured on the left in a happy, sexy pose to match her character, but there is much more inner turmoil in this story. This film also stars distinguished dramatic acters José Ferrer and Aldo Ray, exemplifying the seriousness of the movie's subject. The black-and-white insert photograph depicts Marine Sgt. Ray and a couple of other servicemen (including a not-famous-yet Charles Bronson) escorting Hayworth, to a local Samoan Hotel owned by an expatriate with many part–Samoan children. American lobby card (11" × 14").**

Some of the following Oceanic films with women who carry on this theme may not have the same budgets or production values of the previous films discussed in this chapter, but nevertheless their numbers prove how often prostitutes in the Pacific exist in real life and in South Seas films. Here is a list of a few more: *Victory (1919)*; *The Woman God Changed* (1921); *South Sea Love* (1923); *Driftwood* (1928); *Scarlet Seas* (1929), featuring silent film star Betty Compson as a Shanghai prostitute in a shipwrecked in Samoa story, co-starring a teenaged Loretta Young; *His Captive Woman* (1929); *Dangerous Paradise* (1930)—a remake of 1919's *Victory*; *Girl of the Port* (1930); *Painted Woman* (1932) with Spencer Tracy; *Port of Missing Girls* (1938) starring Betty Compson and Harry Carey; *Sinners in Paradise* (1938); *Seven Sinners* (1940) starring Marlene Dietrich and John Wayne; *South of Pago Pago* (1940); *Isle of Forgotten Sins* (1943), later renamed *Monsoon* (presumably a marketing ploy suggested by the successful films *The Hurricane* and *Rain)*; *South Sea Sinner* (1950) featuring Shelly Winters and Liberace in a remake of *Seven Sinners*; *Big Jim McLain* (1952) also starring Wayne; *Suicide Battalion* (1958); *Twilight for the Gods* (1958) starring Rock Hudson and Cyd Charisse on a ship from Tahiti to Hawai'i; and *The Naked and the Dead* (1958), based on Norman Mailer's novel.

These common scenes and characters of prostitution in the Pacific Islands and sexy grass-skirted Euro-American women from the last chapter are forms of sexualizing not the Polynesian but the islands themselves. Continuing with this concept, the following chapter discusses the tourist industry and one of the main themes of this business, as well as the film industry's "romance on the islands" cliché. This romance can come in many forms, from the person on the plane next to you, to a Native surfer, or a prominent descendant of a Euro-American plantation owner or an indigenous hotel worker at a posh resort, as in HBO's 2021 limited series *The White Lotus*. These possible romances are still promoted today, not on any particular island, but on the sensual islands of Polynesia.

8

The Greetings Continue

Romance in the Tourist Trade

South Seas films and television have perpetuated the notion of romance in the Pacific Islands since the beginning of mass media. Besides the title, a summary of the silent *The Love Trader* (1930) from the popular and well-established film/TV website IMDB (Internet Movie Database) describes this notion that the island itself is to blame for romantic misbehavior, not the visitor or tourist:

> "A woman, raised in the most-strict New England atmosphere, marries a stern, God-fearing sea captain and is thrown suddenly into the romantic, colorful and licentious atmosphere of a South Sea island outpost. With her inhibitions and repressed desires what will be her reaction to the charms of the sensuous of the beautiful tropic nights and the call of love?"

Pacific pictures are heavily derivative of plays, novels, pulp sex magazines, music and paintings, which all share this familiar theme. One of the early public relations stratagems of the 20th century was to develop national contests for free romantic trips to the Hawaiian Islands. The prototypical film for this concept is *Waikiki Wedding* (1937). Its plot has a PR man of a large island pineapple company, played by Bing Crosby, not only coming up with this romantic contest to the islands concept, but also arranging for newspaper and radio associates to cover the winning contestant's experience on the islands. There is a time limit and a disastrous possibility that the contest winner will go home without a romantic experience. If that is the case, it would be very bad national PR for the pineapple brand. Well, Crosby has his work cut out for him because the contest winner, played by pretty actress Shirley Ross, has been on the islands with her friend and escort played by comedienne Martha Raye for a few days and still has no suitors with little time left on her trip. Crosby concocts an outer island trip on a romantic sailboat. With his many local friends, he plots an island full of restless Natives and an erupting fake volcano. In the end Crosby and Ross

Waikiki Wedding (1937, Paramount Pictures). In this American lobby card (11" × 14"), we see escort comedienne Martha Raye on the left with the world's number one singer Bing Crosby in the center and his future love interest Shirley Ross on the right. The two women, wearing their Hawaiian grass skirts, are ready for romance as contest winners of their dream Hawaiian vacation. Miss Ross and Crosby, as the PR man from the island pineapple company that sponsored the contest, end up falling for each other in this island romance.

fall for each other and Crosby saves his job, despite the unethical conflict of interest.

In *Honolulu* (1939) Eleanor Powell meets what appears to be a handsome plantation owner on a ship to Honolulu, but in reality, this man, played by Robert Young, is actually a teen idol and a doppelganger of the plantation owner. The idol is trying to escape his fans and take a long-deserved break. The two identical looking men agree to switch places back in L.A. Now on the island, the movie star, who falls for Powell, tries to act like a local and play host by doing tourist things, like sightseeing and attending a luau. The lure and romance of the islands work, but the problem is the real plantation owner fails to tell the star he is engaged back on the islands.

It's A Date (1940) is similar to *Honolulu*—the romance between a young actress and a Euro-American pineapple king starts on the way over to Hawai'i on a cruise liner. The conflict here is the young actress has a domineering famous thespian mother, and they are not only competing for a part back home, but for the same island man, as well. In most of these pre–World War II films the characters are well-to-do because it was expensive to visit the Pacific Islands. The ships and hotels back then catered to first class travelers. Not so for the next film of romance and tourism.

In *Rhythm of the Islands* (1943), lead Allan Jones deliberately paints himself brown to help the local Islanders entertain the tourists as he runs a scam to sell their debt in the island. Jones and his partner are tricked in the first place by a realtor to buy the island with its potential, so the two go into much debt by borrowing to buy the isle. They soon realize there is no future there, but they owe lots of money. Meanwhile, one rich tourist family enjoys the little South Seas island very much, especially the wife, who says to the husband: "Oh Wilbur, the isle simply breathes romance. Can we buy it?" Jones plays a brown-painted Native chief as he tours the pretty rich daughter around.

In his fake local accent Jones takes her to a romantic setting near the ocean and serenades her in Hawaiian. He later flirts with her in his faux broken English. She responds: "I guess the male technique is the same the world over. The next thing, you know, you'll be wanting to rub noses. That's a funny way to kiss." Jones continues to play the naïve Native, and when he hears the key word, he gets excited: "Kiss. I like." She answers: "You would pick out that word." He starts to force himself on her. She quickly retorts: "Now, wait a minute, you're learning much too fast!" He kisses her anyway. Then, playing innocent, he explains: "Learn tourist boat, me see kiss." She breaks away and yells: "Class dismissed!" and heads for the shelter of the guesthouse. Of course, the truth comes out, all is somehow forgiven, and our Hollywood-imagined couple still gets engaged. Another island tourist finds romance and unbelievably, male Hollywood still gets the girl, despite such a dishonest ruse.

Because of the expense of traveling to the islands, many middle- and lower-class Americans, as depicted in *Waikiki Wedding*, entered the numerous contests sponsored by the tourism industry of the islands. Early television shows, like the movies, reflected this small part of the American historical experience with a variety of plots involving contests for comp excursions to Hawai'i.[1] A notable one was *The George Burns and Gracie Allen Show* (1950–58) in the episode titled "Free Trip to Hawai'i." Gracie hears on the radio about a contest to win a romantic trip for two to Hawai'i. She ponders about her long-time bachelor neighbor and a wardrobe lady at work whom she has also known for years. When she tries to set them up, her neighbor is very uncomfortable about the idea and worse, her co-worker is already married. Also worth noting is that Gracie Allen danced a pretty decent hula in trying to set the mood for her neighbor. She obviously had a good instructor. Hula lessons in her generation were all the rage, as mentioned in Chapter 6. So was Hawaiian music—Gracie's husband, George Burns, sang "A Little Grass Shack," while Gracie danced. Mr. Burns' correct pronunciation of Hawaiian words is commendable as well. From the 1930s till mid-century, one of the many Hawai'i music hits was the "Hawaiian War Chant," written by William Pitt Leleiohoku II and Johnny Noble, who also wrote "A Little Grass Shack." There is an all-Hawaiian lyric version for "War Chant" and surprisingly, many Americans learned that version with proper pronunciation. Various versions of this song can be viewed on the big and small screen.[2]

The next generation in America was epitomized by the music of Elvis Presley. Two of Elvis' big movie hits were set in Hawai'i: *Blue Hawaii* (1961) and *Paradise, Hawaiian Style* (1966). In both films, he sang Hawaiian tunes with a decent accent and with a little of his signature Mississippi and Tennessee intonation. Nonetheless, like almost all of his songs, these Hawaiian tunes could be heard in many American households. During this era, the Elvis generation of the mid–20th century, tourism in Hawai'i skyrocketed. Due to the American empire's ultimate assimilation, statehood and more affordable air travel, Hawai'i was even more accessible and all the rage in America; Elvis' films just added fuel to the fire. Coincidentally, both of these films mirror what was happening in Hawai'i with the growing strength of the tourist industry. In *Blue Hawaii* Elvis tries to persuade his mother to let him work in the growing tourism industry. His father is a pineapple executive and young Elvis wants to transition to a more contemporary Hawaiian business. He ends up driving tourists (all female, but of course) around as a sub-business to a travel agency in the heart of Waikiki.

In *Paradise, Hawaiian Style* Elvis is a helicopter pilot who, with his local business partner, played by actual Hawaii-born and raised James Shigeta,[3] tries to establish a new and original tourism enterprise with helicopters. Of course, Elvis has girlfriends on every major Hawaiian Island, who also work in the tourist trade, so he flies to the outer Hawaiian Islands trying to make deals with them all, offering insincere possibilities of a future romantic relationship. As *Blue Hawaii* was a giant commercial for O'ahu and Kauai, *Paradise, Hawaiian Style* was a commercial for all of the Hawaiian Islands and the state hospitality industry.

Other films exemplified the tourism industry in Hawai'i and

other Pacific Islands during this mid-century period. Another popular title of this era is *Gidget Goes Hawaiian* (1961), in which her gang has the "Waikiki" tourist experience, and the young men and women chase each other for romance. In *Tiara Tahiti* (1962), a British production set in Tahiti involving two British war veterans, one liberal who has gone Native and his conservative friend who represents a huge hotel conglomerate. They seek to build a large tourist hotel on the island, and there is a big clash over the possible change of the quiet island lifestyle.

Romance as a tourist theme continues on the islands, and it continues in filmmaking. Here are a few more relatively current South Seas films that reflect this enduring trend: *Goin' Coconuts* (1978), *Up from the Depths* (1979), *When Time Ran Out* (1980), *Baywatch: The Movie* "Forbidden Paradise" (1995), *Six Days Seven Nights* (1998), *Blue Crush* (2002), *Forgetting Sarah Marshall* (2008), *Nim's Island* (2008), *A Perfect Getaway* (2009), *Couples Retreat* (2009), *Into the Blue 2: The Reef* (2009), *Just Go with It* (2011), *Mike and Dave Need Wedding Dates* (2016) and *Wrong Missy* (2020). A few of these films may not have big romantic plot points, but tourism is a big part of the story. In fact, most current films of the islands are not period pieces but replicate the normal life of middle Americans, including trips to Hawai'i and the tourist experience. Most contemporary film stories include a hotel subsidized luau, a Polynesian review (a mix of dancing from various Pacific Island cultures), surfing, nightlife, and some romantic natural or artificial pool and/or waterfalls.

There is a scene in *Six Days Seven Nights* that sums up this romanticized island tourism concept well. Co-star David Schwimmer is on a romantic trip with his fiancée, played by Anne Heche. He goes all out and takes his betrothed on an expensive South Sea Island getaway to a place called Makatea, apparently a distant and small outlier island of French Polynesia. Although there is a real Makatea[4] in the Tuamotu Archipelago, the Makatea Island in the film is fictional. It seems as if just as they arrive to this paradisiacal getaway Heche is called by her desperate boss to go help produce a photo shoot in Tahiti. Schwimmer is bummed. He goes alone to a tourist dinner with a Polynesian review that he had already prepaid for as a couple. There, sitting by himself at a table for two, he witnesses many tourist couples having a romantic time. BUT all his troubles suddenly disappear when the lead Tahitian dancer is revealed on stage with her minimal outfit, her slow rhythmic movement, what appears to be a direct sexy glare, and the seemingly obligatory hula hand gesture that signifies "come to me" aimed towards our tourist Schwimmer. Schwimmer falls for it and falls for the dancer.

While unaware his fiancée has just crash-landed on a remote South Seas isle, Schwimmer crashes into bed with the lead Tahitian dancer. I guess the romanticism created by the tourist industry may have backfired, but not for the film industry. This sexy Islander scene is just what Hollywood wanted. In real Polynesian reviews these smiles by Native dancers towards the audience (never singling out one person) are for show only. Only in the male imaginations of an L.A. studio would a tourist actually sleep with a Polynesian dancer after the show, and a dangerous notion is set by Hollywood that these dancers are promiscuous and for the taking, like their ancestors of early contact period, and as stereotyped by the studios in other South Seas movies. And of course, true to Tinseltown form, the actress opposite Schwimmer, Jacqueline Obradors, isn't even Tahitian—she's actually Hispanic, the daughter of Argentine parents.

It would be understating the case not to emphasize that romance, for many of today's adults, is synonymous with sex. This chapter focuses on two sensualized island tourist concepts, the first, as just mentioned, is the promoted romance in the islands, and the second is the continued Pacific Island sensualized greeting in the tourist trade as seen in real life and in the movies. As mentioned in Chapter 2, greetings in a Polynesian paradise are a sexual metaphor for an invitation for island conquest and subjugation. Pacific Historian Vernadette Vicuña Gonzalez states:

> Both militarism and tourism rely on sedimented notions of colonized land and people (especially women) as passively there for the taking.[5]

This important concept needs to be emphasized before I continue with the following modern "greeting scene" of contemporary island tourism.

In other present-day South Seas films one can commonly find the trope of the greeting of tourists from the docks to the tarmacs of Pacific Island ports and airports. Almost all visitors to the islands are greeted or treated to leis, sometimes with kisses by beautiful, young and fit Native-like characters from the Islands, all in minimal attire. I call them characters because they are in costumes, usually scant, or attire that these Islanders would not wear in normal, everyday, contemporary island life. This now-modern tourist trade trope is reflected throughout American films of Hawai'i and its South Seas Polynesian Island cousins. But before the common passenger airline became a mainstay of Pacific Island travel, there were the piers of popular Polynesian harbors, with Honolulu having the quintessential Pacific Ocean harbor in American cinema.

The faux image of the "joyous welcoming by the Native" is imagined and produced by the island tourist industry and by the local colonial governments, a very visual scene often accompanied by music and even dance, repeated many times on popular movie screens throughout America. Up until the early 1970s, the local government tourism bureaus and private tourist industry leaders were always amenable to total cooperation with the film industry, providing many complimentary things such as rooms, ships, planes, locations, hotel lobbies, ship entryways or plane tarmacs[6] and even access to restricted military bases (typically predicated upon Pentagon script approval). This generosity was obviously for publicity purposes but more injuriously, it served to solidify mass acceptance of the islands as the settlers' own. The overly hospitable, welcoming scenes not only encouraged visitation and spending but also migration, a huge tool of colonization. They served to dispel anxiety that, perhaps, "the Natives are restless"—indeed, to the contrary, they subserviently welcome intruders with open arms and are ready to accept and serve them.

Early examples of this eager-to-welcome scene go as far back as the very first films shot in South Seas cinema by a Thomas Edison camera crew visiting Honolulu in 1898 and reappear in *Navy Wife* (1935), *Hawaii Calls* (1938), *Pagan Love Song (1950)*, *Jungle Heat* (1957), *South Seas Adventure* (1958), *Diamond Head* (1962), *Tiara Tahiti* (1962), Charlie Chaplin's swan song *A Countess from Hong Kong* (1967), and *Aloha Summer* (1988). All of these films and others like them always display friendly local Natives giving leis and often include the "local boys diving for coins" cliché. This acrobatic act of daring, also lensed by Edison's crew in 1898, is part job and part performance. The risks of high diving from the ship's upper deck, as well as freediving to the harbor's bottom by Natives in these scenes, display the dominance of Western visitors or settlers, as cash-strapped Natives will (almost literally!) jump through hoops for the pocket change of the outsider. While the young island boys may be thinking "what a fun part time job, I get to play in the ocean while white folk are throwing money at me," the "kanakas diving for coins" trope is also emblematic of exploited Islanders dangerously diving for pearls in early period movies.

In the film *Pagan Love Song* (1950), brown-painted star Esther Williams plays a part-Tahitian educated local girl. She reluctantly participates in a Canoe Greeting for a cruise liner coming to town. Her local Tahitian friends convince her to go, just to have some fun. There at the docks a Euro-American visitor aboard a cruise ship throws coins down below towards the Native canoes, but no one moves to retrieve the coins. It's mid-century in this film setting, not the '20s or '30s. Williams' character is disgusted at the gesture, with an attitude like "what are we, monkeys in a zoo?" After all, it is now the '50s, and coins are peanuts, and peanuts are for monkeys.

Soon after, planes filled with middle class (and middlebrow) tourists started to arrive in Honolulu. No film better illustrates this crash-of-class aspect of travel more than *Aloha Summer* (1988), which is based on a true story. In the beginning of the film, the main characters are established. Besides the locals, three families arrive in Hawai'i, two middle-class families by plane and a rich family by a cruise liner. The dock scene of *Aloha Summer* is significant for two reasons, the first being that it illustrates the negligible island costumes the local greeters are forced to wear. Young and fit Natives, who work in the tourist trade, mandatorily wear one- or two-piece sarongs or grass skirts with inauthentic, meager coconut bras, while the young fit males wear lava lavas or simple wraps around their hips and are at times bare-chested. (More on this later in the chapter.)

The second significant act in this scene is the taking advantage of the customary cheek greeting kiss (that modern Polynesians use among each other) by suddenly charging towards the lips of a greeter as she attempts to kiss a cheek of a visitor. I refer to this as "stealing a kiss." Not only does this theft take place in this *Aloha Summer* scene but during airport plane arrivals as well. Perfect examples of this "stealing a kiss" are in the films *Big Jim McLain* (1952), *A Very Brady Sequel* (1996), and *Christmas Vacation 2: Cousin Eddie's Island Adventure* (2003), in which actors Ed Asner and Randy Quaid take "stealing a kiss" of a Polynesian lei greeter to a new level.

This new institutionalized "greeting" by young, fit Islanders again also involves locals wearing the stereotypically minimal Native attire. In fact, in a scene before the lei greeting episode in *Aloha Summer*, the lei greeter (played by beautiful Hawai'i local Tia Carrere) approaches her brother (part-Hawaiian Andy Bumatai) in their small tropical flower farm as she is leaving to go to work in her skimpy, lei greeter, two-piece outfit. Her disgruntled brother looks at her outfit and says (in Island pidgin English): "You know I hate when da kine rich haoles [foreigners] stare at you dressed like that, you know. Daddy would get sick if he seen you in that outfit!" But once more, as in other films, older heavy-set women wear full (missionary inspired) mu'umu'u dresses and are relegated to the back of the stage or behind a check-in or concierge's desk.

Today, because of the exploding numbers of tourists and the cost, labor, and availability of flowers, the handing out of free leis to everyone has ceased and is now limited to upper-class visitors who directly pay for the service in advance.[7] Either way, these contemporary, marginally dressed Native greeters are still displayed to all who land in the islands. Evolving from South Seas and Hawai'i harbors and docks to the tarmacs and terminals of airports, I argue this tourist industry practice of greeting with minimal attire has evolved from the same sexualized tropes of literature and cinema of the Canoe Greeting scene. Hollywood, and its sister industry of advertising, not only have perpetuated these tropes but also developed them into characters of the present-day visitor industry. Ironically, these same customs—not of Indigenous cultures, but of tourism, as demonstrated—can be seen throughout the archives of Hollywood's South Seas cinema genre as well.

A very significant television skit was aired on *Saturday Night Live* in March 2009. It was a scorching introspective look at the real life of island tourism employees. Titled "Hawaiian Hotel," the skit starred Dwayne Johnson and Fred Armisen. They both, as Hawaiian brothers, sing, dance and play the ukulele in a touristic Hawaiian-style restaurant and sometimes they talk to the patrons. Here are some samples of the dialogue: Newlywed wife: "It must be fun working here?" Armisen: "Oh it's great, they make us wear grass skirts." Johnson: "We play the same song over and over." Armisen: "We make $7.00 an hour—it's a dream job." Wife: "Well, Hawaii, is a beautiful place to live." Armisen quickly retorts: "Yeah, you should have seen it before it was covered in hotels." They sing and dance at another table where a lady tourist says: "This place is so peaceful; you guys must love living here?" Armisen: "Peaceful? People here in your oceanfront resort cause my brother and I to live 15 miles inland. Yah, there's a rusty pickup with weeds growing out of it ... that's our house!" Johnson: "You want to visit? It's real easy to get to. You just drive through the shantytown, make a right at the meth lab, and you'll see a 15-year-old girl, who got pregnant by an out-of-town businessman, then ask for her brother—that's me!" There is no laughter in the audience until they see the shocked reaction of the tourist couple.

It seems likely that the memorable skit was influenced or at least supported by the part-Samoan Johnson. Now the highest paid actor in the world, he was partly raised in a modest apartment building near Waikiki. Either he worked in the tourist industry, or he knew people who did. He knows the plight of many modern Polynesians who work in the tourist trade. They need to pay rent, insurance and many other bills in this supposedly better life of the Western world. Hawaiian scholar and activist Haunani-Kay Trask fittingly writes about this dilemma: "Burdened with commodification of our culture and exploitation of our people, Hawaiians exist in an occupied country whose hostage people are forced to witness (and, for many, to participate in) our own collective humiliation as tourist artifacts for the First World."[8]

Another large film (literally extra-widescreen Cinerama) is *South*

Seas Adventure (1958), which seems like one big commercial for the tourism industry. The great actor/director Orson Welles narrates this optical extravaganza and in the opening scene says: "To most of us, the South Seas represents an unfulfilled dream of paradise on earth. Now the enchanted archipelagos await the present-day explorer—you." This is a beautifully lensed docudrama in which stunning views are seen from many Pacific Islands. The "docu" part of the film consists of the many shots of scenic and cultural events that are displayed from various Polynesian and Melanesian locations. The "drama" part is a story narrative that follows a single girl, Kaye, from Ohio, looking for and finding—what else?—romance.

Kaye arrives via an ocean liner and is, of course, greeted with leis. She is escorted around Oʻahu by a *Kamaʻaina* or one who has lived in Hawaiʻi for a long time, regardless of race, as opposed to *Kanaka Maoli* or a person who is Indigenous to an island. Kaye's blonde Euro-American escort shows her the sights, by car and by air. Apparently, he is a pilot from an upper-class local family. At the end, Kaye marries her local escort with a complete modern Hawaiian wedding fit for a royal Hawaiian couple, with many Kanaka and Kamaʻaina guests honoring the couple. The ceremony includes a Hawaiian choir and tapa cloth covering the couple to represent respect and unification. The preacher is from an American Christian religion, but the event is supplemented with appropriated Hawaiian ceremonial, though contemporary, rituals and much Hawaiian vocabulary. The whole scene goes beyond the appropriated grass skirt from Chapter 7. It is one thing for a whole ancient and beautiful culture to be assimilated into a colonial society but quite another thing to have your culture used by colonizers as their own. This film subject, Kaye from Ohio, travels to Hawaiʻi to find romance as a tourist, a visitor, but she ends up in Hawaiʻi appropriating the whole society and inadvertently adding to the overwhelming colonial hegemony, claiming the islands and now claiming their culture.

Today, Hawaiian or other contemporary Indigenous wedding ceremonies are performed as a mainstay of the travel industry (for a price, of course). It is part of the visitation experience for newlyweds, but this immersion into the culture is temporary; the damage is the permanency of the experience. I should mention that it is also rather another experience for a visitor to fall in love and marry a Kanaka Maoli and be accepted by the Pacific Islander family.

9

Breaking the Cycle
How to Change the Course

The chicken-or-the-egg question for film studies is: Does a film influence society, or does society influence film? I believe it is a little of both. The general contents of a whole body of film work and data on audience attendance and viewership in a specific period does reflect society as a whole. Equally so, I believe that a single, exceptional and popular film, made at a given time, may influence a given society or individuals on some level during that period. In regard to South Seas cinema, the genre's whole body of tropes in many films does influence society in general—but not for the good. With the content of these current and past South Seas movies full of false Polynesian representations, this incorrect perspective will continue as reality in the thoughts and minds of today's young and old American and worldwide audiences. This inundation of erroneous facts and representations will lead to misjudgments, stereotypes, tropes, and even prejudices or dangerous sexual miscues for current and future American movie audiences. The evidence is there, and so the real question is: How can we break this cycle?

I must reiterate that South Seas cinema involves films about Oceania made out of Hollywood, and it also encompasses other motion photography media types such as music videos, TV commercials, episodic TV, TV/cable/streaming movies and cartoons. While music videos do not influence adolescents as much because that production form is not as popular as in the past, on the other hand, cartoons and their countless reruns are still very popular with young Americans. The fact that South Seas tropes are found throughout all of these media types leads one to conclude that Americans, from a very young age, are almost conditioned to believe Polynesian stereotypes are actual and not fictional. It's like "the Big Lie" in that if you say something long enough and over and over, it becomes perceived as being "true." Some of today's young audiences are tomorrow's filmmakers. As they have in past generations, the misrepresentation will continue. Stopping this recycling of South Seas tropes is an urgent pursuit. The following are some sensible methods to break this circle of falsehoods.

First, we must spread the word or create awareness. The use of the term or concept of "educating the masses," although a good ideological notion, has never been quite successful in influencing today's average person in a modern society. The word *educate* signifies to many school, effort, and boredom, with little interest for many. In the same vein, the concept of physical protest[1] only works when the news media are present to cover the story; also, the word *protest* carries a negative connotation, causing many to take a defensive position. But in the term *news media* lies the key—media exposure. Today's average American commonly uses the Internet via smart TVs, smartphones, laptops, and tablets, with social media applications of all types found in these devices. The regular use of this technology and instant spread of worldwide communications are effectively implemented by publicity and promotion departments found in Hollywood studios and in all of corporate America to promote products. Different from advertising departments, publicity departments are usually small corporate branches, but they can create a large buzz or a public awareness, usually free of charge. In the case of South Seas cinema, the organized use of free publicity can create a profitable buzz for the studios but a damaging one as well for the Indigene of Oceania if this false form of representation of the Pacific continues in its current practice. This buzz of creating awareness of false, unexamined assumptions regarding Pacific Islanders and erroneous representations of them in American South Seas films must be fought on the same level in the same way.

Ideally, a small, consistent and committed volunteer group (similar to Media Action Network for Asian Americans—MANAA) can send early letters, with suggestions of possible corrections, to the right studio departments. Then if there is no response, one can (with minimal resources and equipment) bombard the web's popular social sites and send press releases to news outlets, political and community leaders and organizations, stating a position or stance of disapproval for a certain idea in development in Hollywood that may be detrimental to the peoples of Oceania, thus creating their own early counteractive publicity campaign. The early letters to Hollywood entities should use a tone of educating producers, writers and directors by pointing out errors in story points or incorrect representations of Pacific Islanders and suggesting a politically and culturally correct course they should take and why. A point to emphasize in these communications is that these corrective changes should not weaken story points and ideas but augment the story with more quality and depth or authenticism. These letters are influential and powerful if sent early in the creative process, when making changes has a minimal cost. They are also influential if sent to the right personnel and departments, including publicity and promotions, because bad publicity or ill-conceived promotions are what they wish to avoid and to resolve, as negative PR could derail box office, award nominations, and critical response. Such letters can be highly effective in influencing an extremely image-conscious industry. This volunteer group (with the possibility of getting grants and Internet funding) can create their own buzz and a good reputation for themselves vis-à-vis working with the press or the Internet, et al. A public relations university major would be ideal as a member for this volunteer board, as well as a grant writer and a computer/Internet expert with social media skills.

On a political front, this board can lobby local governments to withhold tax breaks and other enticements to shoot on location for disrespectful productions that denigrate Indigenous cultures. This may sound extreme to some, but the simple fact of the matter is that the Pentagon routinely does this, denying access to military installations and personnel unless a pre-submitted script meets the criteria of those in charge and upholds the image and integrity of the Armed Services.

The board of this proposed organization only has to meet as needed. Keeping up with Hollywood's comings and goings is essential. Reading *Variety* and other Hollywood trade magazines, dailies, and newsletters plus the online trade press, such as *Deadline Hollywood*, or film union bulletins, or fee services as in *The Mercury Report* or the *Production Weekly*, will be essential for early correction attempts. This is a "nip it in the bud" approach, while a film proposal is still in its infancy. Obviously, a reactive approach after a film is released is too late. The damage is done, and a film is permanently on record. Experience has shown that a reaction approach does not produce much sympathy and support from the studios or from the masses in comparison to a pre-production approach. This should happen, even though there is hope that a more enlightened and sensitive Hollywood would exist on its own with the adage: "We will do better next time" (especially after the *Aloha* controversy—see Chapter 10). Pessimistically, in regard to proper Polynesian representation on American film, in Hollywood the "will do better next time" paradigm has not worked in more than 100 years of American South Seas plots on celluloid, tape, and disc.

Today, there is no need to recruit volunteers to picket a movie unless staging a protest would be newsworthy—this involves much work and many people to be effective and again, it's a "too late," after-the-fact approach. Now, one can be a lot more effective with a computer and an Internet connection. The important thing here is that whatever this entity does, creating awareness and enlightening the masses should be the highest priority. Creating public service announcements (for radio and TV), having a spokesperson at strategic events and programs, preferably events with news coverage, distributing press releases, and the use of the other aforementioned strategies would be more successful methodologies for making change. This pro–Pacific Islander watchdog and corrections group can also help support authentic Oceanic imagery—maybe not financially but by helping to promote Indigenous filmmaking that, for the most part, does not recycle and display Hollywood tropes and instead exhibits a more authentic representation of Oceania and its cultures. Helping to create a buzz for these productions is what is sorely needed for these independent, cash-limited, Indigenous indie producers.

Marketing a film just to break even is the aspiration for most of these independent producers, at least in the beginnings of their careers. With today's production tools of relatively inexpensive high-definition or ultra-definition cameras and economical editing software on personal laptops—combined with talented young local crews and casts, all working for industry minimums out of love for the cause, or simply to build a resume—an Indigenous filmmaker can work economically in comparison to the high production costs of a Hollywood studio. Some agreeable Pacific countries give out grants to make films, but distribution to get more people to watch them is another story. Many Indigenous filmmakers devote their time and their own resources, not for the sake of profit but to expose their talents and those of other local skilled film craftsmen, and to share their culture with others. Many of these Indigenous features and shorts have high quality production values and fresh stories (whether ancient or contemporary), good acting and good soundtracks—all reflecting their culture in some form. The true Indigenous films should not use or need Hollywood tropes—just the realism of cultural authenticity. Considering Pacific Islanders' rich oral history, full of highly imaginative mythology, Oceania has an Indigenous trove of storytelling treasures.

Not all Pacific Indigenous films are perfect—arguably one of the guiltiest Indigenous-made films that uses Hollywood tropes is *Samoan Wedding* (2006), written and acted by young, talented Samoan men, diasporic Polynesians living in modern Auckland, N.Z. The film's plot, which includes the sexualized and objectified island maiden, reflects the immigrant and adaptive lives of these filmmakers, not the authentic lifestyles of their island origins. Although not mentioned, the story of contemporary immigrant Polynesian life in Auckland is that these innocent young men are exposed to much American popular culture, especially through movies and TV. A genuine film plot about these diverse and, at times, conflicting cultures in a diasporic Polynesian life would be an interesting and still a genuine film. In *Samoan Wedding* this conflict and its consequences should have been more recognized, which would have resulted in a better film. Although it can be argued that their objectification of the Pacific Island female can be used to establish the immaturity of their characters in this comedy, I theorize that the existence of this trope in their film is more a reflection of their diasporic upbringing and their exposure to Hollywood film productions; nevertheless, the results are still detrimental to Pacific Island women, as they perpetuate Tinseltown's clichés. Another example of this outside cultural exposure is in the film *Tongan Ninja* (2003), a satire of the once-popular American martial arts film genre that has Hong Kong roots.

Interestingly, another contemporary Indigenous film entitled *Boy* (2010), by Taika Waititi, is heavily influenced by American pop culture but is actually realistic in its contemporary New Zealand Island setting. This present-day film honestly reflects the American pop culture interspersed within their own Māori society, but it does not reflect Hollywood filmmaking with all of its incorrect tropes, stereotypes and clichés. Whether intentional or not, there is a powerful underlying message in *Boy*—the invasion and influence of American popular culture worldwide and how it is diverting youth from their own Indigenous principles, values and culture. (In 2020 Taika Waititi became the first Polynesian to win the Academy Award for Best Adapted Screenplay. The writer-director's anti–Nazi *Jojo Rabbit* was also honored that year with a Best Picture Oscar nomination.[2])

There are noble Indigenous films which have genuine Native stories with a totally Native cast and authentic settings. If given the chance, these films would also appeal to a worldwide audience, as did NZ's box office hit *Once Were Warriors* (1994) and *Whale Rider* (2002). Some other examples are *The Pā Boys* (2014), set in New Zealand; the aforementioned *The Orator* (2011), which is set in Samoa; and *Cousins* (2021) written and co-directed by and co-starring Māori Briar Grace Smith and set in *Aotearoa* (New Zealand). These, as well as many other Native films, are valuable in that they are the antithesis or reverse of Hollywood-made South Seas productions, which are this book's focus. In fact, in *Cousins*, one of the title characters marries, but her Māori husband soon realizes his bride is sexually dysfunctional. He patiently gives in to her discomfort, and they mutually decide to separate. Again, the opposite of a sensualized scene.

An independent Indigenous film producer has to be aware of his or her product or message. He or she also has to be aware that distributers and financiers can influence one's ideologies and end product. These Islander filmmakers have to be conscious of their ultimate goal— whether the film is made just for the love of their craft, to make money, to be famous, or to also get the world to know and understand his or her people, place and culture better.[3]

It is relatively easy today to self-distribute for free via the Internet on a popular video website or spend the money to create your own website. Some kind of cooperative on the Internet would be ideal. But "free" usually means no monies gained. For the producers of Indigenous shorts, this may be the path and a good way to hone their crafts, gain valuable experience and add to their visual resumes. For island producers of the much longer and costlier film format, feature-length films, some sort of compensation for the producer, cast and crew, who devoted much time to the effort, has to be considered. They must be aware that the "film festival" circuit is not for profitability but for exposure, and there are many hidden costs involved. Either way, this genuine Indigenous methodology of producing film as compared to the Hollywood method is very refreshing, sincere, and original, with ideally no sexualized or other tropes from the male chauvinistic imaginations of Hollywood. This Indigenous filmmaking, whether for shorts, features, or for television needs to be supported.

In chapter summary, a typical plot of a Hollywood South Seas cinema production usually includes all four of our thematic sexualized tropes. In the conventional American film of the Pacific, we would find tropes of the Canoe Greeting scene or the introduction of the stereotypical scantily clad Polynesian; the Lagoon Swim scene with the gaze of Euro-American male characters and simultaneously the gaze of male Hollywood and American audiences; the Sensual Dance scene that is made to sell theater tickets with its sexual exposure and connotations; and finally, the Native First Kiss scene, in which we recognize the damaging racist and sexist practices of Pacific interracial relationships on film. These American films could include the sexy stereotypical dress of a sarong or grass skirt for women of any race or comprise the short lava lava wrap for any man onscreen. A contemporary film could show the sexualized Native tourist host or entertainer onstage or the romance of visitors to the sexualized Pacific Isles on screen. Unfortunately, these scenes represent a multi-layered plot full of sexualized displays.

As also discussed, these films have many other pertinent issues, some overt, some subliminal, and some unintentional. But no matter what the case is, the issues of the Euro-American male bias result in untruths, mental and physical subjugation of Pacific Islanders, racism and sexism, all to the detriment of Polynesian identities, their cultures, and in some cases, their lands. Furthermore, the use of widespread media, in particular popular American film, assists in the promoting and recycling of these incorrect biases and dangerous tropes of South Seas cinema to future generations of Americans and anyone else in the world with the capabilities of viewing Hollywood's biased versions of the Pacific.

The American film industry has a cooperative method of production. However, when it comes to the creative and authentic aspects of story and appearance, only a few roles have corrective controls: the original storyteller, screenwriter, art director, costume designer, director, producer, and studio executives influence the end product, as do the studio's promotional and marketing departments. All bear responsibility for a film's outcome, whether it be uplifting and enlightening or fallacious and damaging. All have some form of culpability in terms of the end product when all is said and done, but this is especially true of the writer, director, producers, and studio executives. We must end the cycle and make the responsible people in the American film industry aware of their incorrect sexualized and other inappropriate representations, simultaneously ending the negative consequences for the people they are supposedly trying to represent. An unfortunate byproduct of America's much-vaunted First Amendment is that it legally protects and enables storytellers to indulge in harmful ethnic misrepresentation. (The current debate about "hate speech" and free speech raises similar questions.) But America's Natives, too, can use their constitutionally guaranteed right to freedom of speech to speak out against cultural inauthenticity and for truthful representations.

Also to be recognized, besides Indigenous filmmakers are other independent film producers in the Pacific who are sympathetic to and understand the aboriginals of the islands. These people make films collaboratively with, and with the approval of, their Indigenous neighbors. Some, not all, of these local island "insiders" understand the plight and history of Pacific Islanders far better than outside writers, directors and producers from Hollywood. Together, all of these Islanders can set the bar for true South Seas cinema.

The final irony is that South Seas cinema is usually a fun, escapist film genre with millions of fans who have come away from these presentations with smiles on their faces, especially the men. But after much contemplation, the so-called happy-go-lucky women of Polynesia, who are sexually objectified and commodified to the masses via inaccurate depictions, may be among the saddest people on earth, and there is little escape for them from this patriarchal exploitation. On any contemporary street, the same millions of men who watch these films may smile at these Polynesian females as they walk by, but because of false sexualized stereotypes of these women onscreen, the innermost intentions or perceptions of these men towards these island women are never really known. The good and bad news is that because of incorrect racial representation found in the great majority of these films, most of these men do not know what a real Polynesian woman looks like.

PART II

Annotated Filmography of Polynesian Sexualized Tropes and Sexual Relationships

The following is an exhaustive catalog of feature films whose storylines involve the sexualization of Pacific Islanders and their sexual relationships with Euro-Americans and Europeans. The motion pictures in this record are primarily American-produced films, but there is also a sampling of feature films originating from other countries to illustrate the pervasiveness of Polynesian sexualized tropes found in other parts of the globe. These few foreign films are labeled as such.

Sample data included in this compilation of films indicate that there are no fewer than *158 relevant feature films, among which 152 titles contain at least one of the four sexualized tropes focused on in chapters 2–5 of this book: the Canoe Greeting, the Lagoon Swim, the Sensual Dance and the Native First Kiss tropes. Twenty-six films exhibit the Canoe Greeting trope or another type of sexualized island greeting scene; 34 display the Lagoon Swim scenario; 74 include at least one scene of a Polynesian Sensual Dance; and the vast majority of these films, 140, include one instance of a literal Native first kiss or its metaphorical equivalent, the interracial sexual relationships between a Polynesian and a person of European descent. The few films that do not contain these aforementioned tropes are included because they exhibit a general aura of sexuality found within a Polynesian Island environment as in a village or throughout the island setting itself.

Another interesting point that can be observed in this filmography is that of the 12 film titles that include all four of the emphasized sexualized tropes, almost all are high budget, popular, and historically significant films. Examples of these films are: *White Shadows in the South Seas*

(1928), *Bird of Paradise* (1932 and 1951), *Mutiny on the Bounty* (1935), *Son of Fury* (1942), *Return to Paradise* (1953), and *Blue Hawai'i* (1961). Interestingly, the release dates of these 12 films are fairly dispersed throughout the 20th century. In addition, with some arguing that South Seas cinema has faded after the 1930s, here, one can observe that eight out of these 12 significant films were lensed after 1940, along with many other titles, which contradicts that argument.

There are many facts of interest and thought-provoking conclusions that can be ascertained with the data contained in this Annotated Filmography. A case in point is the fact that among the films (some with multiple interracial relationships within the story) listed here, combined with over a hundred other South Seas films that have in their content same race romantic couplings, i.e., Pacific Island males coupled with island females, and European and Euro-American males with females of European descent (the latter not covered in this filmography), there are only 11 instances where a sexual relationship is established between a male Polynesian and a European or Euro-American female.

Even more infrequent is a South Seas storyline involving a same sex couple of any race or combination of races. Even though, historically, same sex relationships have occurred for generations in both Polynesian and European cultures, there are no American commercial narrative South Seas film that exhibit this relationship (excluding pornographic films) until recently. An American produced streaming movie by Netflix entitled *Falling Inn Love* (2019) co-featured a biracial (Māori and Anglo) gay couple as some of the interesting local New Zealand characters in the film. Also, this relationship can be found in Indigenous-produced Pacific Island films such as the 2010 release titled *Kawa*, which came out of New Zealand. One can then possibly conclude that historically in Hollywood's film industry, not only was it a Euro-American male dominated business, but a "straight male" controlled industry as well. This generality has changed somewhat since the period when most of the films discussed were produced.

*Note: After many years of research on this subject, it is essential to know that the findings of this filmography are neither conclusive nor by any means complete. Although exhaustive and original, it is important to note that the content of this Annotated Filmography of Polynesian Sexualized Tropes is only complete as to the extent of resources that are available. Unarguably, the most efficient way to ascertain and extract facts and data from any film is to view its contents from first frame to last. Unfortunately, many films are lost due to unforeseen disasters, such as chemical decomposition and fires, but in some cases, films are misplaced or have vanished; this is plainly due to human error or possible delinquency. Through various historical records of story summaries or plot descriptions, critiques and the scrutiny of productions' photo stills and ephemera that still exist, some data can still be collected on a few lost film titles, but because these films do not exist anymore, the data concerning them is by no means absolute.

Another general note: the sexualized tropes and racist relationships discussed in this Annotated Filmography are just two subjects among many other degrading or stereotypical tropes about the Indigenous people of Oceania as seen in American cinema. To name a few: racist characterizations of Indigenes as primitive, violent, unintelligent, lazy, uneducated, childlike, and unambitious.

Filmography Notes: Although there are many film types with the setting of a Polynesian Island in its content, this annotated record examines only film titles that are considered major movie releases by American studios, unless otherwise indicated. Film titles are italicized and listed in alphabetical order with initial articles inverted. The date of the U.S. general release follows in parentheses; then the major U.S. distributor of the film is listed. For a quick reference, at the end of this title line, one will note symbols associated with the four common sexualized tropes found in Chapters 2–5 of this book (see legend below).

ʊ = Canoe Greeting or tourist greeting
||| = Lagoon Swim
✗ = Sensual Dance
Ø = Native First Kiss or an interracial relationship

The next line will have the Screenplay writer(s) and the Director(s) in bold print. Noted stars will follow within the ensuing brief summary.

Most importantly, also contained within the summary are notes of significance to Pacific Islands Studies and other academic disciplines, including one or more of the four tropes tracked throughout this book. Also included in this section will be major and minor roles filled by Indigenous Pacific actors. Subsequently, other general notes of interest appear and lastly the originator of the story (other than screenwriter) as in the author of a book or stage play from which the film plot originated, if applicable.

Final Notes: The film descriptions and analytical comments are my own contribution, often drawing on sources cited in the first part of this book. There may be some repeated facts, translations, definitions and viewpoints or conclusions in some of the title summaries, because as a reference guide this Filmography's summaries can be searched and read independently or together as a whole section. Also, plot spoilers are occasionally exposed.

All the Brothers Were Valiant (1953, MGM)—✗Ø
Screenplay by: Harry Brown. Directed by: Richard Thorpe.

Robert Taylor, Stewart Granger, Ann Blyth, and Betta St. John star in this South Seas adventure/drama with conflict in the relationships of two whaling brothers in the Pacific, their conspiratorial ship's crew, and murderous pearl traders. Granger, as one of the brothers, is sick and stranded at the Gilbert Islands (Kiribati) with Polynesian-attired Natives. On the island, a brownface young Native female (American St. John) tends to him. Then they become lovers, but he's on the first boat out. Granger later ponders, as an American chauvinistic male: "Funny thing I never found out her name." In addition, there are Polynesian Sensual Dance and Native First Kiss trope scenes. The feature is set on various Pacific Islands but shot in Jamaica and on a Hollywood studio lot. An earlier version was a 1923 Metro silent starring Lon Chaney, and remade as *Across to Singapore* (1929), with Joan Crawford and Ramon Navarro.

Aloha (1931, Tiffany)—Ø
Screenplay by: Adele Buffington, Leslie Mason. Directed by: Albert S. Rodell.

Ben Lyon plays a young American in the South Seas who marries a half–Polynesian girl named Ilanu, who is the daughter of the island queen. Lyons then takes her home to San Francisco where he is disowned by his family. They return to the island, where the distraught Ilanu leaps into a volcano, sacrificing herself to the island god Pele. Ilanu is played by Latina Raquel Torres, one of many Latinas to be cast as Polynesians. This film's plot includes an early trope of the Pacific Island volcano sacrifice. An interracial marriage with possible offspring is thwarted due to the sacrifice. Miscegenation, in general, violates the Hollywood Production Code and was a general racist taboo for Hollywood even before the Code was written. Typically, after a proven storyline of escapism, finding paradise, then encountering a beautiful Pacific Island woman and enjoying a sexual relationship unencumbered by Christian morality and a Christian judgmental society, filmmakers in Hollywood would eliminate the possibility of marriage and children in this interracial bond by terminating the relationship by any means possible. Also, in the beginning of the story, Ilanu refuses to follow island tradition by marrying a worthy young island man of her class, instead choosing to marry a foreign American with dire Hollywood racial consequences for a woman who has broken the taboos of two cultures. The story is a remake of the silent movie *Aloha Oe* (1915). Mexico-born Raquel Torres also played Polynesians in *White Shadows in the South Seas* (1928) and in *The Sea Bat* (1930).

Aloha Oe (1915, Ince)—✗∅
Screenplay by: J.G. Hawks, Thomas H. Ince. Directed by: Richard Stanton & Charles Swickard.

This is an early significant silent featurette with Willard Mack and Enid Markey. Unusually titled in Hawaiian words, this classical plot involves a drunken and drugged American lawyer who sails to the South Pacific. There he is shipwrecked, becomes a beachcomber and falls in love with the Native king's daughter. This film contains: faux hulas, grass skirts, paper leis, imitation volcanoes, and imitation moonlight. This is the first film with a trope of the Native female who sacrifices herself in a volcano, though in *Hearts Adrift* (1914), a Euro-American female commits suicide or sacrifice. Both films were produced after the volcano sacrifice trope was introduced in the popular play *Bird of Paradise* by writer Richard Tully in 1908. *Hearts Adrift* starred the legendary Mary Pickford, who jumps in a volcano with the baby that she conceived on a South Seas isle with a married American man. Pickford and the married man were both marooned on this island and were soon to be unexpectedly rescued before her suicide. In *Aloha Oe*, the now pervasive trope of an archetypal virgin Native Island taboo princess has now started in popular American cinema. Tully's play, with the Native volcano sacrifice, was made into a film in 1932 and 1951. *Aloha Oe* was one of the first South Seas films featuring numerous erroneous Pacific representations due to non-location shooting. In other words, it was one of the first South Seas films shot in Hollywood with fake studio sets and faux Polynesians. Unfortunately, this pattern of incorrect Polynesian representation, falsehoods and tropes continues in Oceanic cinema. Nevertheless, the film was praised, not ridiculed, by American moviegoers; along with 1914's *McVeagh of the South Seas*, it opened the way for other "staged" and incorrect South Seas films lensed outside of the Pacific. Also, *Aloha Oe* contains the first onscreen beachcomber, along with another 1915 released film entitled *The Beachcomber*, but not the first in other media, as in literature. *Aloha Oe* was remade in 1931 as *Aloha* by Tiffany Studios.

Aloha Summer (1988, Sam Goldwyn)—ʊ✖️Ø

Screenplay by: Mike Greco, Bob Benedetto. Directed by: Tommy Lee Wallace.

Chris Makepeace and Don Michael Paul star in this story about teen problems and parental prejudices. It is set on Oʻahu in 1959, right before Hawaiʻi became a state. An unusual racially mixed group of six teenage young men with diverse class and cultural backgrounds all share in an unforgettable Hawaiian summer. Local Islanders of Japanese descent, Japanese nationals, and Native Hawaiians are distinguished, with Hawaiians played by Blaine Kia and Andy Bumatai. A harbor greeting scene with sexualized, scantily clad female Native lei greeters can be found in this film. One island female greeter, played by part-Filipino and Hawaiʻi-raised Tia Carrere (who went on to star in *Wayne's World* [1992] and *True Lies* [1994]) receives an inappropriately heavy kiss on the lips from a wealthy male tourist teen. This rich teenager later gets involved with the aforementioned male group and falls deeper for Carrere. The possible relationship is not welcomed by an anti–American older brother played by Bumatai. The story depicts tropes of surfing, natural disaster, drunken sailors in Chinatown fighting locals, hulas, Hawaiian wedding, boys diving for coins, and an outrigger canoe funeral at sea. Two major Hawaiian roles are played by actors of Filipino descent, Carrere and Warren Fabro. Based on a true story by Mike Greco.

Aloma of the South Seas (1926, Paramount)—✖️Ø

Screenplay by: James Ashmore Creelman. Directed by: Maurice Tourneur.

In this 1926 version, Aloma is a Polynesian maiden played by popular shimmy dancer and Polish-American Gilda Gray. Her Native protector, Nuitane, is played by Euro-American Warner Baxter in brownface. Gilda has two American lovers in this film: the first is lost at sea, and the second succumbs to alcohol and the societal racist conventions opposing mixed marriages. The second lover, who becomes a beachcomber, then returns with his American ex-lover back to the U.S. continent. Aloma consequently returns to her Native lover Nuitane. Miscegenation is avoided twice in this story. This popular play and film were satirized by two prevalent cartoons, a Mutt and Jeff short film titled *Aroma of the South Seas* (1931), with very racist looking characters, and a Popeye animated short titled, *Alona of the South Seas* (1942). Like the 1941 version of the film, the volcano curse trope is featured in both animations.

In the 1941 feature, Aloma is played by Dorothy Lamour, but this time her lover is a fellow Native played by part-Tahitian actor Jon Hall. Thus this remake does not have an interracial relationship, so it is not essential to this filmography. Both film versions were based on a play written by John Hymer and LeRoy Clemmens.

Altar Stairs, The (1922, Universal)—Ø
Screenplay by: George Hively, Doris Schroeder. Directed by: Lambert Hillyer.

This silent motion picture stars Frank Mayo as the captain of a South Seas schooner who falls for, but keeps his distance from, a married passenger played by Louise Lorraine, who just left her repulsive husband at the altar (hence the title). Coincidentally, Mayo was recently rescued from island "savages" by the same repugnant husband (Lawrence Hughes). Hughes gets a new post on another island where he influences the Native chief to defile missionary efforts and return to "pagan" ways. While still being legally married to Lorraine, Hughes has an affair with a young female Native. The young Native woman's male island lover kills Hughes in a jealous rage. This frees good guy Mayo to marry Lorraine.

The Altar Stairs was filmed on a Los Angeles studio lot, which typically uses Latinos and Euro-Americans to represent Native roles. In this instance, Native Islander Parete was played by Dagmar Godowsky, who was born in what is today's Lithuania. This movie has a typical South Seas plot for the silent era when interracial relationships were taboo. In this case, depicting the white perpetrator as an immoral adulterer signifies that the relationship is on the whole immoral, not to mention its consequences. Characteristic of a South Seas silent, the hero and heroine end up in marriage because the previous circumstances are worked out in a proper fashion. Death by the former antagonistic spouse is the usual and proper scenario for remarriage in these early films, and of course, our heroes are both Euro-Americans. *The Altar Stairs* is based on a novel written by G. B. Lancaster and co-stars a pre–*Frankenstein* Boris Karloff.

As Man Desires (1925, 1st National)—Ø
Screenplay by: Marion Orth. Directed by Irving Cummings.

Stars Milton Sills as a British army major, John Craig, who flees India because he struck a superior. Sills hit the officer who desired his fiancée, played by Ruth Clifford. The superior officer ends up dead, and everyone, except loyal Clifford, blames innocent Sills. Sills then ends up as a fugitive on a South Seas island. Soon, Sills develops a lucrative pearl trade and ends up ruling the island, where he takes a Native lover. Of course, in this Hollywood plot he is considered the innocent, industrious hero, but from an Indigenous perspective, he is a conniving, greedy, land- and power-consuming foreigner. Our "hero" also converts a former wanton Native woman to a more Christian morality, and they fall for each other. The Natives now attempt to break up his business and steal his pearls. Again, from a perspective of the Indigene, is it a rebellion to restore sovereignty, a labor dispute over the exploitation of cheap and dangerous labor and unjustly huge profits for Sills? Perhaps the Natives are just trying to get back what they feel they deserve and punish Sills for his unscrupulous business practices. Either way, in the eyes of Hollywood, Sills is still the hero, and the Natives are deceitful, uncivilized savages. Meanwhile, during the melee, the Native lover gets killed by gunfire. Sills also learns that back in India he is exonerated and returns to his fiancée there. Here the interracial relationship ends—as usual, in tragedy. Despite Sills' Christian beliefs, there is mention neither of a proper marriage to the Indigenous female nor of the hero's disloyalty to his fiancée back in India. For the male-centric Hollywood film industry our hero's inconsistent and unjust behavior with women is irrelevant. This scenario really is: "As a Euro-American or European man desires—he gets."

Baywatch: Forbidden Paradise (1995, All American & Baywatch Prods.)—✕Ø

Screenplay by: Deborah Schwartz. Directed by: Douglas Schwartz.

This movie, derived from the world's #1 TV show starring David Hasselhoff, Pamela Anderson and their *Baywatch* cohorts, was released straight to video worldwide. In the film, the fit lifeguards travel from L.A.'s beaches to Hawai'i for heavy sea lifeguard training. This TV movie quality production was filmed and set on O'ahu. Generic tropes include surfing bad luck, lava rock and a shipwreck on a remote Polynesian Island with fierce male Natives and a friendly and pretty Indigenous maiden who nurses one lifeguard back to good health. Actually, the Natives are not a lost tribe but a Hawaiian activist group going back to nature and their roots—or an excuse for the exposure of scantily clad, attractive, young adult Polynesians. Later, back on O'ahu, there is a tourist luau scene with the regular *Baywatch* beauties sensuously dancing the clichéd Tahitian tāmūrē and a Samoan fire dance onstage.

There is snorkeling in a Sea Life Park (an ocean-centered amusement park) exhibition tank posing as a real reef, and if there aren't enough barely clad female bodies in the plot, the Hawaiian Tropic bikini girls have a scene. There are many parts for Polynesians: Lee Doversola, Sidney Liufau, Wallace Akeo, Buffalo and Brian Keaulana, Laisene Auelua, Celeste Akeo and Mark Kealoha. Most are Hawaiian, but two are Samoan-Americans. Local Hawai'i surf legend and non–Polynesian Gerry Lopez also has a tribal role.

Beachcomber, The (1915, Paramount)—Ø
Screenplay by: Hobart Bosworth. Directed by: Phil Rosen.

Popular silent star Hobart Bosworth plays the title character in this romance about a U.S. sailor who is washed overboard by a storm in Hawaiian waters. A Native Hawaiian family takes care of him, then a romance brews between Bosworth and the Hawaiian family's daughter, who is a stereotypical carefree temptress. Bosworth struggles with his Christian upbringing. He finally decides to take his Hawaiian girl and her brother home to a proper Christian way of life, regardless of possible inner struggles the Hawaiians will undoubtedly have with culture shock in their new environment. *The Beachcomber* is the first film, along with 1915's *Aloha Oe,* with a beachcomber character.

Bela Lugosi Meets a Brooklyn Gorilla (1952, Border Films)—✕Ø
Screenplay by: Tim Ryan. Directed by: William Beaudine.

This comedy/horror "B" picture stars Bela Lugosi, with rare billing in the title, which is a marketing ploy to attract fans of the aging actor. Also in the title is an erroneous South Seas gorilla (there are no gorillas endemic to Oceania). This film has blatant misrepresentations with a comedic excuse, as Bela plays a mad Dr. Moreau-like character on a South Seas island. It also stars Duke Mitchell and Sammy Petrillo, who use their real names as character names, along with Charlita, a pretty Latina, playing the Native girl who has a budding love affair with Mitchell. Al Kikume also has a main part. The little-known Kikume, born in Honolulu as Elmer Kikume Gozier, has the distinction of being a Polynesian Hollywood actor, with more roles than any other Pacific Island film artist. He had worked in over 70 films. This movie also has hula girls along with Dean Martin and Jerry Lewis copycats (Mitchell and Petrillo). Filmed in Los Angeles, it includes a Hollywood luau scene and

Hollywood Polynesian dance numbers. Later, the famous cartoon character Bugs Bunny, in the short *Hurdy Gurdy Hare*, does an obscure reference to this Lewis-like character, played by Sammy Petrillo. Bugs, with Jerry Lewis–like teeth, is an organ grinder with a giant gorilla as his money collector. Bugs remarks at the end of the cartoon: "I hope Petrillo doesn't find out about this." This refers to a big lawsuit instigated by Jerry Lewis over Petrillo's portrayal of Lewis. Mr. Lewis won the suit, so this film is a rare opportunity to see Petrillo play his very good Lewis-like character, because he could not legally do it again.

Big Jim McLain (1952, Wayne-Fellows / Warner Bros.)—ひØ

Screenplay by: James Edward Grant, Richard English, Eric Taylor.
Directed by: Edward Ludwig.

In the heyday of the McCarthy Era, John Wayne and James Arness are federal investigators fighting a communist ring in Hawai'i. *McLain* was filmed mostly on O'ahu and includes the usual tropes: an airport lei greeting scene, with Arness "stealing" a sudden heavy kiss on a hula skirted lei greeter; an outrigger riding the waves, with Diamond Head in the background; and the "Hawaiian Wedding Song," with Hawaiian lyrics sung by Hawaiians, the highlight of this propaganda picture. There are no major roles for Hawaiians. There is, however, an American woman with a questionable past and behavior and a short scene honoring deceased victims at Pearl Harbor. Part of *McLain* has an indirect ethnographic ambience, with background shots of Tantalus Lookout, Aloha Tower, Honolulu Airport, the Pali Lookout and interiors of the Royal Hawaiian Hotel, all from the early 1950s in glorious black and white. There is an Island romance between Wayne and a local Euro-American clerk. Although not an interracial relationship, this romance with the local clerk, a probable prostitute, along with Arness' big unsolicited lip to lip kiss at the airport, demonstrates the perception of sexuality in a Pacific Island environment.

Bird of Paradise (1932, RKO Pics.)—ひ|||✕Ø

Screenplay by: Wells Root, Wanda Tuchock, Leonard Praskins.
Directed by: King Vidor.

Adventurous and wealthy American visitor Joel McCrea volunteers to stay on a South Pacific island while his yacht mates travel on, although his ship cohorts will return to retrieve him later. While on the island, out of all of the Native women, McCrea falls for the taboo daughter of the chief, played by Latina Dolores del Rio. A brownface island priest decides to sacrifice the princess to the male god Pele (of course, Pele is a goddess for many Polynesians). At first del Rio complies with the visitor's wishes and refuses to kill herself, but in the end, she agrees to the sacrifice. *Bird* features the Canoe Greeting, diving for coins, shark attack, luau with pig and poi tropes. Del Rio performs a sexualized Hollywood hula dance while only wearing leis with double-sided tape to cover her breasts. Moreover, couples run off together after the dance. There are also: a wedding ceremony with ring of fire; nude swim by the seductive del Rio; forced Native First Kiss; mixed-race relationship; and the inauthentic volcano sacrifice tropes.

Delores attempts to speak Hawaiian too rapidly throughout

Bird of Paradise (1932, RKO Pictures). In the lobby card of this film classic with classic South Seas tropes, we see Latina actress Dolores del Rio, playing the seductive Polynesian maiden Luana, and the dominant American hero Joel McCrea. McCrea wants del Rio badly and steals her away to a neighboring deserted island for unbridled lovemaking. The problem is, even though they are passionate for each other, McCrea's ship will soon return to take him back to America, and she is—or was—the taboo virgin island princess who will be sacrificed to the volcano god. Del Rio decides she must abide by her island's beliefs and goes through with the sacrifice.

the picture, and with a Mexican accent. This film illustrates the self-centered American character who ignores Island traditions, laws and deity because of his American ethnocentric view of the world, wherein Americans supposedly have true civilized laws, while Islanders have primitive taboos. The American God is the only true God, and Island worship is paganistic and thus to be ignored. This arrogant view of the "Other" gives American McCrea and the audience the right to steal the princess and hide and make love to her without having long-term intentions, disregarding both tribal customs and his own Christian morality. McCrea knows the ship is returning for him, so he can avoid any consequences. His excuse for his behavior is she swam to him nude, in fun; but his subsequently violent forced kiss on del Rio showed his true intentions were a display of dominant masculine physicality and lust. McCrea, in America, is still the hero despite this brutal scene where the Native del Rio succumbs to McCrea's strength and strange lip-to-lip first kiss (which was not the custom for pre-contact Polynesians). McCrea does fall for del Rio and kidnaps her during her arranged wedding, but again it is only for temporary love, since McCrea again knows that his shipmates will return to take him back to the States.

This film encompasses the first role for the son of the silent screen legend, Lon Chaney, Jr., while Hawaiian Napoleon Pukui also had a major part. There is location shooting at Hawai'i and Catalina Island, plus filming inside RKO's soundstages in L.A. David O. Selznick was the executive producer and famed dance movie director Busby Berkeley was the uncredited choreographer. Del Rio wears a stylized Art Deco South Seas/Hollywood costume for her sacrifice, complete with a Hawaiian *ali'i* (royal) male cape and a feathered head piece. Like many South Seas films, the *virgin* sacrifice still takes place even after a sexual relationship with a foreign hero. Scenes are shot on a beautiful, empty Kaneohe Bay for indirect ethnographic and historical value. *Bird of Paradise* is based on a popular play written by Richard Walton Tully.

Bird of Paradise (1951, 20th Century–Fox)—ᘎ|||Ҳ∅
Screenplay by: Delmer Daves. Directed by: Delmer Daves.

This color remake of the 1932 RKO film stars Jeff Chandler, Debra Paget and Louis Jourdan. It was filmed on the Hawaiian island of Kaua'i with Euro-Americans Chandler, Paget and Maurice Schwartz (a Russian-born actor who founded New York's Yiddish Art Theatre in 1926) all playing brownface Polynesians. Significant roles played by Hawaiians include Prince Lei Lani (birth name Edwin

Kaumualiiokamokuokalani Rose) as the chief and hula dancer Mary Ann Ventura as Chandler's wife (although she was not credited).

Scenes depict a Canoe Greeting, taboo princess, luau feast, and sexualized hula dances, with aroused couples running off to consummate their passions after a dance scene. Jourdan and Paget are bound together with Native rituals, but miscegenation is thwarted, with the scene of Frenchman Jourdan getting asked by his seemingly infertile wife to take on a second wife for offspring. He refuses, and the later volcano sacrifice by his wife obviously ends their interracial marital relationship. Whether married by island or mainland rituals, either interracial marriage ceremony is relatively uncommon in South Seas cinema. This film also features surfing, lei giving, Native First Kiss, Lagoon Swim, the Melanesian and Polynesian ritual of walking on hot rocks, *ki'i* (tiki) images, coconut tree climbing, drum playing, and a big volcanic explosion with sacrifice clichés.

Lani, who was born in Hilo, played the Kahuna in the stage version of the film. There are authentic hulas by Hawaiian *kumu* (master, instructor) hula legend Iolani Luahine (whose name was spelled wrongly in the credits) and lead dancer Lydia Bray. The film has been somewhat sought after by contemporary kumu hula because of Luahine's association with the film, but now the hulas seem dated. One long dolly shot shows Chandler walking through the village with many ethnographic-like or near authentic Hawaiian activities such as poi pounding, net throwing, lei making, mat weaving, and net mending. Here the male outsider is a Frenchman, not a self-centered American (see 1932 version); consequently, in this story Jourdan learns and respects island protocol and patiently hopes he is picked by an island maiden—he does not kidnap her. Of course, the island maiden is the beautiful, mixed-raced taboo princess played by Paget. There is a rare nose flute romantic shot and a large, thatched village set that was built on a Kaua'i bay. This remake, as well as the 1932 version, is based on the popular play written by Richard Walton Tully, who first imagined the virgin volcano sacrifice trope.

Black Paradise (1926, Fox)—✗∅
Screenplay by: L.G. Rigby. Directed by: R. William Neil

This is a typical silent South Seas drama involving a complicated and evolving relationship within an exotic Pacific Island setting. An engaged couple heads for the South Pacific. The man (Leslie Fenton) is a thief and fugitive from the law. Fenton promises his fiancée, played by Madge Bellamy, that he will reform. Also at the island is the boss of Fenton's gang (Ed Piel). The island's atmosphere is sensual, with beautiful female dancers wearing little Native clothing to supply the mood. It works because the allegedly committed Fenton soon falls for a young Indigenous woman. Eventually, pretty Bellamy wears minimal attire on this carefree island. Soon the notorious Piel falls for Bellamy, and so does our newly arrived hero, the ubiquitous detective (Edmund Lowe), who is searching for Fenton. In this pre–Code film, the evil Piel blackmails Bellamy: if she makes love to him, he will spare Lowe's life. She gives in, and as she reluctantly disrobes in front of Piel, the island volcano suddenly erupts violently. In the melee that follows, somehow Bellamy and Lowe are the only ones who survive the volcanic devastation as they are miraculously rescued by a passing American steamer. Compare *Black Paradise* with the satirical film *Joe Versus the Volcano* (1990). The trope of a "Volcanic Ending" is common throughout this genre, not just having to do with a virgin sacrifice, but, in this case, simple utter destruction by a natural disaster, albeit one triggered by lust.

There is no such thing as a paradisiacal life in a Hollywood film. Even though, at times Hollywood does a good job setting up the illusion of a South Seas Edenic paradise, there are many tropes that destroy this escapist delusion, i.e., the law, the arriving fiancée from back home, the local taboos, and in this case, Mother Nature hits one's imagination hard to destroy the illusion. Audience members can go back to their homes, families and nine-to-five jobs after the movie. Also of note here is the moralistic theme in this American film that destroys an island full of criminal refugees—although destroying the seemingly insignificant and innocent Natives along with them is immoral. To some this is a very disturbing concept. Just because they have a non–Christian society with different ways and beliefs, this is not justification for American filmmakers to reduce them to lesser human beings—let alone ashes— and kill them inconsequentially as mere collateral damage.

Black Pearl (1934, Urania Film [Poland])—✗∅
Screenplay by: Eugeniusz Bodo, Antol Stern. Directed by: Michal Waszynski

Also known as *Czarna Perla* in Poland, this feature stars Reri and Count Eugene Bodo in a dramatic Polynesian love story about a Polish sailor (Bodo) returning to Europe with the riches of pearls and a Tahitian wife. Before discovering the pearls in a taboo cave in Tahiti, he fell for his Native vahine (Reri), who nursed him to health after a dirty bar fight. She also danced for him in what he thought was a seductive manner. The dance led to his falling for and kissing her. While on the island, our protagonist adored his Polynesian wife, but back in Europe his attitude towards her changes dramatically. There, Bodo is seduced by a married European woman, who turns out to be part of a gang that is after his pearls. Besides Tahitian stock footage, this film was shot entirely on a soundstage in Poland, including the scenes set in Tahiti. This is a very sad story for the Tahitian wife Moana, played by Reri, which is a stage name. This European produced film is a lesson for Polynesian women urging them to stay home, even after lovemaking with the European hero. Part-Tahitian Reri, who was born as Anne Chevalier, also played in *Tabu* (1931) and *The Hurricane* (1937). Reri lived in Europe for a while and even got married on that continent.

Blue Hawai'i (1961, Paramount)—℧|||✕∅
Screenplay by: Hal Kanter. Directed by: Norman Taurog.

As in real life, Elvis returns from a stint in the Army, but in this fictional story he returns home to Hawai'i. He also returns to his half–Hawaiian girlfriend, his Hawaiian beach grass shack, and his music-jamming Hawaiian friends. It is time for Elvis to grow up and get a job. He refuses to work in the pineapple industry, where his father is an executive. Elvis instead works in the tourism industry. His first tour, of course, is with a handful of pretty teenage girls and their beautiful female escort—and the story conflicts and music begin. Main characters in the film include Elvis' very prejudiced "Southern" mother, played well by British thespian Angela Lansbury, and his half–Hawaiian girlfriend Joan Blackman in brownface. Hawaiian Hilo Hattie (born as Clarissa Haili in Honolulu—not in Hilo) is in the Airport greeting scene along with Blackman and three female hula dancers. Tropes include luau, surf, canoe, hulas on stage, and unambitious Native males with non–Native leader (Elvis). The film also has a *hukilau* (community shared activity of hauling in fish with large nets on shore), a beach scene and a Hawaiian rock musical number, featuring the classic and popular Elvis Presley hip-swing.

This story perpetuates the Hawaiian settler promoting the spurious tourism industry cliché, and Elvis' father is in upper management in the Euro-American male run pineapple industry. Elvis expresses his desire to make something of himself, but his close, easygoing Hawaiian buddies do not. Pictorial notes: the now heavily tourist-laden Hanauma Bay was vacant in this film, as it was pre–1970s, or before the beginnings of the Waikiki buildup and affordable jet travel. The view of Hawai'i's capital city from the Tantalus Lookout offers a nostalgic look at mid-century Honolulu. Furthermore, the tropical resort shot on the island of Kaua'i was the famous Coco Palms Hotel (now abandoned and in ruins due largely to Hurricane Iniki).

There is a mixed-race marriage, but complete miscegenation (having offspring) is thwarted by a simple plot device: the film ends quickly after a rare interracial wedding ceremony and before any pregnancy. Typically, the movie avoids the fact that miscegenation obviously already did occur, due to the fact that Elvis' girlfriend, Maile, is half–French/half–Hawaiian herself, and as the white protagonist's love interest, being part-European looking, is almost a prerequisite in this genre. Maile's Hawaiian mother never appears due to an unexplained early death, helping to prevent the audience from contemplating that miscegenation already had transpired. Hollywood uses this story tactic commonly. Her Hawaiian grandmother is played by Flora K. Kaai Hayes, who was not credited even though she has lines. Also, Elvis' Hawaiian buddies were played well by Hawaiians Frank Atienza, Lani Kai and Tiki Hanalei. The last two names are probably staged or beachboy names, not birth names. The forth buddy was played by a Filipino-American raised in Hawai'i. This movie, filmed on Kaua'i and O'ahu, made a couple of *hapa haole* (half–Western) songs or, in this case, a modern mixture of English lyrics with contemporary Hawaiian rhythms, even more famous. Good examples are the title song and the *Hawaiian Wedding Song*. Other Hawaiian/Presley songs in the movie include *Aloha Oe*, *Rock-A-Hula Baby*, *Ku-U-I-Po* (an odd spelling, presumably to help with pronunciation), and *Hawaiian Sunset*. The story is by Allan Weiss, who wrote a number of Presley pictures.

Bora Bora (1968, American International Pictures [IT/FR]) |||✕∅

Screenplay by: Ugo Liberatore. Directed by: Ugo Liberatore.

In *Bora Bora*, a man is looking for his ex-wife in Tahiti and on its neighboring Society Islands. He ends up having affairs with a 15-year-old Native girl, an older Native mistress and a Gauguin Museum curator of European descent. Meanwhile, his former wife has gone Native and devotedly lives with a Native man, Mani, played by Antoine Coco Puputauki. Obviously, this implausible plot of reconciliation soon after having three recent affairs is really an excuse for an erotic film, which is a known characteristic of the works of writer/director Ugo Liberatore. The ex-wife has adapted to the islands, and the disturbingly violent and prejudiced ex-husband, who stalks her, also stays on the island and tries to adapt to Bora Bora life as well. Initially, the

European ex-husband utters racist words against the Tahitians and always wears long pants, long sleeve shirts and a leather jacket in a tropical environment. This dress is emblematic of a non-conformist outsider. The plot has a bad ending, where inexplicably, despite being in paradise, the estranged couple get back together, leave their Native lovers, burn a beautiful, Tahitian-style, unfinished beach house and leave Tahiti. There is no paradise theme *per se*, and in this story it doesn't make sense for the couple to leave or for the ex-wife to get back together with her possessive and disloyal former husband. *Bora Bora* has the trope of Native women or any local island woman of any age being promiscuous. Beautifully photographed by Leonida Barboni.

Bounty, The (1984, Orion)—ʊ✗∅
Screenplay by: Robert Bolt. Directed by: Roger Donaldson.

    This is another remake of the HMS *Bounty* saga with another great cast. By the end of the 20th century, five male actors in this film had won a major Academy Award: Mel Gibson, Anthony Hopkins, Laurence Olivier, Daniel Day-Lewis and Liam Neeson. Also starring in this motion picture are Tahitian Tevaite Vernette and Māori Wi Kuki Kaa, who plays a Tahitian Chief. The film has a classical escapism of paradise-turning-into hell theme. *The Bounty* is a good example of a feature exhibiting Polynesian nudity during the post–Production Code period and the current liberal self-regulated film industry. The onscreen tropes of Canoe Greeting, European male protagonist falling in love with chief's daughter, luau feasts (one with watermelons and the ubiquitous sexualized banana metaphor), Sensualized Dancing, and Native First Kiss tropes. While only rated PG, this film has two very sexualized scenes: the Canoe Greeting and Sensualized Dance sequences. The director, Roger Donaldson, and the producers can use what I call the "ethnographic reality excuse" for such graphic scenes, but in both scenes the topless, wanton Native females are all fit, attractive, young women, while the elderly, overweight, unattractive and sickly are covered or not shown at all, so it is not an authentic representation. Of all the dances in the repertoire of Tahiti's rich Polynesian culture, Hollywood usually chooses the sexualized procreation dance, as the director did in this sexually intense scene. Here, according to Capt. Bligh's actual logs, the crew was probably witnessing an anomalous ceremony of the Arioi (religious order) coming through town—although this is seemingly lascivious dancing and behavior, it was still not common with the general population of Tahiti. Nevertheless, these sensualized stories from Cook, Bligh and other early European voyagers are augmented later by Hollywood male fantasies and imaginations, contributing to the sexualized tropes of the Pacific film genre. *The Bounty* was based on a book by Richard Hough.

Brides of Blood (1968, Hemisphere Pictures)—✗∅

Screenplay by: Cesar Amigo. Directed by: Gerardo de Leon, Eddie Romero.

This feature stars former "beach" movie actor John Ashley, who is part of a small team of American scientists that arrive on a Pacific Island to investigate strange happenings causing Islanders to sacrifice two virgins daily to appease a slow walking plant monster. Apparently, the monster and other non-moving, man-eating plants were mutated due to nearby nuclear testing. Although not listed as such, this film is a Philippines/USA co-production of "blood and sexploitation." Set in the South Seas but shot in the Philippines, this picture is full of Polynesian cinematic tropes including: the aforementioned sci-fi man-eating plants, Polynesian nude virgin sacrifices, illegitimate monkey tiki idol, sensual and inauthentic dances (with coupling), and an interracial romance between the next virgin sacrificial maiden (who is also, of course, the village chief's daughter) and the visiting American hero. The film's male lead slays the monster towards the end and in doing so saves his island lover. All Polynesians are played by Filipinos. In the final scene and after a faux sensual dance, our American hero cannot resist temptation;, he grabs the island maiden and like other Natives who couple up, they all run into the jungle to begin lovemaking. Our protagonist couple follow the other amorous partners into the jungle, embrace and kiss. The movie ends here, without further development of their relationship. This film demonstrates that these sensualized Polynesian film tropes are perpetuated beyond Hollywood. These South Seas tropes are also in films from Japan, Germany, England, Italy and other filmmaking centers. *Brides of Blood* is AKA *Danger on Tiki Island.*

Brute Master, The (1920, Pathé)—∅

Screenplay by: Ralph H. Dixon. Directed by: Roy Marshall.

The Brute Master stars Hobart Bosworth and Anna Q. Nilsson. While Nilsson is on a South Seas vacation, she receives a telegram requiring her to return home. Because of the urgency, she books passage aboard a questionable schooner with what she feels is a dubious captain. Her intuition turns out to be right, because soon out at sea, the captain (Hobart as Bucko McAllister) begins to brutally attack Nilsson in her cabin. A crewmember, who was recently punished by the captain, burns the boat. Most of those who were on the ship survive on a nearby island. Soon the shipwrecked crew sexually attacks one of the Native women on the island, and in revenge the Islanders assault Nilsson. Hobart comes to her rescue, and in return Nilsson tames the brute master. The Natives are unjustly treated as the villains, not the rapist crew nor the cruel captain, who is now the hero. *The Brute Master* is not to be confused with an earlier film, *Brute Island* AKA *McVeagh of the South Seas* (1914), although both have brutal Euro-American heroes, which was a sign of the times, even within American homes.

Call of the South Seas (1944, Republic)—✗∅
Screenplay by: Albert DeMond. Directed by: John English.

On a Pacific Isle, Allan Lane plays a U.S. undercover federal agent who has enough evidence to put an evil American gang away for exploiting Natives. With what may seem like a simple "an American hero who protects Pacific Islanders from the bad guys" plot, one has to also contemplate that usually the bad guys are other Americans let on the islands through American geopolitical foreign policy in the first place. What that storyline does not suggest is that this movie is actually a Hollywood-sexualized South Seas film. The tagline says it all in this typical Pacific narrative film: "SIZZLING!!! With South Seas Sweeties and throbbing music!!!" This is evidence that Hollywood would rather sell tickets through sex than politically promote its country with this pro–American plot. *Call* is the usual lighthearted comedy/adventure, starring Janet Martin as an island princess who is one-eighth Polynesian. This blood quantum may be the acceptable racist ratio of blood, where if one looks to be of European descent, then that person is eligible to marry a Euro-American and need not wear full brownface makeup. In this genre, being of royal lineage is also part of a discriminatory prerequisite for interracial nuptials. There is also a part for Latina dancer/actress Adele Mara, who plays a Polynesian young woman. Mara has a couple of sensuous dance numbers in the film. Satini Puailoa is the only genuine Polynesian actor with a speaking role. A third sensual quasi-Hollywood/Polynesian dance is performed by a Los Angeles–based Polynesian woman. There are also trope scenes of tiki idol worship, kava drinking, an angry volcano god, and a luau in this plot. But of course, our hero does end up with the one-eighth Polynesian princess.

Captain Calamity (1936, Grand Natl. Films)—✕∅
Screenplay by: Crane Wilbur. Directed by: John Reinhardt.

This actioner stars George Houston, Marian Nixon and Movita. A South Seas trading schooner is attacked by a gang consisting of mostly American cutthroats. This film has a simple plot about a captain with an honest boat business and loyal crew, mostly made up of Natives, but the captain has no money. Houston has a love affair with Native Movita, who as previously stated is actually a Latina actress. Some real California-based Polynesian extras, as well as two Hawaiian dancers do authentic hulas. One of the first South Seas films in color, *Captain Calamity* was filmed in California with many Latinos playing Polynesians as bit players or extras.

Christmas Vacation 2: Cousin Eddie's Island Adventure (2003, Warner Brothers)—∅
Screenplay by: Matty Simmons. Directed by: Nick Bradley.

Eddie (Randy Quaid) is the cousin of Clark Griswold (Chevy Chase from the National Lampoon *Vacation* film franchise). Cousin Eddie unjustly gets fired during the holidays, but to avoid a lawsuit his former boss sends Eddie and his family on a South Seas vacation to a fictitious island called Maluka. While there, their chartered boat is shipwrecked off the shore of an outlier island, where the usually bumbling Eddie actually does well surviving and providing for his family. Perhaps coincidentally, Eddie's family name, Tuttle, is also from another South Seas film, 1942's *Tuttles of Tahiti* (a screen version of James Norman Hall and Charles Nordhoff's novel *No More Gas*). A minimally clad young woman on the outlier is played by a Korean American, but later in the film, she confesses she is from Milwaukee and doesn't know much about the islands. *Christmas* was filmed in Southern California with lots of potted tropical plants and computer-generated green jungles, blue skies, and a blue Pacific Ocean. Mostly Asian Americans represent Polynesian Natives. When first arriving on the islands Quaid and his father-in-law, played by Ed Asner, steal lewd kisses from female, minimally clad, Native lei greeters at the airport. Fred Willard also co-stars, and there's a cameo by Monty Python's Eric Idle.

Couples Retreat (2009, Universal)—ʊ|||
Screenplay by: Jon Favreau, Vince Vaughn, Dana Fox. Directed by: Peter Billingsley.

This comedy stars Vince Vaughn, who, with four couples (including Jason Bateman, Jon Favreau and Kristen Bell), fly to a resort at Bora Bora. Māori Native Temuera Morrison has a part as the French Polynesian island guru's assistant. The four couples go on a discounted group trip for couples therapy on a Society Island, although only one couple has true marital problems; the others go along for the discounts. However, the Americans soon find out they all have to participate in the therapy. As the story progresses, the other couples confess or discover their own issues. This is a good fun comedy, but Polynesia is only the backdrop, with Morrison playing the sole featured Native, although his garb was East Indian at times—thus it's a questionable representation.

There is a giant tiki luau party at the other end of the island with Polynesian entertainers in a typical tourist entertainment blend of females doing Tahitian dancing, a Samoan fire dancer, drummers and a DJ. All the Polynesian entertainers are young, fit and barely clad, like the party attendees, who all wear bikinis and surf shorts. There is the female gaze of a nude male in a Lagoon Swim scene, but the naked and buff swimmer is from Spain. Sadly, this film shows the modern man-made lagoons, waterfalls and pools that are an integral part of today's global tourism industry in an effort to recapture the romanticized and now manufactured aspects of Polynesia's past, so as to sell hotel rooms and seats on planes. As a South Seas cinema trait, this picture has beautiful cinematography, which is not unusual when your Pacific Island location (notably Bora Bora) is naturally beautiful with generally clear weather.

Decks Ran Red, The (1958, MGM)—Ø
Screenplay by: Andrew L. Stone. Directed by: Andrew L. Stone.

There's high drama on the high seas but low production values in this drama. Despite starring James Mason, Dorothy Dandridge and Broderick Crawford, the acting and direction is weak. Famous African American beauty Dandridge plays a flirtatious Māori wife of the ship's cook. This is added to the mix of a new captain and a ruthless crew that wants to kill the captain to sell the freighter, which is based out of New Zealand. The plot features the inevitable interracial relationship. The film had poor reviews but a big audience, who probably wanted to see Dandridge—perhaps in a sarong, which never happens.

Devil at 4 O'clock, The (1961, Columbia)—Ø
Screenplay by: Liam O'Brien. Directed by: Mervyn LeRoy.

This feature has a big-time director and actors Spencer Tracy and Frank Sinatra. Tracy plays an alcoholic priest, and Sinatra, a convict.

They both end up helping Pacific Island children with Hansen's disease (leprosy) escape from a catastrophic volcanic eruption on a small French Polynesian Isle. It's interesting to compare this with the escaping volcano scene in *When Time Ran Out* (1980). Even though it centers on two major tropes of this genre, a leper colony and an exploding volcano, it is well-written, -acted and -directed. *Devil* was filmed in and around Lahaina on the Hawaiian Island of Maui. There's a Native First Kiss scene with Sinatra and a blind wahine played by mixed Latina Barbara Luna. Based on a novel by Max Catto.

Devil Monster (1946, Weiss & Landres)—|||✗∅
Screenplay by: Thelma Brooks, Juan Duval. Directed by: S. Edwin Graham.

This was a version of *The Sea Friend* (1936), obviously retitled and re-released for additional profit. Nevertheless, the film has an interesting plot about a schooner that disappears in the South Seas. Years later, a mother of one of the ship's sailors hears rumors that her son might still be alive. She hires another boat to find him, and they do so on a Polynesian Island—but he doesn't want to leave. He also has a Native lover, who is the ubiquitous chief's daughter character. The hired ship's crew then kidnaps him, but as they return home, he leads the boat to tuna grounds where they strike it rich. However, the eponymous devil monster, a legendary giant manta ray, strikes our newly found sailor and the captain has to amputate one of the hero's arms. At first distraught after his capture, he suddenly changes his attitude and happily returns home to his grateful American fiancée and mother. Besides this interracial relationship, there are also tropes of Native rituals at a luau feast, a faux Sensual Dance, a Lagoon Swim with Native female nudity, and a topless wahine canoe paddling scene. Most Natives are portrayed by Mexican-Americans. *Devil Monster* was shot in Los Angeles with a decent village set, but one has to wonder why the additional stock footage of semi-naked Polynesians was added. At first there is what seems to be a sincere interracial relationship, although full miscegenation was avoided because biracial offspring were not produced, due to the kidnapping and the changing of our hero's mind over who was his true love.

Diamond Head (1962, Columbia)—✗∅
Screenplay by: Marguerite Roberts. Directed by: Guy Green.

As a plantation family head, Charlton Heston stars as a hypocritically prejudiced *kama'āiana* (local Islander of European descent).

Diamond Head also co-stars Yvette Mimieux, France Nuyen, Oscar winner George Chakiris, and James Darren, who returns to South Seas cinema after 1961's *Gidget Goes Hawaiian*. Filmed on the Hawaiian Islands of O'ahu and Kaua'i. There is a luau scene where Darren, a brownface Hawaiian, is shot and killed. *Diamond Head* has reverse racial sex roles because the luau was an engagement celebration between Darren and the Euro-American Mimieux, the younger sister of Heston. Usually in South Seas movies it is the Euro-American male hero who falls for a racially mixed European and Polynesian female, but this film has a Euro-American female engaged to a Hawaiian male, although the romance is short-lived. As Heston is having a secret affair with a Chinese worker, Nuyen, he is hypocritical in disapproving of the interracial engagement of his younger sister. Ironically, the island women, and a few men of mixed ethnic backgrounds, are evidence that miscegenation previously took place, even though interracial family making was forbidden (to all intents and purposes, due to the Production Code, from 1930 to 1956). Chakiris plays a half–Hawaiian character, but his white father does not exist in the movie.

This plot plainly identifies racist issues to audiences through the thoughts and dialogue of Heston and his Euro-American sister-in-law (Elizabeth Allen). Here are a couple of lines, from a scene early in the movie wherein the plantation family argues over Heston's sister's engagement to the Hawaiian Darren. Mimieux: "I've heard all that before: 'Trade with them ... be friends with them ... even sleep with them, but don't marry them.'" Heston eventually retorts in anger: "You look grown up Sloane, act it! Your children will inherit Manulani [the plantation] one day ... all of it, all that goes with it. We've been in the islands over a hundred years ... we've never mixed our blood." As though indirectly giving the land back to Hawaiians is a bad idea. Of course, this is all moot because Darren was murdered before their marriage and children, so miscegenation and a just inheritance were thwarted.

Darren and his half-brother—played by George Chakiris (who won an Oscar for 1961's *West Side Story*)—are both in brownface and well-educated. In fact, Chakiris' half–Hawaiian character is a medical doctor. Still, being of half–European descent and well-educated is not good enough for Heston's character. At the end of the film Heston does father a Eurasian baby and finally accepts the child, as well as the new union between his sister (Mimieux) and now Chakiris. Ironically, although this film has an anti-racist storyline, Mimieux hypocritically ends up with the half–Hawaiian, not the full Hawaiian brother. And Nuyen, the actress who portrays Heston's Chinese lover, is not a full-blooded Chinese person. She is half–Caucasian in real life. Nuyen's character also dies at the end due to complications of childbirth, thus enabling the racist film concept of the minority half of a miscegenetic couple to be disappeared from the story. *Diamond Head*'s anti-racist plot is still mixed with racist undertones and filmmaking. The script is based on a novel written by Peter Gilman. Screenwriter Marguerite Roberts received her first screen credit in 10 years (after being blacklisted during the Hollywood Blacklist/McCarthy era) for adapting *Diamond Head*.

Donovan's Reef (1963, Paramount)—℧Ø
Screenplay by: Frank S. Nugent, James Edward Grant. Directed by: John Ford

Donovan's Reef stars John Wayne, Dorothy Lamour and Lee Marvin. The movie's backstory concerns three World War II veterans who defended the island during World War II and were then taken care of by the Islanders. Because of these actions and their love of the island and its Native inhabitants, all three settled there after the war. This is a good example of contradictory characters who are found throughout this genre: pro–American expatriates. The main plot is that these men have truly adapted to local ways by shedding their deep-bred prejudices about the Indigenous people, but a surprising visit by an older conservative Bostonian daughter (Elizabeth Allen) of one of the veterans (Jack Warden) triggers the uncomfortable idea of hiding the facts about the Bostonian's half–Polynesian younger siblings until the father returns to explain the truth is the main story conflict. *Reef* is comparable to *South Pacific* (1958), *Blue Hawai'i* (1961) and similarly framed movies in that this film avoids a former miscegenetic relationship, complete with offspring, through the convenient plot device of the death of the Polynesian mother before the story starts. The eldest of the three half–Polynesian siblings is the reigning queen of the island. Of the three biracial children, two are played by brownface Euro-Americans and one by a Chinese American.

This is the only Pacific picture with both the king and queen of the genre, Wayne and Lamour, but although they are cast in the same film, they are not a couple. It also co-stars Cesar Romero, the island's appointed governor, who is a womanizer, especially with the Native females. There are bell ringing, conch shell blowing, drum beating, and Christmas pageant scenes plus a diving stunt by local actor David Cadiente. *Reef* was filmed on Kaua'i with lots of Hawaiian cultural influence, while the film was set at a fictitious island called Hale'akaloa, meaning "house of much laughter" in Hawaiian. *Reef* is the last of the 11 movies Nugent wrote for Ford in one of Hollywood's most fabled collaborations.

Don't Go Near the Water (1957, MGM)—∅

Screenplay by: Dorothy Kingsley, George Wells. Directed by: Charles Walters.

Glenn Ford, Anne Francis, Keenan Wynn, Eva Gabor, and Gia Scala star in this World War II South Pacific Island movie about a Naval PR unit stationed on a fictional island called Tulura, which is filled with Naval nurses and attractive Natives. The "simpleminded" Natives, who live in the village of Tanoloa, are descended from Indigenous Islanders and Spaniards and speak the Spanish language, as Tulura is a former colony of Spain. Note the brownface makeup on Scala. Some Indigenes are part-Spanish and educated while others are not. Glenn falls for one with Caucasoid facial features, an educated Native played by the Italian/Irish actress Scala.

Down Among the Sheltering Palms (1953, 20th Century–Fox)—✗∅

Screenplay by: Claude Binyon, Albert E. Lewin, Burt Styler. Directed by: Edmund Goulding.

Jane Greer, Mitzi Gaynor, Gloria DeHaven, Gene Lockhart, Jack Paar and William Lundigan star in this musical. The plot deals with the relationship problems of a base's commanding officer (Lundigan) just after World War II in the Pacific ended. The U.S. troops are being organized to be sent home at this point. The main story conflict is that Lundigan is compelled, by duty, to enforce rules of "nonfraternization between servicemen and the Native women." The problem is Lundigan has three gorgeous women after him: Greer, the niece of a missionary; DeHaven, a war correspondent; and Gaynor, a brownface Native princess. Aside from the full brown body makeup and stereotypical sexually desperate Native woman, this is a good, fun comedy. There is a Hollywood sensualized mating ceremony between Lundigan and the Island princess, Gaynor, but Lundigan doesn't understand the seriousness and implications of the performance. Gaynor is ready to sleep with him after the ceremony, but when Lundigan finally realizes what has happened, he avoids Gaynor like the plague. Nevertheless, Gaynor is a relentless and jealous Native. She wears enticing faux Native costumes and performs Hollywood-created, Sensual Native Dances.

Once the harsh anti-fraternization rule is finally dropped, one can imagine the huge release of sexual tension between the soldiers and Island maidens. Of course, no one notes the frustration and sadness of the Island men. There are roles for Los Angeles–based Hawaiians Al

Kikume and Luʻukia Luana, plus early parts for Lee Marvin, George Nader, and Bob Crosby, all uncredited. Lundigan is also appointed governor—but what about the authority of the Island, the chief? Lundigan oddly sings an imperialistic song "I'm a Ruler of a South Seas Island." *Sheltering* is set in the Gilbert Islands (now called Kiribati) and based on a story by Edward Hope.

Down to Their Last Yacht (1934, RKO)—✗∅

Screenplay by: Marion Dix, Lynn Starling. Directed by: Paul Sloane.

American actress Mary Boland plays the island queen of the fictitious isle of Malakamokalu. A group of rich people are shipwrecked on Boland's South Seas island. Boland, as the queen, forces the survivors to wear sarongs, grass skirts and *malos* (simple male loin wraps), while she wears their expensive European clothes. The queen also wants to marry one of the rich passengers, but he is in love with another ship's passenger. This is an attempt at a forced interracial relationship by a Native woman, not the first instance in South Seas cinema of a man being forced into a relationship by an unattractive female. Compare *Bela Lugosi Meets a Brooklyn Gorilla* (1952), among others.

This musical comedy includes the songs "There's Nothing Else to Do in Ma-La-Ka-Mo-Ka-Lu but Love," sung by Natives, and "South Seas Bolero." This poorly written and badly cast production also suffered from weak and inauthentic art direction. It was obviously shot on a soundstage with no Hollywood illusions otherwise. This film was a legendary financial disaster for RKO that almost bankrupted the studio. AKA: *Hawaiian Nights* (1934) by RKO—not to be confused with 1939's Universal movie of the same name.

Drums of Tabu (1967, PRC/Splendor/Fisa [Italy/ Spain/US])—✗∅

Screenplay by: Javier Setó, Santiago Moncada. Directed by: Javier Setó.

Drums is first set on Fiji, where a Korean war vet and drunken beachcomber (James Philbrook) discovers a beautiful Samoan princess (Seyna Sien AKA Seyn) washed up onshore. In a reverse plot circumstance, it is American Philbrook that nurtures the Polynesian maiden back to health. Sien's character has an unusual double trope-background in that she is a woman with a questionable past (be it in this case forced) and a taboo island princess. Philbrook soon finds out that Sien escaped from a sex slaver based in Malaysia, and he protects her as much as he can. He and Sien, who is a Burmese or part-Burmese actress in real life, flee to her Samoan island of Manu'a. Manu'a (which appropriately means injury in Samoan) is also a small and historically sacred group of three isles. In the 1920s, Margaret Mead did her research for *Coming of Age in Samoa* at one of them, Ta'ū. Using this sacred island name in the story is arguably inappropriate.

As the story unfolds, the two leads characters are falling for each other, but as they travel to Manu'a, Philbrook soon finds out she is taboo and betrothed to Ta'aroa, handpicked by the island's high priest. At Manu'a the sex slaver returns to enslave Sien again and forcefully tries to marry the beautiful princess. But this time Philbrook kills the Asian blackbirder, which frees him to marry the taboo princess. I guess the island warriors were not up to the task that a single Euro-American was able to do—protecting their princess—considering the Islanders are ancestors to a historically powerful warrior dynasty of Manu'a. *Drums* has the usual interracial romance and sensualized Polynesian dancing. AKA *La Vergine Di Samoa* (Italy), *Fugitivos De Las Islas Del Sur* (Spain). European posters of this film amplify a highly sexualized Sien.

Drums of Tahiti (1954, Columbia Pictures)
Screenplay by: Robert E. Kent, Douglas Heyes. Directed by: William Castle

This action film is about a sympathetic American bar owner in 1877 Tahiti (Dennis O'Keefe) who is trying to outwit a French inspector so he can run guns into Tahiti to help a rebellion. The uprising by Tahitian Queen Pōmare (played by American Frances Brandt) and the British was to drive the French out of the islands. Meanwhile, O'Keefe is building a relationship with one of his Tahitian female workers, Mawai'i, played by another American actress (Sylvia Lewis). The plan was for O'Keefe to sail to San Francisco to obtain the guns and ship them back to the islands, but a suspicious local French inspector goes along for the ride. O'Keefe's excuse for the voyage was to marry his fiancée and bring her to his home in Tahiti. The problem is that O'Keefe is not betrothed.

Scrambling in San Francisco, O'Keefe enlists a woman of a questionable past (Patricia Medina) to marry him for $2,000, a fortune in 1877 dollars. She unwillingly does so because a mutual friend of both O'Keefe's and Medina's catches Medina trying to take the money and run. So, she has to choose between getting hitched or arrested. Picking marriage, Medina is still defiant during the trip back to the islands and is curious about O'Keefe's real intentions. At the end, Medina becomes sympathetic to the Native cause, but a hurricane AND a violent volcanic eruption quell the rebellion. Is God or Mother Nature on the side of the imperialist? In the minds of the filmmakers—yes. With her understanding of O'Keefe's honorable intentions and her shared sympathy for the Islanders, they remain married.

The two Natives in the story lose out: the Queen permanently loses her Island sovereignty, and Mawai'i loses her boyfriend. Having a Native woman beaten out by a Euro-American woman is not an unusual racist story device for a South Seas film, but what is unusual here is the American hero in this story has a non-royal Native girlfriend or a woman of lower-class origin. Surprisingly for an American South Seas film, our Yankee hero does not have a sexual relationship with the queen. Perhaps this is a plot device to emphasize the hero's understanding of the Polynesians' ill-fated situation under imperialism and their loss of land and sovereignty, but almost all of that goodwill is negated with our hero's marrying into his own race instead. Directed by William Castle, who was known for his gimmicks, *Drums* could be screened in 3D, so there are plenty of spears thrown directly at the camera and so on to capitalize on this sensationalistic stereoscopic technique.

Enchanted Island (1958, RKO)—Ø

Screenplay by: James Leicester, Harold Jacob Smith. Directed by: Allan Dwan.

A couple of sailors desert their whaling ship, which is commanded by an evil captain, while the whaler is anchored at the Marquesan Island of Nuku Hiva (although the film was actually shot on location at Mexico, in part at Acapulco). The two crewmembers then make a run for the island jungle. They were forewarned that two tribes live in the inner jungles, one friendly and the other cannibalistic. *Enchanted* stars Dana Andrews, who, with his shipmate (Don Dubbins), find what they think is the friendly tribe. Andrews falls in love with a Native girl and loves the Polynesian lifestyle of this tribe. The island lover Fayaway is played by a brownface Jane Powell, who is *hapa* (biracial) and the granddaughter of the chief. Quite dramatically, we later find out that the two deserters have actually settled in with the tribe of cannibals.

The high drama is set when Dubbins is homesick and wants to leave the valley of human-eaters and is forbidden from doing so. He later escapes and possibly becomes dinner, later that day, for the tribe. Andrews doesn't consider this scenario until later. Apparently, one is either in or out of the tribe and becomes either an enemy or possible sustenance for the group. In that case, it's lucky for Andrews he was comfortable with his new environment and not homesick. Andrews could see the beauty of the chief's granddaughter and of the life of the tribe and equally so, the tribe recognized Andrew's genuine good intentions towards them. One wonders what happened to Powell's European and Polynesian parents. Note of interest: the chief was played by the tall and very fair Friedrich von Ledebur, an aristocrat and cavalry officer from Austria. Ledebur had played in two other Polynesian roles despite not having the physical characteristics of a Pacific Islander. All three parts were within three years, with Von Ledebur also playing a Native chief in *Voodoo Island* (1957), and the famous tattooed Māori harpooner, Queequeg, in John Huston's *Moby Dick* (1956). *Enchanted Island* is a mediocre adaptation of Melville's popular 1846 novel about the Marquesas Islands entitled *Typee: A Peep at Polynesian Life.*

Ensign Pulver (1964, Warner Brothers)—Ø
Screenplay by: Joshua Logan, Peter S. Feibleman. Directed by: Joshua Logan.

This is a sequel to the popular 1955 film *Mister Roberts*, but with a different cast. Folksinger Burl Ives, Walter Matthau, Tommy Sands and Robert Walker, Jr., as the titular ensign, co-star in this version. The setting is among some fictional islands called Elison and Apathy. The island where the Ensign and his captain (Ives) land, after going overboard in a storm, is called Ramos, a real Pacific Island located in the Solomons, which borders Polynesia. Ramos is filled with sexy, barely clad Native women who greet the near-dying men that washed up on their shores with leis and kisses, without first rendering aid. In the next scene, one of the sassy main Native women, played by classical stage actress and African American Diana Sands, does nurse the men to good health in a grass hut. That pretty, younger Island women do the nursing instead of older men or women, who are well-versed in traditional island medicine, is yet another South Seas film trope.

Diana Sands is not related to co-star Tommy Sands, but she does have a resemblance and similar disposition to Hawaiian actress Varoa Tiki (born Shirley Kaluahine Piliwale Bither), who could easily have played this part. There is a scene in which characters drink kava. Also, there are early pre-stardom bits by Jack Nicholson, Larry Hagman, James Farentino, James Coco and others. Exterior scenes were shot in Acapulco, Mexico, which partly accounts for the improper Pacific Islander representation. Al Freeman, Jr., another African American actor, plays a key Native role—perhaps because the Indigenous people of the Solomon Islands are Melanesians, who are darker and have curlier hair than Polynesians. From a Hollywood perspective, there is no difference between a sexualized Melanesian and a sexualized Polynesian. Interestingly though, in the Western perspective of the exploration era, there is a huge racist difference in the historical accounts between these two Pacific Island peoples. *Ensign Pulver* is derived from the play *Mister Roberts*, written by Thomas Heggen and Joshua Logan, which was based on the novel written by Heggen.

Fallen Idol, A (1919, Fox)—Ø
Screenplay by: E. Lloyd Sheldon. Directed by: Kenean Buel.

A Hawaiian princess and composer visits California and is courted by the wealthy host's nephew, resulting in prejudices being exposed. Evelyn Nesbit plays Princess Lanoe, surprisingly not in brownface—either way, it's a false representation because Hawaiians are generally not so fair-skinned. This film also contains a scene in which, on her way home, the princess is forced to have sex with an evil ship's captain. He threatens that he'll throw her to the crew, who is also lusting after her, if she doesn't comply with his libidinous demands. There are underwater swim shots of a young Hawaiian girl, played by an American of European descent, Thelma Parker. In the end the princess and nephew reunite. This is one of the earlier plots involving a royal Polynesian guest on the continent as a social equal or a delightful spectacle, until there is a romantic relationship with a Euro-American—then true racism is revealed. Compare this film with *Never the Twain Shall Meet* (1925) and its 1931 remake. Island scenes were filmed in Miami.

Flaming Signal (1932, Invincible)—Ø
Screenplay by: Charles E. Roberts. Directed by: George Jeske, Charles E. Roberts.

Noah Beery, Sr., stars in a story about a daredevil pilot who is forced to land on a small South Seas island in the middle of a Native uprising. An evil German trader tries the reputation of a young and pretty Native woman named Manu. This German is also a hotel owner and seems to rule over most of the Natives. The pilot saves a missionary daughter from the uprising, but all other foreigners (most are bad people) are massacred. This actioner also stars a dog named Flash.

Historically, during the early days of flight, there were flying contests to Hawai'i, with a few crash landings in the Pacific. The subject of crash landings on a Pacific Isle was represented in other South Seas films. In the early days of manmade flight, the odds would not favor a successful flight to a small island in the middle of the Pacific. In Hollywood movies, American pilots always survive and become the island hero in some form. See Dorothy Lamour and Ray Milland in *Her Jungle Love* (1938), also *Air Devils* (1938) and *Forced Landing* (1941), as examples. Of course, Amelia Earhart is believed to have been lost while trying to cross the Pacific by plane in 1937. Her last known coordinates were somewhere on the border of Micronesia and Western Polynesia.

Flower of Hawai'i (1933, Ro-Film GmbH [German])—Ø

Screenplay by: Heinz Goldberg, Alfred Grunwald. Directed by: Richard Oswald.

AKA: *Die Blume Von Hawai'i. Flower* stars Martha Eggerth as a Hawaiian queen disguised as a waitress in a Paris café. The island waitress is suddenly kidnapped and taken back to Hawai'i to marry the king. However, Eggerth had already fallen deeply in love with an American officer, so the king then nobly stands aside. This is yet another interracial relationship with Native royalty and a Native man submitting to the advances of the American protagonist. The Kilima Hawaiians were credited as singer/band in this pro-colonial picture. *Flower* is the film version of the 1931 operetta by Paul Abraham. Remade in 1953 with Maria Litto as Princess Lia and William Stelling as Lilo-Taro.

Gidget Goes Hawaiian (1961, Columbia)—✗

Screenplay by: Ruth Brooks Flippen, Fredrick Kohner. Directed by: Paul Wendkos.

This popular "beach party" movie with Deborah Walley, James Darren, Michael Callan, Peggy Cass, and Carl Reiner features a dream vacation for the Californian hip and young surf crowd that loves to emulate Hawaiian culture and appropriate it as their own. Hawai'i was a Mecca for this young, West Coast pop culture group from the 1950s through the 1960s. The movie is set and filmed in glorious Eastman-color at the Royal Hawaiian Hotel. Darren sings the snappy and popular title number "Gidget Goes Hawaiian" with a Hawaiian band. The song is full of jealous innuendos alluding to Gidget's promiscuity with the Native men: "...'cause when the Gidget goes Hawaiian, she catches each Hawaiian's eye." This is the polar opposite of the common and documented trope of an American male visitor coming to the islands and flirting with promiscuous Native females. In a trope surf scene, Gidget is tandem surfing while Honolulu's landmark Diamond Head is in the background.

One scene depicts a touristic entertainment show and luau on the lawn of the hotel, with provocative Polynesian dance numbers, throbbing drumbeats and plenty of alcohol. The dancers, as well as the local wait staff, are scantily clad, as though they're wearing traditional costuming. This is a Hollywood scene that includes the sexualized trope of the ubiquitous Polynesian feast but in a modern setting between high-rise tourist hotels. At this contemporary luau, the clichéd roasted whole pig gets carried in, like royalty. In reality, cooking pork throughout Polynesia is done in dugout earthen ovens. The gutted and ti-leaf-wrapped pig is buried or semi-buried and stuffed with hot rocks, then covered with many coats of big damp banana leaves, and a final layer of dirt for a sealed covering. It is similar to a giant sealed pressure cooker, but underground. Meat cooked in this method falls apart after a few hours. There would be no "whole" pig and definitely not one with a ripe apple in its mouth.

Interestingly, this Hawai'i-set feature has sexual undercurrents dealing with whether or not Gidget and Abby are virgins, plus spouse/partner swapping and infidelity. True or mere rumors, these scenes, as well as the lyrics to the hit title song, help sell sex and romance on the islands for the Hollywood film and the Pacific Island tourism industries.

Girl in Every Port, A (1928, Fox Film Corp)—Ø
Screenplay by: Seton I. Miller, Malcolm Stuart (Titles). Directed by: Howard Hawks

This silent comedy stars Victor McLaglen and Robert Armstrong, with Louise Brooks and a bevy of beautiful actresses, as the title indicates. The two male leads are American sailors traveling the world and their pastime is picking up girls in every harbor town. One of their conquests is played by actress Natalie Kingston, who is of European descent but plays the South Seas Native girl. *Port* was directed by a young Howard Hawks who, according to Hollywood insiders, had a sharp eye for good-looking female talent—apparently regardless of representation.

Girl of the Port (1930, RKO-Radio)—Ø
Screenplay by: Beulah Marie Dix, Frank Reicher. Directed by: Bert Glennon.

In this Pacific movie, burlesque girls are stranded in Suva, Fiji, where we find an English lord turned beachcomber. An American barkeep (Sally O'Neil) is sexually harassed by a racially mixed local. This is an uncommon occurrence in this genre, as the sex and race of these character types are usually reversed. The Anglo beachcomber (Reginald Sharland) saves her, and she then saves him from the bottle (ironic for a barkeep). The cause of his drinking is a fear of fire, so there is a fire-walking scene set up by the Indigene, and Sharland passes the test. The famous Hawaiian surfer Duke Kahanamoku has a part. *Port* includes the age-old trope of the exiled woman of questionable past or prostitution and is based on the story *The Firewalker* by John Russell. Note: Suva is located just outside of Western Polynesia, but in this case, from a Hollywood perspective, there is no difference.

Hawai'i (1966, United Artists)—ΰΧ
Screenplay by: Dalton Trumbo, Daniel Taradash. Directed by: George Roy Hill.

This is the movie adaptation of James Michener's uncommon tell-it-like-it-was account of the 19th-century missionary influence on the Hawaiian Islands. Julie Andrews, Max von Sydow, Richard Harris, Gene Hackman and Carroll O'Connor star with Manu Tupou (of Tongan descent), playing a young Hawaiian Island chief. The epic film chronicled this chapter of Hawaiian history of American religious settlers, including many who turned into covetous landowners, then powerful politicians. This story is told through the eyes of one missionary family.

Included in the plot of this movie is the rare depiction of the devastation of the Indigenous Islanders caused by diseases brought by explorers, whalers and other outsiders, mostly from America and Europe. This film also shows the large contrasts between Hawaiian versus missionary practices and customs. Issues include Islander semi-nudity, incest, commonplace sex, idol worship, vivid procreation dances, infanticide, etc. On the other side of the cultural clash are outsider intolerance, impatience, greed, selfishness, attitudes of racial and national superiority, insistence on Western education, including learning the English language, the elimination of much of the Hawaiian so-called "pagan" culture (dance, language, traditions) and the imposition of full, modest clothing in a hot climate.

Interestingly, Michener also includes in his story the sharp contrast between the zealous and conservative early Christian missionaries and the free-spirited and sexually active whalers who used Hawai'i as a major port-of-call. Both outsiders took advantage of the local Indigene, one for conversion and greed, the other for sex. Here, as well as in other Pacific Island nations, the missionary settlers' zealous determination to convert and educate the Indigenous or to assimilate them into American culture is exploited to inject colonization among Pacific Island sovereignties and elsewhere. This massive, cost-free missionary effort, the unregulated intrusion of Western business interests, and the threat of U.S military might all contributed to the calculated colonization of the Hawaiian Islands. These efforts along with introduced diseases and the concealment of the Indigenous perspective from the mass U.S. voting population, while promoting a false narrative of native willingness and welcoming in mass media, degraded Native self-worth. This all augments the formula that many imperialistic countries used in conquering small nations in the last 270 years. This film boldly exposes many of these colonization efforts..

Coming right at the end of the strict Production Code era of Hollywood, *Hawai'i*, which was lensed in beautiful widescreen color, showed lots of bare Hawaiian skin of both sexes in the trope Canoe Greeting scene and in the Seductive Dance scene. But of the many dances and accompanying chants of Hawai'i, the director selected the very sensual dances of procreation with symbolic copulation to represent a narrow and sexualized view of the Hawaiian culture. Compare the sexual mating Native dances with *The Bounty* (1984) or to a lesser extent *Miss Sadie Thompson* (1953) and *Bird of Paradise* (1951). Perhaps the half-nakedness of the Natives and the copulation-simulating movements of their dance in front of the missionaries was a liberal Hollywood message to the conservative Christian right, but it was at the expense of the Hawaiians. In fairness, at least director Roy Hill shot topless whole families, including heavier and older women, as well as the fit young adults, unlike other similar Polynesian scenes in other films, who only used the latter. Trivia: this was first time a young Hawai'i-born and raised Bette Midler appeared onscreen. The Jewish-American actress/singer plays (in a non-speaking part) a young missionary wife onboard the arriving Christian proselytizers' ship and in the streets of the old Honolulu harbor set.

Two-time Academy Award-winning screenwriter Dalton Trumbo co-adapted this epic based on the novel of the same title by James A. Michener. Daniel Taradash, who won an Oscar for writing that other Hawai'i-set classic *From Here to Eternity*, co-wrote the three hour-plus *Hawai'i*. Major Polynesian roles for Jocelyne LaGarde and Manu Tupou.

Hawaiian Love (1913, World's Fair Stock Co. / Universal)—Ø

Screenplay by: Unknown. Directed by: John Griffith Wray.

This is an early one-reeler about a sea captain who woos a pretty young Hawaiian woman. Shot on O'ahu, this is probably the first Hollywood narrative film with a mixed-race romance and a Euro-American actress playing a Hawaiian in brownface makeup. It stars Virginia Brissac, a leading stage actress who was in a theater production in Honolulu at the time. John Griffith Wray, the director of this short film, also directed that same play.

Wray and Brissac lensed another Hawaiian film while in Honolulu that year with the same American cast from the play, but this time set in a pre–Western contact Hawaiian setting. The second film was entitled *The Shark God*. *Shark God* also used Americans of European descent as leads, playing Natives. Unfortunately, both of these films were viewed by millions of visitors at the 1913 World's Fair, the vast majority of whom had never seen real Polynesians, let alone on film. For *Hawaiian Love* and *The Shark God* to be the introduction to the culture of Hawai'i and its Indigenous population to millions of people—this was a huge travesty of misrepresentation and a terrible precedent to be set by Hollywood to American and worldwide audiences. The actress and director married back in California two years later.

Hell Ship Mutiny (1957, Republic)—ʊ✗Ø
Screenplay by: DeVallon Scott, Wells Root. Directed by: Lee Sholem, Elmo Williams.

Tagline: "AN EXCITING STORY! Of Passionate Love ... and High-Adventure in the South Pacific!" *Hell Ship Mutiny* stars Jon Hall, John Carradine and Peter Lorre in a tale of a ship's captain helping to prevent Natives from being exploited. Found in this film are a giant monkey head tiki, a luau trope scene with the almost mandatory Tahitian tāmūrē dance and the Samoan slap dance, as well as the Native Kiss trope. Hall marries Native princess Mareva (brownfaced Roberta Haynes) at the end after killing bad guys Carradine and Mike Mazurki. In *Return to Paradise* (1953) Haynes played a Native beauty named Maeva. Also in *Hell Ship* is a role for Tahitian actor Charles Mauu, who plays Tula. While Texan Roberta Haynes portrays a Polynesian princess, part-Tahitian Jon Hall plays an American sea captain of European descent. Either way, their characters—onscreen—have an interracial relationship. Worth noting is that the film starts with Captain Hall's noticing, as their ship nears the friendly generic Polynesian Island, that the Islanders were not enthusiastically paddling out in their canoes to greet them as they customarily did. Hall knew, with the absence of this trope behavior, that there was something amiss on the island.

Hidden Pearls, The (1918, Paramount)—✗∅
Screenplay by: Beulah Marie Mix. Directed by: George H. Melford

In this silent movie, Japanese-born and successful silent film star Sessue Hayakawa plays a half–Hawaiian son of a Hawaiian princess who was raised in the Continental U.S. While still on the mainland, Hayakawa learns that his island family's fortune is gone, and his mainland fiancée refuses to marry a poor man. Hearing that his mother has pearls hidden on her isle, he departs for the island to retrieve them. While there, he is treated well by his fellow Indigenes, who recognize him as their rightful king. A Native woman, played by brownface American actress Margaret Loomis, falls for the new king. Hayakawa finds the pearls and travels to Honolulu, where he meets his fiancée. There, he realizes she is just a materialistic gold digger, and he feels guilty about abandoning his people, who are now angry because their new king has left them. Hayakawa then returns to his new and rightful home to marry his true love.

This is likely the second time an actor of Asian background portrayed a Polynesian, with Hayakawa himself playing a Hawaiian just a year before in *The Bottle Imp* (1917). Later in Hollywood history, Asians representing Polynesians on film or TV became a commonplace practice. Hayakawa was pigeonholed to play non–Euro roles; even though a fine and popular actor, Hollywood could not put him in a serious romantic film with a white leading lady without some kind of consequences, in this case not marrying his Caucasian fiancée at the end. He later started his own film company because he was tired of playing every race but his own. Even though *Hidden Pearls* was filmed in Hawai'i, it still contained lots of Hollywood-Hawaiian culture, including Euro-Americans as Islanders and a Hollywood hula with Hayakawa.

Latinos and brownface Americans of European backgrounds were the norm to play Polynesians in Hollywood until an unofficial social organization or network of Los Angeles–based Polynesians saw the need to fill the call for extras, musicians and day players in many of the South Seas films Hollywood was producing between the '30s and early '60s. After this *hui* (group) dissolved and the use of brownface was finally deemed politically and socially incorrect, the Los Angeles studios started to use Asian-Americans for Polynesian parts in film and television. Because of this false representation in American mass media, it is unfortunately very difficult for an average continental American to distinguish a Pacific Islander from an Asian. Consequently, American directors mistakenly cast an actor of Asian descent as a Polynesian, though they be from ethnicities of distinct cultural backgrounds with distinguishing appearances, customs, etc. To this day Polynesians, Micronesians and Melanesians are lumped together with people of Asian ancestry, with terms such as "AAPI (Asian American and Pacific Islander) Community" and the "Pacific Rim."

His Majesty O'Keefe (1954, Warner Brothers. [UK])—✗Ø

Screenplay by: Borden Chase, James Hill. Directed by: Byron Haskin.

This is a huge production—and a huge mess of misrepresentation. In the title role, Burt Lancaster plays an overthrown and thrown overboard captain of a mutinous ship. Lancaster soon washes ashore on the Micronesian Island of Yap. There, the opportunistic American tries to export copra and to get the Natives to help his enterprise. He marries a biracial (half–European/half–Micronesian) girl from Palau, played by a brownface Euro-American, Joan Rice, and defeats the notorious buccaneer Bully Hayes, who is bullying the Natives. The Natives in turn make him king. After many lessons, Lancaster finally learns Island ways.

Based partially on a true story, *Majesty* was filmed in Fiji on the island of Viti Levu. The movie was also set in Palau, with the Micronesians portrayed by indigenous Fijians, who are Melanesians, a different and more ancient race. The large stone money used by the Yapese called Fe' in the movie or more commonly known in Yap as Rai was heavily featured. There were also Hawaiian *ki'i* and Rapanui *mo'ai* (tiki images) incorrectly represented. Lancaster first kisses a very innocent and startled Native woman, played by Rice. But unlike other similar scenes of this type in this genre, Rice does not give in to Lancaster's advances, and, in fact, she is very disturbed by them. In turn, Lancaster is sincerely apologetic, and they soon marry, but shortly afterwards he has eyes for a pretty Yapese woman, played by part-Afro-Jamaican beauty Tessa Prendergast made up and costumed with a Fijian appearance to resemble the Fijian (Melanesian) actors portraying other Yapese (Micronesian) characters. This unusual double misrepresentation, Afro-Jamaican for Melanesian for Micronesian, is characteristic of the film. In another Fijian part, New York Afro-American dancer Archie Savage plays a Micronesian, and another Micronesian part is depicted by veteran Jewish-Burmese character actor Abraham Sofaer. Savage also played a Melanesian in *South Pacific* (1958) on the isle of Bali Hai. Admittedly, *His Majesty* is neither a story about Polynesia *per se* nor about its inhabitants. It is about their Pacific Island neighbors who are arguably an amalgamation of distant Southeast Asian and Polynesian islands. *His Majesty O'Keefe* also demonstrates the same tropes and misrepresentations to which Oceanic neighbors are subject. The story is influenced by Gearld Green and Lawrence Kingman's book of the same title.

Houla Houla (1959, Les Films Corona [FR])—∅
Screenplay by: Maurice Griffe. Directed by: Robert Darène.

This French comedy co-stars Fernand Raynaud and Tahitian Maea Flohr as his Tahitian love interest. A film poster also shows Raynaud's other love interest, Rita Giannuzzi—a beautiful blonde back home in Europe. Raynaud plays a shy and nerdy-looking teacher in France who falls for the lovely older sister of one of his students. Her father hates him because he makes little money teaching. Our timid protagonist then gets transferred to Tahiti by mistake, and Raynaud ends up on an outlying fictional island called Houla Houla, populated by "fanatical Polynesian Mormons and Catholics." Meanwhile, the girl he left back home realizes she loves him no matter what, so she travels down to the island to save her shy future boyfriend. Before Giannuzzi's arrival, Raynaud gets along with the Natives and loves it there. He is even cultivating a romance with a beautiful Native young woman. Suddenly this shy teacher has two very attractive women after him. *Houla Houla* illustrates the imagination and gall of men in the male-dominated worldwide film industry. According to this Hollywood and apparently European chauvinistic trope, an unappealing European or Euro-American male can always win a young, beautiful Polynesian woman—and apparently a young, beautiful European woman as well. Giacomo Puccini's *Madame Butterfly* is another case in point. In the 1904 opera, a mediocre Westerner successfully woos an exotic beauty. The work was partially based on an 1887 novel by Pierre Loti, who also wrote the 1880 Tahiti-set *The Marriage of Loti*.

Hula (1927, Paramount)—|||✗
Screenplay by: Doris Anderson, George Marion (Titles). Directed by: Victor Fleming.

Giant silent screen star Clara Bow plays the title character, and legendary film director Victor Fleming (*The Wizard of Oz*, *Gone with the Wind*) shot this Hawai'i-set story in Hollywood. Bow plays the daughter of a wealthy, but often drunk, American plantation owner. Not only is he a drunk, he is also a widower, and because of these circumstances, the father is happy with Hula being raised by his wiser, older, Hawaiian head ranch hand, played by Italian Agostino Borgato. This film is an example of a stricter use of interracial coupling during the silent era. Bow has a Hawaiian name, is raised by Hawaiians, and has a more stereotypical carefree attitude towards life and dress, without the social constraints of American society. She would rather eat poi with the Hawaiian workers and not socialize with the wealthy conventional people of her own race and class. There is even the trope of her bathing nude in a lagoon, which is usually reserved for Polynesian maidens.

All this eliminates an interracial love relationship, because later in the story, our hero is a handsome Euro-American engineer who comes to Hawai'i to build a dam. Hula falls for the engineer after ignoring a local American socialite. She also does a supposedly sensual Hollywood hula (totally fabricated without any authentic Hawaiian origins) at a luau, arousing both white suitors until the two are very hot-tempered and jealous towards each other. Although not credited or easy to spot, Duke Kahanamoku is in this film as probably one of the many Hawaiian ranch hands in the poi scene.

Part of the opening title of this silent film reads: "...where volcanoes are often active, and maidens always are." The problem is that our male hero is married, with a wife back on the continent. There's a happy ending though, with the gold-digging wife finally granting him a divorce. The plot is from the novel *Hula, a Romance of Hawai'i*, the first book written by Maui-born Caucasian Armine von Tempski.

Hurricane (1979, Paramount)—℧⊥⊥⊥✗∅

Screenplay by: Lorenzo Semple, Jr. Directed by: Jan Troell.

This is a multimillion-dollar remake of the 1937 film classic *The Hurricane* starring Jason Robards, Mia Farrow, Max von Sydow, Trevor Howard, Timothy Bottoms, and Hawaiian Dayton Ka'ne, along with Manu Tupou of Tongan descent, both playing Samoans (though the film was shot on location in French Polynesia). Besides the updated cast, this version has a male Samoan prince (Ka'ne) paired with the pale American captain's daughter (Farrow) in an interracial relationship, instead of the all-Islander love relationship of the 1937 film. There is still a Canoe Greeting trope scene, but the vessels are large metal-clad American naval ships from a more modern era, and the Native canoes have very Hollywood stylized sails of different, solid colors. Although to some this could be a beautiful image, it is nevertheless very inauthentic. However, like its predecessor, the film features good hurricane special effects. (Note: This is the movie Roman Polanski was set to direct before he was charged with rape.)

As mentioned, there is an interracial relationship between Kaʻne and the blonde Farrow, but it is a reverse-gender relationship, which is not the norm in this genre. Farrow is also the daughter of the U.S. Navy ship captain (Robards), who is assigned to protect the island. Robards is not happy with this cross-cultural and cross-racial romance between his daughter and the island prince. Notably, there is a unique reverse-gender Native Sexual Dance trope scene, where Kaʻne woos Farrow directly with his sensual dance movements, while she watches from the audience, next to her not-so-happy dad. She is embarrassed and curiously aroused at the same time. Based on the novel by significant writers on the Pacific, James Norman Hall and Charles Nordhoff. Filmed on the island of Bora Bora.

Hawaiian Dayton Kaʻne was discovered on Oʻahu by Dino De Laurentiis. Soon after the completion of *Hurricane* the famed Italian producer cast Kaʻne a second time in another South Seas movie titled *Beyond the Reef* (1981), opposite beautiful part-Hawaiian model and actress Maren Kawehilani Jensen. Samoans protested the use of Tahiti, Tahitian people, and Tahitian culture doubling as American Samoa in *Hurricane,* as well as a controversial deflowering scene. De Laurentiis set his next release *Beyond the Reef* safely in French Polynesia, where he also owned a luxury resort. But in *Reef* the majority of main Tahitian roles were played by Hawaiians, imported from Honolulu and, in Miss Jensen's case, Los Angeles. *Hurricane* was later retitled *Forbidden Paradise* for TV release.

Idol Dancer, The (1920, 1st National)—✗Ø.
Screenplay by: Stanner E.V. Taylor. Directed by: D.W. Griffith.

The pioneering director D.W. Griffith filmed this South Seas love triangle. American Clarine Seymour, who plays the *hapa* (half Polynesian/half Euro-American or biracial) heroine, is involved in a budding relationship with two male Euro-American visitors, one a beachcomber and the other a strict missionary's nephew. Both fall in love with Seymour's Native charms, enticing minimal clothes, and inauthentic hulas. Seymour plays the two suitors to the hilt, until the nephew of the missionary dies in an attack by a brutal American trader and his Native henchmen. In this scene the bad trader and his thugs are trying to kidnap island women. There is a dancing to an idol scene, with again an imagined Hollywood dance routine. Seymour later throws the tiki idol into the Pacific.

This silent film was lensed in Florida and the Bahamas, and it shows. Erroneous representations of the South Pacific and its peoples and their cultures were everywhere. The Natives were a mix of brown-face Euro-Americans, African Americans and African Bahamians. There are also jerry-rigged outrigger canoes, incorrect costuming and bad, ad-libbed hulas. This inaccurate representation was common after 1914 when director/writer/producer Harry Carey decided to shoot *McVeagh of the South Seas* in Southern California, instead of the real islands—an obvious measure to save money. Both *McVeagh* and *Idol Dancer*, as well as other South Seas movies that were shot outside of the Pacific, were successful, despite the rampant falsifications. With their own ignorance about the Pacific, American movie audiences had no clue otherwise, and these faux representations continued to be reused in Pacific films for future generations. Thus, tropes and stereotypes of the Pacific were now mainstream in, and because of, the popular medium of film. These incorrect tropes are now perceived as common knowledge by the general American and worldwide public, while having no basis in fact.

Griffith did manage to get the sexy grass skirts in his silent movie, even when our Native heroine's Euro-American father objected to them. He told his daughter to cover up, and our idol dancer responded that she detested missionary clothes. The two-piece outfit and the grass skirt with full leg exposure were very erotic at the time for Western audiences, but also prevalent in other Pacific films. Also, as in other South Seas cinema, one parent of an interracial relationship is nonexistent so as to not remind the audience that the racist American taboo of miscegenation had already taken place. Based on a novel by Gordon Ray Young.

In Harm's Way (1965, Paramount)—∅
Screenplay by: Wendell Mayes. Directed by: Otto Preminger.

John Wayne, Kirk Douglas, Henry Fonda, Patricia Neal and many others star in this story of a World War II U.S. Navy captain based at Pearl Harbor. It was filmed partly on O'ahu with the Kaneohe Bay Marine Base used as one of the featured locations. Though the film is set in the middle of the Pacific Theater during World War II, one can still find classical South Seas movie tropes in this war plot. Although it features a heavy, dramatic storyline, has many rich character developments, and is well-directed, this summary primarily covers the character played by Kirk Douglas because of his character's significance. Douglas starts off as a straight-up naval officer in Hawai'i—then something dark happens. The life changing event is not shown, but the film establishes that Douglas was with a female WAC officer on a romantic, secluded Hawaiian beach location. Later we learn she was found murdered, without any evidence as to who the perpetrator was. Douglas then begins to exhibit strange behavior; for example, he gets in a fight at a Hawaiian bar for little reason.

Douglas is then transferred to the South Pacific. Later the audience meets up with him again in a Polynesian port town, with the local women soliciting servicemen on the streets and Douglas living the wild South Seas life of a naval officer. He sports a beard, a young vahine live-in girl, a bottle of booze, and leis. Now he is a man with a questionable past, escaping to the South Seas, or in this case, a lucky military transfer. In this South Seas port, there is a scene in a naval harbor with outriggers, Natives and Douglas on a canoe with an unrealistic tiki post on the front. The idol is more for the Hollywood camera and obviously not for ethnographic purposes.

Also worth mentioning, in the context of this annotated list, is that Preminger created a very sexual tone for the film, which is set at the dawn of the war, with a sensual scene of a naval officer's wife being dunked at the famous officers' pool party on Ford Island, which is in the middle of Pearl Harbor. Today, this party is organized every year as a tradition on the island to memorialize the filming of this movie. The famous director of the film also lenses a nude swim scene at Kualoa Beach in Kaneohe Bay and a beach love scene between two military officers as the Japanese planes fly overhead to attack Pearl Harbor. Although these earlier sexualized scenes are not centered on Polynesians as the objects of desire, they nevertheless still associate the sexualization theme to tropical locations of Hawai'i and the other Pacific Islands on the big screen. As mentioned, Doulas' character does have a live-in young Polynesian female lover later in the plot. Based on a novel by James Bassett.

In Love and War (1958, 20th Century–Fox)—∅
Screenplay by: Edward Anhalt. Directed by: Philip Dunne.

Robert Wagner, Jeffrey Hunter, Hope Lange, Sheree North, France Nuyen, Mort Sahl and Bradford Dillman star in this film about fighting and life experiences of three U.S. soldiers during World War II in the South Pacific. One of the Marines falls in love with Hawaiian nurse Kalai, played by Nuyen, a half–Chinese, half–French actress. Bradford Dillman plays her boyfriend, who is from a high society background and has to choose between a sincere and modest nurse or a rich, materialistic woman back home. Dillman chooses the Hawaiian nurse, which is a very different scenario from others in this genre. Usually in World War II action dramas, it is Euro-American nurses and prostitutes who entice the American G.I. away from his all-American girl back home, or they stay loyal, but rarely stay for an Indigenous girlfriend.

One of the three featured soldiers doesn't survive the war. In the Anton Myrer novel *The Big War*, from which the film's script was derived, it is Dillman who dies to avoid miscegenation. The screenwriter changed the dead Marine to be Hunter, who dies and leaves his fiancée, Lange, and new baby to survive alone back in the States. Possibly it is a sign of post–World War II times, the beginning of acceptance of interracial marriages, but in this case, there are no racially mixed children. That is also the big message in the movie *South Pacific* of the same year (1958), co-starring France Nuyen playing a Tonkinese immigrant and young love interest of American Lt. Cable.

In the Wake of the Bounty (1933, Chauvel Prods. [AU])—℧‖‖✗∅

Screenplay by: Charles Chauvel. Directed by: Charles Chauvel.

The second of five feature films about the ill-fated HMS *Bounty*, this one from Australia is by filmmaker Charles Chauvel. While his motivations for his early filmmaking (this film and *Uncivilized* in 1937) were questionable, Chauvel's career, in general, ended up being very respectable. Seemingly to avoid enforcement of the Hollywood Production Code, Chauvel played the ethnographic card in both *Wake* and *Uncivilized*. In *Wake*, Chauvel managed to put together a hodgepodge film of various styles, with his own silent documentary footage of Pitcairn Island and interior sound stage scenes in Australia plus exterior sexualized scenes shot in Tahiti showing Polynesian female nudity. Another possible motivation to finish the film in haste was possibly to exhibit *Wake* before the American studio giant MGM released the same story in a much more spectacular style with far higher quality and a much bigger budget movie.

But the race for exhibitionism is pertinent here. *Wake* contains tropes of Canoe Greeting, Lagoon Swim, and Sensual Native Dancing—all with topless Tahitian vahines. Some of these gratuitous shots were distinctly posed and choreographed for Chauvel's lens (as the director, writer and producer), also for the gaze of paying Western audiences. These scenes in Tahiti are much less accurate depictions of Polynesian life as an ethnographic observation or realistic representation. Ironically, MGM, which had a very different film with big Hollywood production values, bought out and contained the exhibition of Chauvel's version of the *Bounty* saga and even used some of its footage in the promotion of the award-winning version of their 1935 *Mutiny on the Bounty*. Chauvel did discover Tasmanian Errol Flynn, who played Fletcher Christian. Despite the film's being Australian produced, Chauvel initially had serious release complications with the Australian censoring authorities.

Island Captives (1937, Falcon Films)—Ø
Screenplay by: Al Martin. Directed by: Glenn Kershner.

This B-picture stars Eddie Nugent and Joan Barclay and is produced by Stephen Tabor. A plantation owner in Tahiti is murdered by thugs hired by a cannery company boss and his handsome son. Coincidentally, the same son is traveling to Tahiti on the same cruise liner as the daughter of the deceased plantation owner. Although it seems as if they will fall in love, she falls instead for the ship's communications officer. The ship wrecks on a reef, and the main three characters are stranded on a remote Polynesian Isle. This island is also home of a large smuggling ring with an evil leader and a wahine (played by a Latina) who has a stereotypically immature and undignified affection for the ruler. *Captives* uses stock footage of Tahiti with Hawaiian steel guitar music.

Isle of Destiny (1940, RKO)—Ø
Screenplay by: Arthur Hoerl, Robert Lively, M. Coates Webster. Directed by: Elmer Clifton.

June Lang and Gilbert Roland star in this dramatic film. A wealthy adventurer (Lang) is flying around the world. En route, Lang decides to stop on a Pacific Island to visit her brother, who is in the U.S. Marine Corps. There on the island, a local smuggler tricks Lang into letting him fly with her to escape from the island, but they crash on a neighboring island. On a speedboat, the handsome American hero (Roland) races to save them. The smuggler has a jealous Native wife (American actress Katherine De Mille) who kills him, because she finds out he was going to leave her. This presents an entirely different conception of a Polynesian wife, who is not submissive and docile, but possessive and homicidal. (This film is not to be confused with the movie *The Isle of Destiny*, produced twenty years earlier by Rialto Studios.)

Isle of Escape (1930, Warner Bros.)—✕Ø
Screenplay by: J. Grubb Alexander, Lucien Hubbard. Directed by: Howard Bretherton.

Monte Blue, Myrna Loy and Betty Compson star with Duke Kahanamoku, who plays an exotic South Seas head-hunting Native. The Hawaiian Duke kidnaps Compson on the orders of the evil American ruler of the island, played by Noah Beery. Monte resists temptations from Moira (the Islander depicted by Loy), and he saves Compson. Loy boasts to other Native women that she can sleep in Blue's hut. She had entered it earlier, but Blue kicked her out before he could relent to the seductress. Despite this, the studio's promotions department plays up Loy's relationship with Blue very differently. With a "sex sells" undertone, a released poster has Native Loy in the arms of Blue and a still of a sexy Loy in her Islander costume with a long black wig. For good measure, there is also the inevitable Native dancing and semi-nudity of female Indigenes. In 1923, the famous silent actress Compson donned the hula outfit as a half–Polynesian in *The White Flower*, while Blue starred in 1928's film classic *White Shadows in the South Seas*.

Isle of Forgotten Women (1927, Columbia Pictures)—Ø
Screenplay by: Norman Springer. Directed by: George B. Seitz.

Conway Tearle stars in this silent about a Euro-American man on the run in the Pacific. While on the lam, he falls in love with a sensuous Native girl, played by brownface American Dorothy Sebastian. Not only does Sebastian get killed saving Tearle from a drunken fellow American, but our hero's faithful fiancée, who always believed in Tearle's innocence, lands on the island to claim him because he was found innocent back home. Typical trope of a South Seas affair with a Polynesian woman, while our so-called hero has a faithful fiancée back home. Tearle is still the good guy in the eyes of his fiancée and the American audience, despite his unscrupulous sexual relationship with another woman, because she is "just" a Pacific Islander. *Isle* appears to be filmed on a Hollywood soundstage. Compare this film to *As a Man Desires* (1925). The story for *Isle of Forgotten Women* was originally written by Louella Parsons, who was a B-picture actress and screenwriter before becoming one of Tinseltown's top gossip columnists.

Just Go with It (2011, Columbia)—IIIX
Screenplay by: Allan Loeb. Directed by: Dennis Dugan.

Adam Sandler, Jennifer Aniston, Nicole Kidman, Rachel Dratch and sexy Brooklyn Decker star in this comedy/romance. Decker is a former *Sports Illustrated* bikini model who also starred in 2012's sci-fi movie set in Pearl Harbor, *Battleship*, due to her sex appeal. *Just Go with It* is minimally applicable for this book because none of the main characters are of a Pacific Island racial background; hence, there are no interracial relationships. This picture does illustrate the sexualized contemporary tourism industry, incorporating a Waterfall/Lagoon Swim scene, a commercialized mixed Polynesian dance review complete with scantily clad Tahitian dancers and a hula contest. The contestants of the hula competition are objectified and superficially judged by how sexily the tourist women dance for the audience. Older and heavy-set contestants are quickly voted off the stage, and the finalists are Aniston and Kidman, who both don the ubiquitous, but sexy, coconut bras and grass skirts. As a matter of interest, Nicole Kidman, who is known as being from Australia, where she was raised, was actually born in Hawai'i, while her Australian father did research as a biochemist at the University of Hawai'i at Mānoa at the time of her birth.

King of the Islands (1936, Vitaphone/Warner)—✗∅
Screenplay by: Joe Traub. Directed by: Ralph Staub.

This big-budget, 20-minute short was shot on the Warner Studios backlot. It is the only South Seas cinema title featuring Hawaiian musical star Wini "Leimomi" Shaw. The short also starred popular actor Warren Hymer as a shipwrecked sailor who lands on a Polynesian Isle. There he's seduced by the charm of the Natives and their dancing, but more so by the allure of lead dancer and singer Shaw. Their grass skirts, showing lots of leg, and small bikini tops were a big draw in the '30s. However, Shaw is the princess and taboo. When Hymer thinks he can overcome the customs of the taboo, he becomes a willing participant in a tribal marriage ceremony. Afterwards, he readies himself for the honeymoon with Shaw, but Shaw suddenly says "Aloha" to him and leaves. When Hymer goes after her, the chief scolds him and tells him he just married the island volcano—not Shaw. Definitely no miscegenation here.

Although filmed in Hollywood, this short featured many diaspora Polynesians living in the Los Angeles area. Most of these Southern California Pacific Islanders were musicians and dancers, and their talents are showcased in this short film, as in many other features of that era. Compare *Flirtation Walk* (1934) with many of the same musical numbers, Polynesian performers, and the same studio, which made this possible and legal. I suspect that *King of the Islands* was a very early color film, and that Warner Bros. was eager to release such a project, but in an eye-catching way. To save time and money, the reuse of a part of a pre-shot Busby Berkeley (uncredited) directed musical spectacular short would suffice. Winifred Shaw was an Irish-Hawaiian actress raised by vaudeville Hawaiian entertainers in San Francisco. She learned the hula and the ukulele before taking her singing talents and good looks to Hollywood in the '30s. Shaw is best known for her huge hit, "Lullaby of Broadway," which she crooned in the Busby Berkeley-directed *Gold Diggers of 1935*, which won an Oscar for Best Music, Original Song in 1936. Although she was in over 30 films in the '30s and part-Hawaiian, like many other Indigenous actors Wini rarely portrayed a Pacific Islander and only played a Polynesian in this short film. Dropping her middle name and being part-Irish, she could "pass" and play a tanned Euro-American and was typecast as such.

Land of Fury (1954, Rank Film Org. [UK])—|||✗∅
Screenplay by: William Fairchild. Directed by: Ken Annakin.

Set in 1821, when British settlers were first arriving to Aotearoa (New Zealand), this adventure film stars Jack Hawkins, Glynis Johns and Noel Purcell as the main English settlers and Inia Te Wiata (a Māori opera singer and actor) as the benevolent Māori Chief. Chief Te Wiata spares the Europeans and gives them tracts of land on which to settle. Wiata also has a beautiful Māori wife, who is portrayed as seductive and lascivious. She and the married Hawkins rendezvous to have an affair, and the chief, hidden in a nearby forest, witnesses the romance. Instead of violence and anger, the chief weeps and retreats into the darkness. At the end of the story, a rival tribe attacks the settlers and a battle with Wiata's tribe ensues because the chief and his tribe are sympathetic to the settlers. A very pro-colonization statement by a European film company.

The libidinous chief's wife is played by German born actress Laya Raki, who, in real life, was an exotic dancer, which arguably makes Raki suited for the character, despite her incorrect racial casting. Raki has a huge Sensuous Dance scene that is more of a modern dance, without any Māori authenticity. Although the film was largely shot on location in Aotearoa, many scenes were filmed on a soundstage in London, where Māoris living in Britain actually staged a protest against Raki's casting.

Fury has a Polynesian death scene or an "Auwē" scene. Auwē is a common cry or lamentation of sorrow found throughout Polynesia and in a few South Seas films. Thanks to filming partially on location at New Zealand, the artwork on the sets (Māori cravings, architecture, canoes, weapons, etc.), props and costumes were excellent, as is the usage of the Indigenous Māori language. Because of this, one is perplexed by the inclusion and intent of the nonauthentic Sensual Dance scene. There is also a Nude Swim trope involving Raki and Native maidens offering themselves, for the night, to the European visitors. This British production also features the same Polynesian sexualized tropes as American cinema. Also known as *The Seekers* in Commonwealth countries, the movie is based on a novel titled *The Seekers*, written by John Gutrie.

Last of the Pagans (1935, MGM)—ʊ|||✗
Screenplay by: John Farrow. Directed by: Richard Thorpe.

Stars Mala and Lotus Long, as competing Tahitian village members in a rare Indigenous Islander-centered film. After a raid and bride hunt by a rival island tribe, Mala captures Long. She hates Mala for a while, but then falls for him after realizing he is a kind, giving and responsible human being who has also saved her from a wild boar attack. An evil American slave trader breaks up the romance, and Mala is enslaved on a faraway island to do forced labor in mining. Meanwhile, Mala's chief wants to marry Lotus. We know he's a mean chief and had something to do with Mala's capture. At the end, the two lovers reunite and survive a hurricane together. They then find an unoccupied island where they can begin anew. There is an underwater battle with a giant swordfish, a wild boar (monsters in the paradise cliché), and a hurricane ending (the natural disaster in paradise trope). There is also a vahine Lagoon Swim trope, with rival Native males and the ever-present gaze of the male Western audience also watching the Native women bathe. Set and filmed in French Polynesia, *Pagans* has real Indigenous extras and authentic Polynesian dialog with English subtitles. Mala is part-Jewish and from an Alaskan Native tribe and has played more Polynesian roles than Native American (and Jewish) roles. Lotus Long has a mixed ancestry with Chinese, American and possibly Hawaiian lineage. The two non–Tahitian leads did a reputable representation in their Tahitian speech and cultural nuances.

The film also contains a Canoe Greeting trope and the bell ringing cliché. The film includes parts for Indigenes Rangapo A. Taipoo, Ae A. Faaturia and Teio A. Tematura. The credits include some of the same MGM crew who worked on the second unit scenes of *Mutiny on the Bounty* in the same year and location. The story is by John Farrow, who married actress Maureen O'Sullivan (Jane in the Tarzan film franchise) and was the father of Mia Farrow, who would star in another movie shot on location in French Polynesia, 1979's *Hurricane*.

Also of note: Today, the word "pagan" or "savage," especially in a title, would be considered politically incorrect. As recently as 2009, an independent filmmaker came to Hawai'i to film a biopic of the young and beautiful Hawaiian Princess Kaiulani. The working title was "The Savage Princess," but because of much protest the project was retitled *Princess Kaiulani*. Although the semantics between the words "pagan" and "savage" may differ, the connotations are the same—an inferior, uncivilized race or being.

Leopardess, The (1923, Paramount)—Ø
Screenplay by: J. Clarkson Miller. Directed by: Henry Kolker.

This romance drama was set in the South Seas, with many Native roles played by Euro-Americans, including Alice Brady as the half–Polynesian Tiare. A millionaire finds the South Seas maiden Brady, who believes in the Native religion and customs. Montagu Love plays the millionaire who wants to marry and tame the wild biracial Polynesian, whether she wants to or not. The captain of Love's yacht, Edward Langford, doesn't like this forced marriage and gets thrown overboard for his convictions. Later on, in New York, Langford catches up to them, but Love releases his pet leopard on Langford. However, the big cat attacks Love instead. The captain and Tiare return to the island together, starting a nonstandard, committed interracial relationship. Strange title with a strange story by Katharine Newlin Burt.

Loved by a Māori Chieftess (1913, General Film Company)—Ø
Screenplay by: Edmund Mitchell. Directed by: Gaston Méliès.

The Chieftess referred to in the title was possibly played by Ma'ata Horomona. What could be the first South Seas film with an interracial relationship is based on a local New Zealand story. This two-reel drama is about a Māori princess being told by a Native sorceress that she will marry a tall white man with fair eyes and a beard. Soon a white trapper is caught by the Māori, who plan to devour him as the main course for dinner, but the princess realizes that he is the one she must marry. The problem is there is a betrothed Māori prince who disagrees. After some hardships, her father, the big chief, relents and the outsider is accepted by the tribe as a chief, who is now free to wed the princess. A feast is made to celebrate the occasion.

Gaston Méliès was French, so there is no American miscegenation stigma. This was one of a number of short Tahitian and Māori stories (along with early documentary and travelogues shorts) filmed by Gaston Méliès during a 1913 voyage to the South Pacific, Australia, Java, Singapore, Cambodia, and Japan. He shot about 64 films (now mostly lost). In contrast to early American films of the period, the Méliès films—which were shot on location—had much better representation and participation of Polynesians and other Indigenous people. Gaston Méliès worked for his famous and talented film pioneer brother, Georges Méliès, via the American Branch of Georges' company, Star Films. Georges is the fabled motion picture pioneer who directed classics such as 1902's *A Trip to the Moon* and was depicted by Ben Kingsley in Martin Scorsese's 2011 *Hugo*. Unfortunately, Gaston's South Seas/Asia film adventures almost bankrupted his brother's company because of the costs of traveling to authentic, distant locations.

Love Trader, The (1930, Tiffany)—✕∅
Screenplay by: Harold Shumate. Directed by: Joseph Henabery.

Leatrice Joy plays a prudish wife of a puritanical South Seas captain who moors his boat offshore and keeps his wife onboard, away from the "indecent" Natives. One day, on a canoe, a stereotypical half–Polynesian Native hears beautiful singing from the ship and investigates. The singer is Joy, and she and the Native fall for each other. The next day, as part of an Indigenous plot, the Islanders sneak her ashore to witness a celebration of their shark god and for a night in the Native's hut. She returns to the ship before her husband, but after many days below deck, Leatrice can't stand being away from her Native lover anymore, so she finally jumps overboard. Unfortunately, she jumps right outside of Bedford, New England. He—or she—who hesitates is lost…. *Trader* features an early example of reverse sex interracial romance. All of the Islanders are played by Euro-American cast members. Released in Britain as *Island of Desire.*

Lt. Robin Crusoe, U.S.N. (1966, Buena Vista/ Disney)—|||✕∅
Screenplay by: Don DaGradi, Bill Walsh. Directed by: Byron Paul.

Dick Van Dyke stars as the surviving pilot of a plane wrecked during World War II. Like the namesake of the title, Van Dyke survives on a tropical Pacific Island. Also, similar to the later *Island of the Lost* (1967), *Call It Courage* (1973) and the 1980 and 1991 *Blue Lagoon* films, this island is sacred to Pacific Islanders, one where banishment, survival, and sacrifice take place. As in most of the other films mentioned, a sacred large stone tiki with idol worship a sacrificial *ahu* (platform) are present, but, of course, in this Disney version there, is no bloodshed, just an escapist comedy. In this amusing family film, a female Polynesian played by half–British, half–Chinese actress Nancy Kwan is banished to the island for refusing—like a good, self-assured and independent princess—to participate in a prearranged marriage. Compare this to *Bird of Paradise* (1932).

She is found by Lt. Crusoe, and after they establish a trust for each other, Crusoe gives Kwan a name, not "Friday" as male Natives are given in the original Defoe story, not "Saturday" as the female Native is dubbed in the 1932 *Mr. Robinson Crusoe* film, but "Wednesday." In some way, all of the Crusoe "day-of-the-week" Native characters are saved by the American or European hero, so they are indebted and thus subjugated to him. Why do the Natives have to learn English, why are they given names and not the other way around?

The male Natives in *Lt. Crusoe* are portrayed as clumsy, unintelligent and uncivilized. The female Natives are portrayed as man-hungry and chase Van Dyke all around the island. As in all Crusoe stories, the main European protagonist is a super tropical survival genius, demonstrating that in two or three months he can learn and do what "primitive" Pacific Islanders have taken generations to learn to do (except for navigating off the island or building a seaworthy boat), exhibiting a so-called European or Euro-American intellectual superiority. The audience forgets how the Natives navigated and arrived by their own designed and built canoes to the remote Crusoe island in the first place. In this Crusoe version, not only does Wednesday get there alone by canoe, but also her many island girlfriends get there later in the story, and Kwan's mean father and his warriors also get there via canoe—all with no problem. But as with all Crusoe stories, our American or European hero has no clue how to get off the island.

In *Lt. Robin Crusoe, U.S.N.*, there is the Waterfall/Lagoon Swim trope with the Polynesian female beauties who join Wednesday on the island. All the Native women, who are apparently conscientious objectors against their home society and political refugees, want Van Dyke, the only male. Before the arrival of the other Native women, Van Dyke stays loyal to his girl back in the states, although he's tempted by the presence of beautiful Kwan, with her minor advances and small, tight-fitting sarong. When Wednesday's angry father, who is also the high chief, lands on the island with fierce warriors, Van Dyke is prepared to defend himself and all the Native women supporting him. Van Dyke uses surplus gear from a nearby Japanese sub wreck and integrates this gear to the interior of the large mo'ai-like sacred tiki image to try to scare away the Native invaders. Although funny for a Western audience, this could be considered insulting and sacrilegious to Indigenous Pacific Islanders— even more so, given the inept representation of the Polynesian invading force. The chief, played by Russian-born Armenian actor Akim Tamiroff in brownface, arrives on the island in the ubiquitous Native-carried rattan, pheasant throne chair. Large Melanesian–like masks are worn by the island warriors, while the women wear contemporary Polynesian sarongs. *Lt. Robin Crusoe, U.S.N.* features red carpet clichés: conch shell blowing, tiki worship, along with the sensualized Native female dance. The story by Retlaw Yensid (Walter Disney spelt backwards) is obviously influenced by Daniel Defoe's *Robinson Crusoe* novel.

Lure of the Islands (1942, Monogram)—|||✕Ø
Screenplay by: Edmond Kelso, George Bricker, Scott Littleton. Directed by: Jean Yarbrough.

Robert Lowery, Kahala, Odetta Bray, and Santini Puailoa co-star with Gale Storm (of the popular 1950s TV series *My Little Margie*) in this film. Also, former stripper Margie Hart plays a half–Polynesian, half–Irish island princess named Tana O'Shaughnessy, who is taboo in this "B" movie. Federal agents posing as victims of a shipwreck land on a tropical island to expose a criminal war gang. The fictitious island's name is Tanaukai. A seductive Native dance is performed, a simple hula with swaying hips and a wanton stare by the dancer. Two songs, "Tahiti Sweetie" and "Lure of the Islands," are performed, plus a Tahitian number, which is similar to the Bugs Bunny number in the 1943 cartoon *Wackiki Wabbit*. Tana tries to seduce Lowery, so he can take her off the island. The film includes a Lagoon Swim with a Western gaze, a luau feast, and many female light Seductive Dance tropes. Lots of the usual sexy grass skirts exposing lots of leg. The Texas-born Storm plays a character named "Maui."

Maeva (1961, Cascade)—|||✕Ø
Screenplay by: Maya Deren. Directed by: Umberto Bonsignori.

This 90-minute drama, shot on location in French Polynesia (Tahiti), stars Tumata Teuiau, who plays the title character, Maeva (which is Tahitian for "welcome"). The film's lobby card reads, "Young and pretty but she brings out the fury between men." The small poster also shows a dead man. Horror in paradise. Taglines on a larger movie poster read: "She was wild! She threw herself with abandon into dancing, flirting … and love!" "Her desire was always there—and nothing and no one could cool down her burning!"

Also, the poster exhibits Maeva's character in a revealing sarong, dancing the Tahitian tāmūrē, kissing a man, posing naked for an artist and swimming nude. Usually, a poster over-exaggerates the story, but the point is clear: the sexualization of a young Polynesian woman for the consumption of the American and European male gaze. AKA: *Pagan Hellcat, Wahine* & *Terror en Tahiti* (Mexico). Judging by the credits of the majority of the film crew, this is an Italian production. Possible sexploitation with multi-national distribution, including the United States. Screenwriter Maya Deren was one of cinema's great avant-garde, experimental filmmakers, creating poetic works such as 1943's *Meshes of the Afternoon*.

Māori Maid's Love, A (1916, Vita Film Corp [AU/NZ])—∅

Screenplay by: Lottie Lyell, Raymond Longford. Directed by: Raymond Longford.

This is a lost silent film about an unhappily married surveyor who is sent to New Zealand to work on a project. There, he falls in love with a young Māori woman. He stays on the island, and they have a child together, but the mother dies giving birth (compare this with 1953's *Return to Paradise*). The father gives the baby to a Māori man, who later kills the father. This is an early foreign film about the subject of miscegenation. The New Zealand/Australian-produced film may be the first with a plot that produces biracial offspring, although out of wedlock. The story has dire consequences because of it, as the Native mother dies giving birth and the father is later killed.

Marriage Cheat, The (1924, First Nation Pictures)—∅

Screenplay by: C. Gardner Sullivan. Directed by: John Griffith Wray.

In this drama, Percy Marmont plays a handsome missionary who fights off the advances of a Native woman portrayed by American Laska Winter. Marmont does fall for a Euro-American woman (Leatrice Joy), whom the Natives saved after she jumped from a yacht full of promiscuous, drunk Americans. Joy is adopted into their tribe. The problem is the yacht owner is still her husband and Joy just gave birth to his child. Her husband finds Joy and the baby on the island, but soon after they board his yacht, a tempest hits the local harbor and sinks it. In rough seas Joy has the choice of saving her baby or the dreaded husband. Joy chooses the baby, but Marmont saves the husband from drowning. The husband does not survive the ordeal, so our Euro-American heroes are free to marry. Brownface Winters plays a stereotypical Polynesian woman chasing desperately after European and Euro-American men. Also costars Adolphe Menjou. Stock, background and second-unit shots filmed in Tahiti. Story by Frank R. Adams.

McVeagh of the South Seas (1914, Progressive Motion Pictures)—✗Ø

Screenplay by: Harry Carey. Directed by: Cyril Bruce, Harry Carey.

Before becoming a legendary Hollywood character actor, Harry Carey directed a handful of silent pictures, including this confusing love story set in the South Seas on a faux island in the Solomons. *McVeagh* has poor art direction and representation, with some Afro-Americans playing Natives and Euro-Americans in brownface playing lead Pacific Island characters. This is the first South Seas Hollywood film shot in Southern California, which is the likely reason why the incorrect depictions are so evident.

McVeagh is a bitter and brutish bad guy who runs everything from guns to gin. He even runs the local chief. He picks a Native woman by making a few of them dance sensually. Like the whole film, the dance is very inauthentic. The island woman he picks soon loves McVeagh and is devoted to him, but McVeagh's first mate lusts after her and causes a Native uprising to kill McVeagh. Before the revolt, McVeagh's old fiancée arrives on his island. She cheers him up, apparently ignoring his infidelity, and at the end he sails off with the fiancée back to San Francisco, abandoning the Native woman who loved him. Although McVeagh treated her and all of the Natives badly, he did love her, too. Nevertheless, he sails off with his own kind. Unfortunately, tropes of false representation inundate and miseducate the moviegoing masses with the impression that this representation is genuine and what to expect from the Pacific Islands and its peoples and customs. AKA: *Brute Island.*

Melodia Prohibida, La (1933, Fox [Spain])—Ø

Screenplay by: Enrique Poncela, William Kernell, Paul Perez. Directed by: Frank R. Strayer.

Conchita Montenegro is a star from Spain who was known in the English-speaking world. *Melodia* features an all-Spanish cast in a South Seas story of love between the island prince and his Native bride-to-be. One day, before the wedding, a ship arrives with wealthy European and Euro-American passengers. One of the newcomers is a beautiful, fair woman, and the prince falls for her. He flirts with the visitor and sings a sacred Native song to her. From then on, his life falls apart. He ends up dying alone in San Francisco after recording his now-a-hit sacred song. Quite a lesson in interracial relationships: don't try it. It is not just a matter of differences of culture and race but a matter of class. Even though both people are considered high class in their respective societies, the upper crust on the mainland U.S. and Pacific Island royalty are not the same because the European/American culture is considered dominant in European/American films. Either way, this is a rare attempt of a Native male courting a European/American female, especially in a foreign film. However, in this masculine European/American film industry, the dejected former Native bride-to-be is considered insignificant in this Spanish/American plot. AKA: *La Cancion Prohibida*.

Miss Sadie Thompson (1953, Columbia)—✕Ø
Screenplay by: Harry Kleiner. Directed by: Curtis Bernhardt.

This famous movie stars Rita Hayworth, José Ferrer and Aldo Ray in the third major adaptation of W. Somerset Maugham's classic short story, following the silent version *Sadie Thompson* (1928) with Gloria Swanson as the title character and *Rain* (1932), a talkie with Joan Crawford as Sadie. This film is about a temptress named Sadie Thompson who is a woman with a questionable past (prostitute). Sadie is running to Asia via the South Seas from Honolulu. With a stop in Samoa, Sadie finds a bunch of sexually hungry U.S. Marines and a self-righteous preacher who judges her harshly. Not the environment she was hoping for, but as in the story and its other film versions, the main character, Sadie Thompson, is full of sensuality. Also of note: this iteration of the Sadie story includes a scene in which the preacher and his prudish wife witness a Samoan sensual coupling dance.

The American woman of a questionable past is a common trope of South Seas cinema and another sexualized product of this genre. In addition, one of the focus subjects of this book is the hypocrisy of the zealous Christian right found throughout Polynesia in film and in history, but what makes the story of Sadie Thompson so powerful is that at the end, the overzealous, self-righteous, pious preacher rapes Sadie and then commits suicide.

More appropriate to this section of the book is that in all three

Sadie films there is also an interracial relationship between American expatriate innkeeper Joe Horn and his Native wife Ameena, but in this version, the couple have 10 biracial children. This is a rare instance in South Seas cinema, but there are only a few seconds onscreen where Joe, his wife and at least one child are together in one shot. A common cinematic characteristic of South Seas film is that filmmakers or the studios try to avoid the visual appearance of miscegenation. Ameena was played by Latina Diosa Costello, who was born in Puerto Rico. This popular plot was based on the short story *Rain* by W. Somerset Maugham. Before any of its film versions, it was first made into a play expanded by writers John Colton and Clemence Randolph.

Miss Tatlock's Millions (1948, Paramount)—Ø

Screenplay by: Charles Brackett, Richard L. Breen. Directed by: Richard Haydn.

Barry Fitzgerald, John Lund, Robert Stack, Monty Woolley and Wanda Hendrix co-star in what today would be considered an insensitive and appalling story about a mentally challenged heir who disappears. The guardian of the heir then hires a look-alike to appear in the rich family mansion in Los Angeles, but there, the imposter falls in love with the heir's sister and is about to confess to her that he is a fake so he can date her. However, that confession would destroy the mentally handicapped son's chance of inheriting anything because he had to be home on a certain date to sign papers pertaining to the will, the reason for the ruse in the first place.

Fortunately, the real son shows up on the assigned date—but he brings a big surprise home with him. We find out he's been in Hawai'i for a while, got married to a Hawaiian wife (Hilo Hattie), and has two biracial little boys. He brings all of them home to the L.A. mansion. Needless to say, everyone is in shock. Here is a rare film, made in Hollywood, that not only features an interracial marriage but also the full fruition of miscegenation, biracial offspring. The question here is: Are the filmmakers trying to say that miscegenation is permissible in this case, due to the fact that the male Euro-American spouse is not of sound mind? Or is a mentally challenged Euro-American on the same level as a normal Polynesian person? These human scales of racist imbalance have been used often in South Seas cinema, i.e., a Euro-American commoner is equal to an island prince or princess, or an older and/or unattractive European or American sailor is equal to a gorgeous young Polynesian woman in the prime of her life. *Miss Tatlock's Millions* is based on a play titled *Oh, Brother!* by Jacques Deval. Co-screenwriter

Charles Brackett, ironically, wrote classics such as Greta Garbo's 1939 *Ninotchka*, 1950's *Sunset Blvd.* He also made uncredited contributions to Dorothy Lamour's first Sarong Girl movie, 1936's *The Jungle Princess*.

Mister Roberts (1955, Warner Bros.)—℧Ø

Screenplay by: Frank S. Nugent, Joshua Logan. Directed by: John Ford, Mervyn LeRoy.

Big budget production with big Hollywood male leads, Henry Fonda, James Cagney, William Powell (his last film) and Jack Lemmon. Lemmon, who was a relative newcomer compared to the other cast members, won the Best Supporting Actor Oscar for this performance. Set in World War II, the plot revolves around an ambitious and spiteful naval commander (Cagney), who wants to captain a larger, fighting ship—not the old cargo hauler that he presently commands. He takes his frustrations out on his crew. Mr. Roberts (Fonda) risks his neck to be a buffer zone between the captain and crew.

This popular film continues older tropes of the genre and mirrors the *Bounty* saga. These include a Canoe Greeting scene in which the Natives, in their outriggers, greet a naval ship. But this time, the ship is a large, modern, steel military ship. However, the Natives, with females, still manage to climb aboard and ignite the crew into a frenzy. As a South Seas cinema naval tradition, the lower-ranked swabbies go nuts over the Native women, while the officers maintain their composure. Cagney plays the World War II version of Captain Bligh, while Fonda has the Fletcher Christian role. Like most World War II liberty privileges in the Pacific, the festive dance scenes are replaced with dances in a bar, with liquor replacing the feast of food and local prostitution replacing promiscuity. In other words, Western civil behavior with the opposite sex in the Pacific is still absent. Sex is a commodity traded during the war. The ship's crew usually get drunk and have their way with some of the local women, and as a part of the film trope, the swabbies are almost always escorted back to the ship by MPs. *Mister Roberts* includes such a scene. Duke Kahanamoku has a small part as the local Polynesian chief.

The sequel, entitled *Ensign Pulver* (after Lemmon's character), was released by Warner Bros. later in 1964 with a different cast. In *Roberts*, the Polynesian Island of Elysium is fictitious, and Kaneohe Bay, on the Hawaiian Island of O'ahu, was the shooting location for Elysium (which is, of course, is a word derived from Greek mythology that's synonymous with "paradise"). Local Hawaiians and Hawaiian koa wood outrigger canoes were used for the film. For indirect ethnographic purposes the pre–1955 Kaneohe Bay is beautifully green without the numerous homes covering the shores and hills of Kaneohe today. Nominated for the Best Picture Oscar, *Mister Roberts* was based on an equally popular play written by Thomas Heggen and Joshua Logan, which was based on a book, also written by Heggen. *Roberts* is the first of two South Seas cinema collaborations between the famed screenwriter Frank Nugent and director John Ford. This duo also teamed up for 1963's *Donovan's Reef*. Joshua Logan, who was uncredited as a *Roberts* director, helmed another World War II-era South Seas classic, *South Pacific* (1958), as well as the *Mister Roberts* sequel, *Ensign Pulver.*

Moana: A Romance of the Golden Age (1926, Paramount / Famous Players-Lasky)—✕

Screenplay by: Robert Flaherty. Directed by: Robert Flaherty

This film is an early docudrama classic, shot on location in Savai'i, Samoa, that depicts Samoan lifestyle and values. It was produced and directed by Robert Flaherty. *Moana* is the first of three South Seas films directed/co-directed by the famous Flaherty, but the only one he completed. *Moana* has a simple plot about the daily life of the titular Moana (played by Ta'avale), a young Samoan male, and his girlfriend. Towards the end, Moana becomes a man through a tattoo initiation ritual. Also noteworthy is that while reviewing this classic, John Grierson, film critic of the *New York Sun*, is credited with coining the word "documentary." However, *Moana* has a fictional romance plot combined with shots of Native life of a contemporary documentary style, so in reality, it is more of a "docudrama," a more modern term. There are valuable semi-ethnographic shots of early Samoan life in this film: in harvesting edible plants, coconut tree climbing, food preparations, tattoo making, conch shell blowing, and other customs.

Moana also stars Fa'amgase, who played Moana's young girlfriend, Pe'a, and T'ugaita played her mother. One criticism of the film was the constant showing of Fa'amgase's breasts throughout the film, while other Samoan women were covered. In reality, missionaries had covered Samoan women by the 1920s, and the women back then may have felt uncomfortable to be topless, unlike their ancestors. The exposure of Fa'amgase's breasts may have started the argument over what is ethnographic and what is staged body exposure for a male gaze by the filmmakers and for the audiences. Grierson, the reviewer, also had only one criticism: "Lacking in the film was the pictorial transcription of the sex-life of these people." In the same vein, after viewing the first cut, from the masculine Hollywood perspective studio heads criticized the fact that Moana and his girlfriend didn't do anything sexual with each other. AKA: *Moana of the South Seas.*

Note: the name *Moana* means ocean in most Polynesian cultures. Moana is also the female title character in the hit animated Disney film of 2016. All Polynesian names are unisex.

Molokai: The Father Damien Story (1999, Era Films [BE/AU/US])—✗Ø

Screenplay by: John Briley, Hilde Eynikel. Directed by: Paul Cox.

This co-production boasts a big cast: Peter O'Toole, Sam Neill, Kris Kristofferson, Tom Wilkinson, Derek Jacobi, Leo Kern, and Alice Kruge, with the then-unknown lead David Wenham from Australia. The script is based on the famous story of a Belgian Catholic priest who volunteered to work in an unorganized and underfunded "leper colony" in what was then the Kingdom of Hawai'i (pre–American Annexation). During the time when Father Damien served there, ignorance and trepidation ran rampant worldwide about this long existing and well-known disease. Appallingly, no one had dared to check on the conditions of the Hawaiian colony. Needless to say, they were deplorable when Damien arrived. It was a savage, every-man-for-himself survival situation.

This is the brave, fact-based saga of Father Damien who, with the aid of a few others (most importantly, Hawaiians), brought the colony to a civilized state. Hansen's disease (the proper name for this disease of nerve damage and skin and limb disfigurement) had no cure back in the time of Father Damien. Although not fatal, the latter stages of the disease are gruesome to some, debilitating, and very infectious. The movie was actually filmed on Molokai's Kalaupapa Peninsula, where the "leper colony" still exists, and some of the last generation of residents with Hansen's disease were used as background patients in this period piece set in the 19th century.

The location was critical to the story, a relatively flat peninsula jutting from the base of the world's tallest sea cliffs, and the rest of the peninsula is surround by one of Hawai'i's roughest seas fifty weeks of the year. Although a spectacular and beautiful location, it also forms a perfect natural prison. The inhabitants, thinking that God and others had abandoned them and that they did not have long to live, created an environment of utter chaos until Father Damien's arrival. There are many subplots of personal change in this film, but there are also three scenes worth discussing here.

One, there is a faction of Hawaiians who took the "primitive" and "savage" route of sexual abandon and the worshiping of ancient Hawaiian gods with procreation rituals. The camera lens did not attempt to show this, but the audience has a sense of shock owing to the Father's reaction to this faction's behavior. Judging by Wenham's response to the physical activities of this group, whatever they were doing was deplorable to his priestly eyes. Two, somehow in all of this chaos, some other Hawaiians constructed a bar with moonshine, topless dancing and other wanton acts. Three, suddenly one of Father Damien's faithful young Hawaiian women followers thinks the Father is strong and handsome and wants to have sex with him. He angrily refuses and makes her leave. I imagine these vices took place in some form or another, and Father Damien rebutted temptations of some kind, but these semi-fictional sexualized scenes, written to build the moral character of our protagonist European Priest, were at the expense of Hawaiian integrity, reputation, and dignity, given this narrow and sexualized representation.

Molokai was theatrically released only in Europe but distributed on tape and disc elsewhere in the fall of 2000. Notes of interest: Academy Award winner Daniel Day-Lewis was actually scheduled to play the "Leper Priest" but hurt his back on his previous film and had to decline. Also, Robin Williams was also set to play the Priest in a big budget Hollywood studio production shortly after this film was completed, but it never materialized—perhaps due to the surprisingly high quality of this low-budget version of the Damien story and its surprisingly (because of said budget) famous cast. David Wenham, who at the time of this film's release was only popular in Australia, later became known around the world due to *The Lord of the Rings* movie series.

Molokai's official poster features four men of European descent. One only played in the first part of the film, and a second only appeared at the end. Where are the conscientious Hawaiians who historically and heroically assisted the Father and were instrumental in changing the attitudes of many of the patients of the colony? And where are the women who had crucial roles in this story, such as Princess Liliuokalani and Mother Marianne Cope? Yes, it is a marketing tool to sell theater tickets and DVDs to mainstream audiences with the big-name performers featured on the posters. Why not have an image on the poster that represents the intriguing story itself, not who is "sort of" in it? The plot is based on a book by Hilde Eynikel, who is from Belgium. Hawaiian actors of note: Kate Ceberano, playing the Hawaiian Princess Lili'uokalani, Keanu Kapuni-Szasz, Henry Kapono, Curtis Crabbe, Norbert Palea, and Verona Tiki.

Moon and Sixpence, The (1942, United Artists)—Ø
Screenplay by: Albert Lewin. Directed by: Albert Lewin

This is a film that will not admit that it is based on the life of the infamous (or famous, depending upon your POV) painter Paul Gauguin. The main character in *Moon* is called "Charles Strickland." George Sanders stars in W. Somerset Maugham's story of an Englishman leaving "civilization" to paint in Tahiti, after being influenced by a small Tahitian tiki he bought in Paris. He cohabitates with a Native girl, paints masterpieces and dies of leprosy, even though, as discussed above, Hansen's disease is not fatal. There's an odd twist at the end when Sanders makes his Native wife burn all his works.

Earlier in the film, the young Polynesian bride to be (Ata) is played by a very young (17 at the time) Latina actress Elena Verdugo, who is a servant of an elderly and educated biracial Tahitian woman, Tiare Johnson. Johnson treats Ata like an object, passing her off to Strickland because Johnson advises Strickland that he needs "a good woman" on the island. Ata is much younger than Strickland, but there are no concerns about age. Strickland does, however, worry that Ata might not want him. But Ata, being a "good" Polynesian girl, would love to marry Strickland. Then Strickland tests her by telling her: "I shall beat you; you know." Ata responds with a small smile: "How else shall I know you love me." Sign of the times. Also, Tiare Johnson is played by talented, educated (math and law degrees), and Texas-born character actress Florence Bates. Bates, who had a late but successful career, has played many character roles, but interestingly she played three Polynesian woman in two years during this time. She also played Queen Liliha in 1944's *Tahiti Nights* and Emily in *The Tuttles of Tahiti* (1942). Luckily, Miss Bates was not locked as a typecast mature Polynesian woman, and she went on to an enjoyed a fulling acting career playing many acting types.

The Native Feast trope scene is found in this film. Stock footage was shot in Tahiti and used for the movie, but the rest of the film was lensed on a soundstage. It is shot in black and white, but interestingly, Tahiti scenes are shot in sepia tone, and one scene is in color: the artist's very colorful Gauguin-like works are shown at the very end as they are being burned. Besides the artwork, there are huge similarities to Gauguin: both the main character in *Moon* and Gauguin are European stockbrokers, both paint and are miserable in Paris, both end up in Tahiti painting young, minimally clad Tahitian females and both physically suffer miserably. Like the real Gauguin, Sanders here exploits the Polynesian young woman for the sake of sexualized art—similar to Hollywood studios (which could be why Gauguin is so celebrated, besides his beautiful use of color).

One can categorize the paintings as art, but either way huge profits were made in exploiting and exporting the sexualized image of the Polynesian maiden. The imagery emanates from the mind of a European or a Euro-American, from an actual painted pose to filmed scenes, with all decisions of dress and/or undress made by the artist or director. At times, it's not an ethnographic observation of authentic images and representation but imagined sexualized images for commercial gain or the commercialization and marginalization of the Polynesian female. To be fair, this may not have been the original intention of Gauguin or the character Strickland; after all, Strickland eventually destroys all his work, and as for Gauguin, the riches paid for his canvases were reaped by others after his death in the Marquesas. Legendary producer/director Stanley Kramer gained experience on this film, earning an associate producer credit.

Mr. Robinson Crusoe (1932, United Artists)—✗∅
Screenplay by: Thomas J. Geraghty. Directed by: A. Edward Sutherland.

During a private cruise to the South Seas, Douglas Fairbanks, Sr., bets his fellow wealthy, socialite friends that he can survive on a South Seas island like the real Mr. Crusoe. He then jumps off the yacht and swims ashore to a paradisiacal island. Here he proves to his friends and American audiences that he can do anything "primitive" Islanders can do, although in reality, the real Robinson Crusoe (believed to be Scottish castaway Alexander Selkirk in the early 18th century) took years to master tropical living. In this movie, like all films, the shelters are built by a stage crew, with modern tools, along with other unrealistic Hollywood conventions of non–Indigenous creatures—such as an intelligent monkey somehow living in Polynesia. There is also a trained turtle in the film.

Unlike the real story of finding a Native male friend named Friday, Fairbanks' tale involves saving a Polynesian female beauty, who is running away from her betrothed. This time the Polynesian runaway is named Saturday and is played by Latina Marie Alba. Male Natives are treated as ignorant and brutal. Being of the opposite sex, particular tensions arise between our two lead characters. There are scenes of Native First Kiss and brief nudity. Notably, when in Fairbanks' hut for the first time, one of the first things Saturday does is look around and then, being a female, she naturally, washes the European and American-like dishes. This is a sexist trope found in many other genres. In Polynesia, the "dishes" are made of bamboo, wood, coconut shells, and dried gourds, not like the Western-looking cooking gear made of natural tropical materials found in this film. It's a wonder Native Saturday not only knew what these kitchen utensils were, but also what to do with them in the accompanying Western sink and water faucet.

Mr. Robinson Crusoe was filmed in Fiji, Tahiti, Samoa, the Marquesas, and in the United Artists lot in Hollywood. The future hit song *Moon of Manakoora* plays throughout film, five years before Dorothy Lamour famously sung it in the intermission of the film *The Hurricane* (1937). Native First Kiss is reversed in this film. When Fairbanks wants to kiss Saturday goodnight, she demands that they should do it her way, by *honi*, or rubbing noses, not via the touching of lips. At the end of the movie Saturday is entertaining onstage in a big American city. When she finishes, she and Fairbanks, who is in the audience, throw each other *honihoni* (nose rubs), not kisses. An unusual, inconclusive ending with their undeveloped relationship. Also, there is an unusual scenario for an Islander in this genre: Saturday is actually happy and well-adjusted living on the mainland. The story is by Douglas Fairbanks.

Mutiny on the Bounty (1935, MGM)—ʊlll✕Ø
Screenplay by: Talbot Jennings, Jules Furthman, Carey Wilson. Directed by: Frank Lloyd.

This classic *Bounty* film, which won an Academy Award for Best Picture, remains the only feature set in the South Pacific to do so. Although another Best Picture Oscar-winner was the 1953 *From Here to Eternity*, *Eternity* was set in Hawai'i, which is located in the North Pacific, even though in the genre Hawai'i is commonly referred to as being a South Seas island. This *Bounty* featured the biggest star at the time, Clark Gable—"The King of Hollywood"—plus British actor Charles Laughton and Franchot Tone of the legendary Group Theatre. All three were nominated in the Best Actor Oscar category (a record), but none won. Although the MGM epic received eight Oscar noms in total, *Bounty* scored only one win, the grand prize of Best Picture. Laughton's performance was so powerful that many caricatures of him playing Bligh were developed by comedians and cartoonists.

Unlike the previous *Bounty* film by Charles Chauvel in Australia, the Hollywood Production Code and its enforcement were in full effect in 1935, so this version of the *Bounty* scarcely displayed, nor needed to display, the full temptations of a half-naked and wanton Polynesian female as did the 1932, '62 and '84 *Bounty* films. Granted, this feminine impact is important to the storyline and a large reason for the mutiny later in the film, but the love of Polynesian females, in this version, was just as strong as it is in the other films, even without much exhibition of skin: the attraction of the women in this picture was not just physical but also emotional. Christian truly loved Maimiti, his Tahitian mate, whom he holds in high esteem, and his marriage to her was genuine, which is unusual for this genre.

There are the major tropes of the Canoe Greeting without female nudity, topless swim scene suggesting but not exhibiting bare breasts, dancing but not sensually and a first kiss with love and mutual trust as its base, not lust with personal and national conquest motives. In a deck scene with Natives, there is actual fighting and jealousy between the Native men and the Western sailors. With fewer women than men, this conflict in some form is naturally almost bound to happen, but not in this genre, in which, usually, spoils or the objectified Native woman goes to the white men without dispute.

But the most uncommon item in the movie is that actual miscegenation had taken place between Christian and Maimiti, culminating in parenthood. There is a unique shot of the couple and their biracial baby girl together onscreen. Truly significant and historic. How did they get away with it? The producers were not censored by the Production Code staff because of the little known "Polynesian exception," which makes it permissible to marry and bear offspring with a Polynesian, but with no other non–European races. Seemingly, more than ninety percent of the writers, producers and directors did not know of this exception, because miscegenation leading to marriage and children was in some form avoided in the vast majority of South Seas films. From any perspective, this exception or permission of miscegenation is still a very racist concept.

The two female leads of the film were Mamo Clark, a Hawaiian with some English heritage, who was an out-of-state student attending USC (although she earned a cinematography degree from UCLA, much later in life, in 1965), and Movita who is a Mexican-American, born Maria Castaneda. Movita made a career from playing Polynesian roles, thus her name change. Ironically, she was married to Marlon Brando, who always had a fascination with Polynesian women. One wonders if he thought Movita was a real Polynesian when they first married. After divorcing Movita, Brando then married a real Polynesian, his *Mutiny* co-star, Tarita. Interesting note: the other Fletcher Christian, megastar Clark Gable, like Brando, also had the South Seas acting bug since his teenage years after watching the stage play *The Bird of Paradise* when it hit the theatre in Akron, the closest city to his small Ohio hometown.

Because he is bilingual, the part of Tahitian leader Hitihiti was played by Tahitian Bill Bambridge, who in 1931 was a local liaison and assistant director on *Tabu* with director F.W. Murnau. Bambridge also had a small role in *Tabu* playing a local policeman. His role in this *Bounty* as Hitihiti parallels with his own life as a bilingual film crew liaison much like the real Hitihiti, who was a bilingual Native and liaison aboard another early British ship of discovery, the *H.M.S. Resolution*, captained by James Cook. Both were happy and eager to do their part. In this film, Hitihiti is portrayed as the Tahitian chief, but in the real history, King Tu (who later changed his name to Pōmare) was the high chief, and Hitihiti was one of his representatives. This film, *Mutiny on the Bounty*, was based on the bestselling book by Charles Nordhoff and James Norman Hall.

Mutiny on the Bounty (1962, MGM)—ʊ✖Ø

Screenplay by: Charles Lederer. Directed by: Lewis Milestone, Carol Reed.

This movie was famous not just for its content, but for its controversies during filming. Marlon Brando, the legendary actor, had real obsessions with Tahiti. There were many issues over control, with Brando inserting himself over many aspects of the film, which reportedly had the first director (Reed) quit and the second director Milestone wanting to leave. Lots of rain and Brando's insistence on questioning every line and camera angle, along with his tardiness, allegedly caused storied delays in filming in Tahiti.

Nevertheless, aspects of the film were astonishing, especially the cinematography (filmed in glorious Ultra Panavision 70 Technicolor) and the people of Tahiti. The highly respected Robert Surtees received a Best Cinematography Oscar nomination, while the epic received a total of seven Academy Award noms. The onscreen customs, costumes, culture, the handsomeness of the Polynesians, and Tahiti itself were jaw-dropping. Thousands of Indigenous Tahitian extras were used in the filming process, especially in the Canoe Greeting, in the Native feast scene, and in dance scenes of spectacular imagination that were probably larger than real-life Tahitian fetes. While still filming during the Production Code era, Native women were just barely covered by the ubiquitous and strategically placed flower leis and double-stick tape. The use of this tape was an old Hollywood innovation, which didn't leave much to the sexual imagination. As with all *Bounty* films, exposure of this anatomical nature left the lower rank and file crewmembers of the *Bounty* in a testosterone frenzy, while the officers behaved with decorum relative to their positions.

188 **Part II—Filmography**   *Never the Twain Shall Meet*

Besides stupendous trope scenes of Canoe Greeting and Sensual Dance, there is also the Native First Kiss scene, under the ferns, between Christian and Maimiti, who was played by Tarita. Captain Bligh, played by Trevor Howard, catches them in the act and reminds Christian that the Native woman he is with is Chief Hitihiti's daughter. In the real *Bounty* encounter, there was no chief Hitihiti *per se*. Tu (later renamed Pōmare) was the high chief or king. Historically, Hitihiti was Pōmare's bilingual representative and official greeter of the *Bounty* because of his experience as a former British/Tahitian liaison on-board an earlier British ship during Captain Cook's second Pacific voyage. In this film, the Chief's assistant is a fictional character, Minarii, played by Latino Frank Silvera, but his role was based on the real Hitihiti. High Chief Pōmare, in real life, never did come to the beach to greet the *Bounty*. Perhaps his doing so onscreen was an attempt by the American filmmakers to embellish the importance of a European ship's arrival. Also, Maimiti was not Pōmare's daughter, but probably of some high rank. The fictionalized chief Hitihiti was played by Matahi, the former star of *Tabu* lensed some 31 years earlier in French Polynesia. His full name was Matahiarii Tama, and he claimed he was a humble fisherman. With a name like Matahiarii (ari'i means some kind of chiefly ranking), however, there may have been royalty in his veins somewhere. The Canoe Greeting scene begins with the cliched conch blowing. This *Bounty* saga is also based on the 1932 novel by Charles Nordhoff and James Norman Hall.

Never the Twain Shall Meet (1925, MGM/ Cosmopolitan)—Ø

Screenplay by: Eugene Mullin. Directed by: Maurice Tourneur.

The tagline on the movie poster reads: "The Famous Romance of South Seas Love." But in reality, as its title derived from an 1889 Rudyard Kipling poem suggests, the theme of this movie is the negative consequences of interracial marriage. In this early version of the plot, a Euro-American husband returns to an island with his half–Native princess wife Tamea, played by New York-born, Euro-American Anita Stewart. Note that two requirements are fulfilled in this genre pertaining to a Native Islander love interest—royalty and part-European. The couple return to the island after the rejection of Tamea by his family.

Soon after arriving back on the archipelago, her husband (Bert Lytell) turns ill with rock fever (claustrophobia and/or homesickness). Then the friends of the husband and his former fiancée pay a visit to the island. The husband leaves with his former fiancée, and his friends stay behind to comfort the distraught Native princess. Not a very romantic South Seas love story. Miscegenation is thwarted because the husband simply leaves. Did Tamea not need an annulment or divorce proceedings because she was "just" an Indigenous Islander? This suggests some kind of lesser human of lower significance. Confusingly, the marriage to an Indigene wasn't even recognized in the end of the story, although they did get married on the continent where legal papers do exist. The message here is: Don't look for romance in the South Seas; it will only lead to problems. There is no appearance nor mention of the princess' parents or of their biracial relationship. There was some location filming in Tahitian. Based on a novel by Peter B. Kyne.

Never the Twain Shall Meet (1931, MGM)—|||✕Ø
Screenplay by: Peter B. Kyne. Directed by: W.S. Van Dyke.

This talkie remake of the earlier 1925 silent movie co-stars Latina Conchita Montenegro as the Tahitian love interest and Leslie Howard. A good drama in which it is established that Howard has a platonic relationship with a proper (same race and social status) fiancée. This story begins with socialite Howard taking care of his dad's friend's 'afa (half) Polynesian daughter in Tahiti. Howard gets caught up in her raw sexuality, directness and simple ways. He returns to the continent but drops everything to return to live with the 'afa popa'a (half-white or biracial person) back on the South Seas island. In Tahiti, Howard finds the food and lifestyle of the islands are too hard for him and most importantly, his Tahitian dream girl continues to be sexually active with other Native men. He gets angry, hits the Polynesian girl and becomes a drunken beachcomber until his former fiancée comes to rescue him. Howard, in turn, rescues a fellow drunken beachcomber, to whom Howard swore earlier that he would never become a degenerate. Ironically, the second beachcomber had earlier warned Howard he would be trapped in paradise and also become a drunken degenerate.

This film has the classic "paradise-is-hell plot." The lure of the island, as it does in many cases, includes the tried-and-true trope of the sexualized *vahine* (Tahitian woman). In this film, the unwarranted stereotype is that Polynesian women are licentious before and after marriage. In most Polynesian cultures, a commitment to coupling or marriage is a serious taboo to break. Pre-marital or pre-committed life may not have the same taboos unless a female is of chiefly rank or a descendant of a god where her virginity is of high importance—proof of which can be a matter of public display. Offerings of virgin girls to members of early-contact European ships were more of the erroneous

Never the Twain Shall Meet (1931, MGM). The title comes from Rudyard Kipling's "Oh, East is East and West is West, and never the twain shall meet," Kipling's colonial take on how two diverse cultures can never coexist, which is precisely the theme of this story. The film stars Leslie Howard as a young heir, who, due to unfortunate circumstances, takes on a beautiful half–Polynesian ward, played by Latina female star Conchita Montenegro, and they fall in love. This film not only exposes hypocrisy and prejudices of the American upper class, but also exposes Hollywood's misrepresentation of the Polynesian female as a promiscuous person.

construct and belief by Pacific Islanders that Europeans were gods or contained much *mana* or godlike power that could be passed down to offspring. The Europeans took full advantage of this error. *Twain* was filmed in Tahiti with Feast, Dance and Waterfall/Lagoon Scenes by W.S. Van Dyke, who specialized in shooting films at "exotic" locations with an ethnographic-type approach combined with Hollywood drama.

North Shore (1987, Universal)—✗Ø

Screenplay by: Tim McCanlies, William Phelps. Directed by: William Phelps.

Arizona's wave-pool surf king (Matt Adler) learns Hawai'i isn't easy for a "fresh off the boat" *haole* (Euro-American or foreign outsider) who wants to ride the waves at the famous North Shore of O'ahu. He falls for a local girl played by part-Filipino/mainlander Nia Peeples (who replaced a fired part-Hawaiian/California actress). Peeples' pidgin English and hula are good, but another "haole" North Shore board shaper's pidgin is hilariously bad. Gregory Harrison plays a retired surfer with a Hawaiian (Loke Lau) as his wife. They have three biracial young children together. Miscegenation is no longer an issue by the late '80s and finally reflective of social reality on the islands. Compare this film with *Ride the Wild Surf* (1964). At a family luau, Hawaiian entertainer Bruddah Iz Kamakawiwo'ole plays his ukulele and sings his famous rendition of "Somewhere Over the Rainbow." Also at the luau, Peeples dances her little sensual hula directly to Adler, and there, one of her little brothers tells outsider Adler to: "Go back to Arizona, haole. Leave local girls alone." In addition, the film portrays notorious North Shore surfer thugs, the "Black Shorts," as themselves. Produced by and story by Randal Kleiser, director of *Grease* (1978), two *Blue Lagoons* (1980 and 1991) and others.

Nude Odyssey (1961, PCM/Francinex [FR/IT/US])—Ø

Screenplay by: Golfiero Colonna, Ennio De Concini, Franco Rossi, Ottavio Alessi. Directed by: Franco Rossi.

Part-Hawaiian Elisabeth Logue (co-star of 1966's *Hawai'i*) plays Matae in this story about an Italian filmmaker who heads for Polynesia to shoot a film but ends up helping an American woman find her husband. The filmmaker has hot romances with Tahitian women, lives with two women in a mansion, then befriends a boy and a priest. He feels guilty and returns home. I don't know how much "nudity" is in the film, but its title is undeniably a marketing ploy. Being a popular subject for American and European males, certainly there must be Polynesian nudity of some kind.

There's some location shooting in Tahiti. There are other Italian-produced films with other European countries attached to it as distribution partners, because unfortunately there is a market for this kind of Polynesian sexualized specialty film in all these countries. Note that the writing was done by an all-male committee. Tahitian actor Charles Mauu is also credited in this film. It won a Silver Ribbon for Best Cinematography by the famed Allessandro D'Eva. The movie is also known as *Odissea Nuda* (Italian) and was later rereleased as *Aventure a Tahiti*, perhaps to lure the larger general market audience.

Omoo Omoo the Shark God (1949, Lippert Pics.)—✗

Screenplay by: George Green, Leon Leonard. Directed by: Leon Leonard.

The film is set on the fictional Polynesian Isle of Taviti, where a cursed captain returns to retrieve giant black pearls that he'd stolen. The pearls were the eyes of a sacred tiki statue of a shark god. The captain buried the very valuable pearls near the tiki image. The skipper's even greedier first mate kills the captain for the chance to keep the pearls for himself. Meanwhile, an ethical sailor and the captain's daughter want to return the pearls to the local Natives. Unfortunately, the curse is passed on to the daughter when the captain is murdered, which complicates things, because she is the only one left who knows where the pearls are buried. Erroneous Oceanic representations of monkeys, snakes, and tigers are displayed in this low-budget film. Also look for tiki idol worship, cursed taboo and pearl greed tropes in this "B" movie. More specifically, one can view in this film a very inauthentic Sensual Dance as part of secretive tiki idol worship. The maiden's first mate is viewed gawking from the bushes at the island maidens dancing, but the viewing of this sexualized dance is really for the European and American audience. Very loosely suggested by Herman Melville's 1847 sequel to *Typee, Omoo: A Narrative of Adventures in the South Seas*. Omoo is a Polynesian word for "wanderer."

On the Isle of Samoa (1950, Columbia)—∅

Screenplay by: Harold Greene, Brenda Weisberg. Directed by: William Berke.

This movie stars Jon Hall, but this time the "Sarong Boy" is playing a Euro-American. After stealing money from his partner, Hall crashes his getaway plane on a South Seas island. There he meets and falls for Native brownface American actress Susan Cabot, playing the part of Moana. On the island there is also a missionary who's actually friendly (rare for a Hollywood South Seas film). At first, Hall plans to leave with his riches, but his repaired plane is permanently wrecked by a volcanic eruption. Cabot is hurt, also. In his remorse, Hall decides to return the money and come back and live with Cabot. Hence, their interracial relationship develops. Al Kikume plays the chief, and the story is by Joseph Stanley.

Operation Pacific (1951, Warner Bros.)—∅

Screenplay by: George Waggner. Directed by: George Waggner.

John Wayne and Patricia Neal star in this World War II naval story. *Operation* has strong submarine action sequences, as well as a shore leave drama, with the Duke (Wayne) trying to win over ex-wife (Neal), a nurse at Aiea Heights Naval Hospital located above Pearl Harbor. There is a fight between a drunk and rowdy naval crew and some Hawaiians in a bar. Apparently, Al Kikume's character is the Hawaiian bar owner, who wants compensation for damages. In a funny scene on board the naval vessel, sailors watch another Warner Brothers submarine film, *Destination Tokyo* (1942), with Cary Grant captaining a sub in Tokyo Bay—something that never happened. The chief petty officer rolls his eyes, and a lieutenant leaves the room because he can't take the Hollywood version of the war anymore, even though this officer is really an actor in another Tinseltown version of the war.

Besides Euro-American males dressed in sexy hula outfits for comic relief, *Operation* is on this list as an example of many others South Seas films that skirt the World War II issue of rampant and unofficially sanctioned prostitution in Honolulu and other parts of the Pacific. There are many drunken soldiers and sailors on leave, and who knows where they go? John Wayne, in another film, had a serious and obvious prostitution scene, even though there was no direct mention of a transaction for sex. *Sands of Iwo Jima* (1949) was set in Honolulu, but that is a very rare scene. There are many white women of questionable pasts in South Seas cinema, and one presumes they were Honolulu prostitutes, but it is rarely if ever enunciated as such unless the film precedes a novel in which prostitution is spelled out clearly in print. Of course, the Hollywood self-regulated Motion Picture Production Code between 1934 and 1968 did prohibit such activity and related vocabulary on film, which the film industry was forced to do by the U.S. government. One would not see this adult activity in newsreels or schoolbooks. The U.S. did go out of its way to suppress the fact that the "sex for hire trade" was widespread among our greatest generation of servicemen, who exchanged services with a majority of Euro-American prostitutes and some Islanders during World War II. At times, these soldiers were also being "entertained" onscreen by young Polynesian women, who, like their predecessors of an earlier era, are portrayed as wanton, licentious, half-naked characters. The official movie poster of this film illustrates this, albeit in subliminal small print. *Operation* includes O'ahu location shooting.

Orator, The (2011, NZ Film Comm. [New Zealand])—|||

Screenplay by: Tusi Tamasese. Directed by: Tusi Tamasese

Set in a small village in Samoa, *The Orator* stars Fa'afiaula Sagote, Tausili Pushpara, Salamasina Mataia and Ioata Tanielu. Saili (Sagote) is born a small person in a society inhabited by mostly large Polynesian people. Saili must find himself, accept who he is and go beyond his self-imposed limitations. Directed and written by Tusi Tamases and associate produced by Samoan actor Maiava Nathaniel Lees, this is an example of an Indigenous Pacific film and is not within the scope of this filmography. However, *The Orator* is listed here as an example of a film from the Pacific region, made by Native Pacific Islanders, that illustrates the contrast between a simple and real Indigenous story and a sexualized Hollywood storyline in the same setting.

A case in point: this film contains the Lagoon Swim scene trope, but it is lensed very differently than in a Hollywood South Seas film. In *The Orator*, Native women do bathe together in a beautiful lagoon, but the characters here are from different stages of life: They are middle aged and elderly and heavyset. Most importantly, they bathe in the village bath fully clothed. These realistic Polynesian women are not all nude or semi-nude, they are not all young and fit, frolicking with carefree laughter, but with the aches, pains, and stresses we all have in life. There is no indication of any kind of sexualization in this scene, just real life in a Polynesian "Women's Only" bathing area. AKA: *O Le Tulafale*.

Other Halves (1984, Finlayson Hill [New Zealand])—Ø
Screenplay by: Sue McCauley. Directed by: John Laing.

At first this movie has a similar plot about an interracial encounter in a hospital setting as in another New Zealand film, *The Whole of the Moon*, lensed later in 1997. Love breaks color, age and class barriers in urban, contemporary Auckland in *Other Halves*. The main cast includes Mark Pilisi as the young and socially troubled Polynesian male and Lisa Harlow as a 30-something *pākehā* (Euro-New Zealander) housewife, who is in the hospital because of a nervous breakdown. In the mental ward, she meets drug addicted, 16-year-old gang member Pilisi, and Harlow is attracted to him. After their release they live together.

Maybe Harlow should have had more treatments because the story's dilemma is not just about race, but about age and class, which Harlow should have recognized in a better state of mind. Two problems are evident in the film. The first problem is that Pilisi treats Harlow worse than her husband did. Besides the story's being nonsensical, Pilisi portrays a one-sided stereotype of violent Polynesian men, as in the domestic violence movie *Once Were Warriors* (1994). The other problem concerns the age difference, which can be better understood as a question of age in a sex-reversal role. What if a 30-something Polynesian-New

Zealander man, with a history of mental illness,, took home a young Caucasian 16-year-old street girl to have an affair? Temuera Morrison has a small part in *Other Halves*, which is based on a reportedly autobiographical novel also by Sue McCauley, a pākehā New Zealander who also wrote the screenplay.

Other Side of Heaven, The (2002, Excel Entertainment Group/Disney)—Ø

Screenplay by: Mitch Davis. Directed by: Mitch Davis.

Heaven is an indie that was picked up and distributed by Disney. Young stars Christopher Gorham and Anne Hathaway, as well as many Native actors, notably Joe Folau, Nathaniel Lees, Miriama Smith, and Alvin Fitisemanu, appear in this contemporary missionary drama. It is a big-hearted true story about an early "Mormon" missionary proselytizing at the outer islands of Tonga. If one isn't biased against Mormonism, this can be an entertaining film. There is great photography and charming acting by the local Indigenes, as well as the outsider missionary.

There is also a hurricane scene or natural disaster trope. A rare heart-filled Polynesian farewell scene occurs, as opposed to a sexualized Canoe Greeting scene. In another cliché, with the help of her mother, a young Native woman tries to seduce the young American missionary by isolating herself with him and dropping her clothes to tempt him, but he stays loyal to his girlfriend back on the mainland and to his religion. He persuades the pretty young lady to think not of physical gratification but of eternal love from above. Compare this with Father Damien's temptation in *Molokai: The Father Damien Story* (1999) and Van Dyke's temptation in *Lt. Robin Crusoe, U.S.N.* (1966). *Heaven* is based on John Groberg's autobiographical account titled *In the Eye of the Storm.*

Pacific Banana (1981, South Australian Film Corp [AU])—|||Ø

Screenplay by: Alan Hopgood. Directed by: John D. Lamond.

Two Australian pilots working for a small South Seas airline are trying to find love at different Polynesian islands. Manuia Taie co-stars as one of the girls on an island. The plot is similar to clichéd maritime storylines with merchant seamen or military crew members, with "a girl in every port." Later, with the invention of passenger airplanes, the adage should be changed to: "a girl in every airport."

This objectification of women is a worldwide trope, and the Pacific is not an exception. The film holds the general sexist notion that a man can have multiple women in different locations, while each woman stays true and stays put, waiting for her dishonest and disloyal man to occasionally return. While these types of plots are generally comedies, we see in retrospect that there is nothing funny about them for the women involved. Another good example is Elvis' *Paradise, Hawaiian Style* (1966), in which Presley has women on every Hawaiian Island. At times in *Pacific Banana*, the women know of the others, but it seems not to concern them much, as though they are fixated upon or obsessed about one man, and nothing else matters. This demonstrates the incorrect assumption that women are not independent and cannot think or function on their own. Males dominate Hollywood and other modern global film centers in executive hires, screenwriters, and in film directors.

Female nudity and the nude swimming trope are included in this picture. This softcore sexploitation "R"-rated movie was filmed in different South Pacific locations, including Huahine. *Banana* is comparable to older South Seas films like *A Girl in Every Port* (1928) and *Girl of the Port* (1930).

Pagan, The (1929, MGM)—|||Ø
Screenplay by: John Howard Lawson, Dorothy Farnum. Directed by: W.S. Van Dyke.

This hit movie stars well-tanned Latino actor Ramon Novarro (who also played the title character in the 1925 silent epic *Ben-Hur*). *Pagan* is about a happy-go-lucky *hapa* (half–Polynesian) young man sunning, swimming, lovemaking, and singing with an operatic voice "The Pagan Love Song." The film also features another beautiful hapa (Euro-American Renée Adorée), who is the ward of a strict missionary (Donald Crisp). Both hapa (no plural "s" in Polynesian languages) fall in love with each other. Both pairs of miscegenetic parents of the main characters have all died before the story begins, but in Novarro's case, he inherited a huge copra plantation. Novarro is portrayed as a stereotypical Polynesian, lazy, with no cares for wealth and money. He has neither any ambition nor any clue about running the plantation.

The missionary on the other hand has business dealings on many islands, not ministerial but material. Working with the bank, the evil missionary tricks Novarro into reopening his plantation and adding a general store. To do so the missionary tells the naïve Novarro he just simply has to borrow money from the bank. The so-called Christian knows that Novarro has no sense for money or profit, due to a very different, culturally based economic system. Novarro soon goes bankrupt, and the missionary buys the debt from the bank as he had planned. The missionary now owns the plantation, and then suddenly and forcibly marries his pretty and protesting young ward Adorée.

Before this forced marriage is consummated, Novarro kidnaps Adorée, and they live deep in the jungle, until the evil, land-grabbing missionary recaptures her and takes her aboard his ship. Novarro is in fast pursuit and a fight commences. At the end, the evil missionary falls into water full of sharks. This part-talkie was filmed in Papeete, one of several movies lensed on location in French Polynesia by W.S. Van Dyke. Co-writer John Howard Lawson went on to become the first president of what is now the Writers Guild of America and interestingly, in 1947, one of the blacklisted Hollywood Ten.

Pagan Island (1961, Cinema Syn. / Century)—✗Ø
Screenplay by: Barry Mahon. Directed by: Barry Mahon.

Part-Hawaiian Nani Maka plays the character likewise named Nani Maka, who is a princess on an all-woman Pacific Island. Filmed in Florida, this sexploitation or soft porn flick uses mostly local Euro-American women to play Polynesian women and Afro-American Floridians to play neighboring Melanesians. The plot is about a Euro-American man who shipwrecks on this "pagan" island where the women—except for Nani Maka—hate all men. The stranded male falls for Maka, but the taboo princess is to be sacrificed to the tiki sea god. Instead, Nani Maka and the man paddle away in the survivor's raft. The underwater scenes were shot in the Seaquarium at Miami.

There is the cliché warning bell. All women are fairly young (excluding the middle-aged chieftess), fit and topless. There are not only no men but also apparently no elders or children on the island as well. Fresh leis are always present to cover some breasts but not all. In one case the leis remain fresh even after days in the hot ocean adrift in a life raft. There is tiki idol worship with a very inaccurate statue of a Pacific Island deity image, which can be construed as offensive to some. There are also giant monster clam and Sensual Native Dance tropes. The sexy hula worship dance is for the audience's lens and to excite the loins of our shipwrecked visitor. Nani Maka is obviously a hula dancer in real life, so her hula movements are proper, but the purpose of her particular dance was improper (not for idol worship). There is a Native First Kiss trope, but for an island of only straight women, Nani seems to be an experienced kisser—not an uncomfortable or innocent female with her first lip-to-lip European/American style kiss, which runs contrary to the naïve-Native First Kiss trope of this genre. As our interracial couple tries to escape, the giant clam mortally wounds Nani Maka. Pretty Nani dies in their escape raft days later and right before a rescue ship comes along, which obviously kills the plans for a miscegenetic family.

Pagan Love Song (1950, MGM)—ʊⅢ✕Ø

Screenplay by: Jerry Davis, Robert Nathan, William S. Stone. Directed by: Robert Alton.

Along with Rita Moreno and Howard Keel, Esther Williams stars in this musical romance set in Tahiti. Of course, there is a water ballet by a brownface Williams, who plays a wealthy *'afa* (half) Tahitian woman who lives with her high society Caucasian aunt. We never see or hear about her interracial parents. Interestingly, in this film the standard Canoe Greeting trope has been updated from the greetings of early contact European and American wooden sailing ships to a much larger steel cruise liner full of tourists. Like most films of this genre, the Islanders wear new, bright, colorful tropical printed attire and fresh leis, which is clearly a cinematic trope. There is a diving for coins trope scene initiated by Keel, but our Polynesian heroine, Williams, can't believe tourist Keel's ignorance of contemporary island culture. Keel, who inherits a plantation on the island, is still trying to practice this European and American convention of treating Polynesians as if they belong in a lower-class position by throwing cheap coins into the water for amusement and to assert his status as master and Pacific Islanders as poor, uneducated labor. Williams' educated character is either thinking this or thinking that Keel is just an old-fashioned cheap tourist because he's only tossing coins, which does not take inflation into account. Later, there is a forced First Kiss scene by Keel until the Native Williams gives in.

Exteriors were filmed on the Hawaiian Island of Kaua'i. There is also a key role for Tahitian Charles Mauu and the featured Polynesian dancers Tani Marsh and Freddie Letuli, the Samoan knife and slap dancer. The then-teenaged Moreno plays Mauu's little sister; although Latina, Moreno is also brownfaced. The feature includes big Hollywood/Polynesian production numbers mixed with Tahitian and Samoan dancing, all done on a Los Angeles soundstage. Many local Polynesians had lines in the film but were not credited.

Paradise Found (2003, Lionsgate)—Ø

Screenplay by: John Goldsmith. Directed by: Mario Andrecchio.

Unlike in *The Moon and Sixpence* (1942), the character Kiefer Sutherland plays actually is Paul Gauguin. In this version, it is not so much that Gauguin goes insane but that he gets angry at the French government, which is colluding with the Christian church to suppress Island values and beliefs. The two groups are categorically and catastrophically destroying the ancient and rich culture of Tahiti and its associated art and artifacts—an act similar to the Taliban's destroying of the Bamiyan Buddhas. One may not believe in Buddhism, but one knows that was a terribly wrong thing to do.

In this version of the Gauguin story, the famous artist sees beauty in the Tahitian culture and in their tiki images, but the church and government see heathenism and the devil. Sutherland will paint what he can't save. Gauguin's craze for underage nude Polynesian girls is downplayed in this film. The plot is focused on an anti-colonization theme instead. Also, in this film, Sutherland's beautiful Tahitian lover is depicted as being in her late 20s, not the early teenaged sexual partner of the real Gauguin. The actress playing Sutherland's lover Tehura is Sarah Lina Brown, who does have a nude scene. In the scene Brown is not posing for a painting but being nursed by Sutherland, because she is very ill with a high fever. The scene is not sensualized in intent but still sexualized in visualization. To portray a high fever does not necessitate the display of the young woman's nude body. What would be the odds in American script and film of Sutherland nursing an elderly heavyset Tahitian woman or man in this manner?

Paradise, Hawaiian Style (1966, Paramount)—Ø
Screenplay by: Allan Weiss, Anthony Lawrence. Directed by: Michael D. Moore.

Paradise stars Elvis and James Shigeta as new owners of a helicopter charter air service, with Presley having a girl on every island. Of course, the drama or dilemma here is what to do with all of these women. This is a predicament only Elvis could have, which a normal man can only fantasize through this Hollywood lens. Almost all of the women are incorrectly represented as Hawaiian—two are of Asian descent and two are Euro-American. Even fine Asian-American actors Shigeta and Philip Ahn play Hawaiians, and Shigeta's Hawaiian daughter is portrayed by a Euro-American. The most prominent female in this film, Suzanna Leigh, may be the only one in the film who is represented correctly as a person of European descent. However, in the finale, Elvis gets to perform at the Polynesian Cultural Center, where many Polynesians are well represented. Most are student performers working their way through college next door at Brigham Young University's Hawai'i campus. Elvis' presence there is legendary to this day.

Paradise Island (1930, Tiffany)—Ø

Screenplay by: Monte M. Katterjohn. Directed by: Bert Glennon.

This is a totally racist story about Marceline Day traveling to Tonga to marry her fiancé. When she arrives, she finds her fiancé is a total drunkard. She also finds that she is the only Euro-American female on the island, whereas there are many men of European descent. Most of these men have a questionable character and past. Suddenly all of the outsiders on the island try to court Miss Day. The only Euro-American man on the island that has a possibility to be worthy of Day's interest is an adventurer/trader played by hero Kenneth Harlan. Near the end, all bets are on with a poker game in which the winner gets half of Day's fiancé's debts. Harlan knows the deck is marked by an evil saloon owner and takes advantage of it. Meanwhile, the bad European bar owner sends Poppi, played by American actress Betty Boyd, a brownface island female, to seduce Day's fiancé in order to make him start drinking again. She successfully does, and Day catches them in the act. Then the engagement is off for sure.

There are so many things wrong with this film. Our hero is engaged in trading with the Islanders and is known to give the Natives a better deal than others. In other words, he takes less advantage of them but still exploits them with unfair trade. He also engages in high stakes gambling. Is this the man Day really loves? Why doesn't she just get on the next boat and go to the continent to find hundreds of additional choices for a suitor? Only on a white male-fantasized South Seas island do you get this male Hollywood imagination. Not to mention that Poppi and all the other Tongan *fefine* (women) are mostly portrayed by Latinas, who are all over every man of European ancestry. There is easy sexual accessibility on the island, but the white men drop everything to covet the fair, modest, and engaged Miss Day when she arrives. The sexualized female Polynesian stereotype and racist tone run throughout the film and throughout this book.

Also, the captain who brings May to the island gives her an "orientation" about the location before they dock: "Natives are too lazy." In one scene, an American sailor has seven Tongan fefine who all want him. The sailor comments: "This would be a good country if I can get this to work." He wants them all legally. The sailor also mentions to his captain that a couple of the "wahines" got in a fight and he just "smacks them down." The hero captain laughs. A sign of the times in America. Also, clichéd Hawaiian steel guitar music is played in the background, even though they are purportedly in Tonga. The Hawaiian steel guitar background music is commonplace throughout South Seas cinema, no

matter where in the Pacific a plot is set. *Paradise Island's* story is by
M.B. Deering.

Paradise Isle (1937, Monogram)—Ø

Screenplay by: Marion Orth. Directed by: Arthur Greville Collins.

Paradise stars Latina Movita and Warren Hull. A blind artist (Hull)
is shipwrecked on a South Seas island, where Native girl Movita saves
him by nursing him back to health. The successful painter was on his
way to Java to restore his sight, hoping to continue his career. Later the
loyal Movita dives into shark-infested waters for pearls so she can afford

Paradise Isle (1937, Monogram Pictures). **Shown in this American title
lobby card (11" × 14") is Latina actress Movita, wearing a revealing Hollywood sarong, and Warren Hull, TV's future Green Hornet. In *Paradise
Isle*, Hull plays an artist who has recently lost his sight. Hull shipwrecks
in pursuit of a medical cure and lands on Movita's island. All this makes
Hull's character indignant, despite Movita's love and caring for him as a
typical Polynesian maiden. She also ignores her Native boyfriend. Movita
dangerously works to retrieve pearls so she can afford to get Hull to the eye
doctor. Before Hull departs, he feels her face with his hands, realizes she
is beautiful, finally falls for her and appreciates her efforts. Hull's eyesight
returns, and he returns to Movita.**

to send Hull to the eye doctor. A jealous but understanding Native boyfriend is found throughout, witnessing the new romance between his island girlfriend and the shipwrecked survivor; although he is saddened, he does not intervene.

In American films it's very rare to see Native males with vested emotional involvement with lead Islander females. Most of these beautiful Indigenous females are conveniently unattached because of some taboo or other lucky circumstance and have no entrusted love interest. Some island women have just an early, unconsummated non-romance or perhaps a non-committed relationship set up by parental agreement only. In South Seas cinema, these non-emotional island relationships, although unrealistic, justify European and Euro-American men's claims to island women, even though the relationship intent of these foreign men is short-term and nonbinding. Furthermore, one can suppose there are naturally many Native male significant others of our Polynesian heroines throughout South Seas cinema who are not revealed because they are just assumed or inconsequential to American audiences and to our American onscreen heroes. *Paradise Isle, Land of Fury* (1954) and *Through the Breakers* (1928) are just a few South Seas films in which the Native male lover is recognized.

Paradise was shot in Samoa and was later retitled *Siren of the South Seas*. There are two credited Native roles for Tau Mana and Malia Makua. There is a Native Kiss with the blind man that evolves into Movita and Hull's interracial relationship. Hull's eyesight is later saved, and he returns for Movita. The story is by Allan Vaughn Elston. Compare this plot to the silent motion picture *Soul-Fire* (1925)—but in *Soul-Fire* the shipwrecked foreigner is a composer, not a painter. Each finds his Native muse and lover.

Paris Playboys (1954, Allied Artists)—Ø

Screenplay by: Edward Bernds, Elwood Ullman. Directed by: William Beaudine.

Leo Gorcey, Huntz Hall and the rest of the Bowery Boys return to the big screen. This must be some kind of a Hollywood record, with a total of 48 films featuring this cast of New York City characters. *Paris* is the 33rd film in this B-picture film franchise. At least one of these films was bound to be set in the South Seas. In this film, Hall (as Horace Debussy "Sach" Jones) is mistaken for a missing French scientist lookalike, who is almost finished inventing a new rocket fuel. A NATO agent whizzes Hall to Paris to take the place of the missing scientist, and Hall's gang comes along with him. There's good and bad news. First the good news: the real scientist has a beautiful French girlfriend of whom Hall takes advantage. The bad news is that the bad guys want to kidnap Hall, thinking he is the scientist.

What happened to the real scientist? Well, he is self-exiled on a Pacific Island and is lying atop a hammock surrounded by faux Polynesian beauties. Poor Huntz plays both roles. Although only a small part of the movie is set on a Polynesian island, Hall, as the scientist, for the most part lounges on the island while pretty Polynesian women (all brunette Euro-American Hollywood beauties) see to his every need, including the cliché of hand feeding Hall grapes. Importantly, Hall kisses any one of them anytime he wants. The women enjoy their roles as subservient and sexualized partakers in another imaginary male-dominated Hollywood fantasy of the South Seas. Just as degrading and perplexing is the fact that when the French scientist character discovers that an impostor is taking advantage of his beloved girlfriend back home, he is suddenly gallant and faithful, and Hall jumps on the next plane out, instantly dismissing all of his island beauties as if they were merely objects like the grapes he was eating. How about the feelings of his French girlfriend, whom the scientist heartlessly left in the first place, subsequently having simultaneous affairs with pretty island maidens? Despite all this, the scientist gets one last kiss from each wahine before he leaves. Male Hollywood fantasies to the fullest.

Passion Fruit (1921, Metro)—Ø
Screenplay by: Edward T. Lowe, Jr. Directed by: John Ince.

Passion Fruit stars Doraldina (Dora Sanders of San Francisco) who was a "hula hula" stage dancer in the *Frivolities of 1920* and in *Road to Mandalay.* Doraldina plays a half–Hawaiian daughter of a plantation owner whose father is subsequently murdered by an evil plantation overseer. This bad plantation overseer also wants to marry Doraldina to complete his plans to own the island, but Doraldina is in love with the new Euro-American manager. The overseer stirs the Natives to revolt and tries to kill Doraldina, but Doraldina's faithful Native maid kills the overseer, and everyone lives happily ever after.

The film has location shooting on Oʻahu and the important issues of murder and an attempted forced marriage for material gain. It seems a man can think he can get away with anything on a remote Pacific Island—but this bad man could also get killed on such an island with the same premise.

There are two reoccurring thematic issues here: First, the Euro-American plantation owner has a half–Polynesian or biracial daughter, but the Native mother is nonexistent. Second, there is no mention as to how Doraldina's father acquired the whole island in the first place or how he had all the Indigenous Islanders working in servitude to him. A supposition by the American writer, filmmaker, and audience is that this is the norm for a so-called superior race—to own and run an entire island including all its Native inhabitants, with no explanation as to how, justified or not, this man acquired this island. *Passion Fruit's* story is by Carey Wilson.

Pearl of the South Pacific (1955, RKO)—✖Ø
Screenplay by: Jesse Lasky, Jr., Talbot Jennings. Directed by: Allan Dwan.

Virginia Mayo stars in a sarong within a murder plot involving a treasure of black pearls guarded by a cliché giant octopus. Mayo, a woman with a questionable past, joins two fellow American opportunists to find black pearls on an undisclosed South Seas island. They find the island, and on the island, they find an American posing as a high priest. The parties know each other's game, so they play it conservatively. The priest has a half–Polynesian son (Euro-American Lance Fuller in brownface), and the son is attracted to Mayo. Mayo, like Francis Farmer in *South of Pago Pago* (1940), will take advantage of this attraction. Also, like Farmer, Mayo dons a sexy sarong and turns on the charm to get information about the pearls. It's a rare reverse Native gender relationship, even though the sincerity of this relationship is dubious.

Mayo does find out where the pearls are, but as in *Wake of the Red Witch* (1948), the treasure is placed deep on the bottom of the lagoon and guarded by a similar giant octopus. At the end, Mayo confesses that she is really in love with one of the men she came with, and after their ship explodes, only she and her true lover survive the mishap. The foreign couple have become sympathetic towards the Natives and sorry for their earlier intentions. In compassion, the Polynesian tribe accepts them, which means there is no longer an interracial relationship, and the fair and blonde Mayo can keep wearing her short and shapely sarongs.

There are also rather decent representations of large tiki images from throughout Polynesia, but the problem is they are from throughout Polynesia. Many Polynesians had their own distinctive carved images, so to see many of different styles in one place is unrealistic. This mixed Polynesian culture phenomenon can be found in a museum or in an American tiki bar or on an American film set like this one. *Pearl* features tikis, canoes, sarongs, luau, and Native Dance tropes, along with

Al Kikume as a spear-hurling extra—all the ingredients of an archetypal Hollywood South Seas movie. The story is by Anna Hunger, and the film is directed by Allan Dwan, who also helmed *Enchanted Island*, the 1958 adaptation of Melville's *Typee*.

Quick Before It Melts (1964, MGM)—Ø
Screenplay by: Dale Wasserman. Directed by: Delbert Mann.

Melts stars Robert Morse and George Maharis. Morse plays an ordinary-looking photographer on an unordinary assignment to the South Pole. On the way there, however, he runs into and falls for a beautiful part-Māori young lady as he runs away from a bar fight in New Zealand. They become a couple, even though she is gorgeous, and he is, well ... ordinary looking. It's as if his being of full Caucasian blood is an equalizer, compensating for his unattractive or plain appearance in this romance equation. The Māori girlfriend's character is named Tiara Marshall and is played by Texas-born brunette Anjanette Comer. A quote from the official trailer for the movie calls her "exotic Tiara, the new heartthrob from the South Seas." Also, according to the trailer, produced by the studio's publicity department, *Melts* is about "women, women and women." Hollywood produces sexualized representations of women, especially Pacific Island women, but the publicity departments from the studios intensify these sexualized tropes even more on the basic theory that sex sells theater tickets. The movie is based on a novel of the same name by Philip Benjamin.

Quiet Earth, The (1985, Anchor Bay Entertainment. [NZ])—Ø
Screenplay by: Bill Baer, Bruno Lawrence, Sam Pillsbury. Directed by: Geoff Murphy

From the "doomsday" sub-genre of sci-fi films comes a New Zealand version starring Bruno Lawrence, Alison Routledge, and Pete Smith. A middle-aged Euro–New Zealander (Lawrence) is a seemingly lone male survivor of a nuclear holocaust, who then finds that he is not alone. Also surviving is a beautiful young woman (Routledge) who is, like Lawrence, of European descent. But soon the two survivors discover an alive, dark, and brawny Māori man with a violent past. This interracial triangle has a lot of tension—not just due to race, but also due to class and age differences. Of course, the older Euro–New Zealander male survivor is educated, while the Polynesian man is a blue-collar worker. The lone female has sexual relationships with both. While race is a big issue in contemporary New Zealand, many Indigenous Māori are a Euro-British mix. Case in point, the dark Māori actor in this film was born Pete Smith and continues using his very British birth name. This post-apocalyptic movie is based on a book by Craig Harrison.

Ragged Edge, The (1923, Distinctive Pictures/ Goldwyn)—none

Screenplay by: Forrest Halsey. Directed by: Harmon Weight.

This silent film stars Alfred Lunt and Mimi Palmieri. Lunt plays an American fugitive running throughout Asia. There, he has bouts of depression and alcoholism. But he also meets and falls in love with a missionary's daughter. They marry, and Lunt then gets a job on a South Seas island. While there, he is tracked down by an aunt to tell him that his uncle did not press charges and there are no police coming after him. She wants him to return home. Why is this movie in this filmography? Simply because, as author Larry Langman writes in *Return to Paradise: A Guide to South Seas Island Films*, "At least one critic points out that, to its credit, the film avoids the usual clichés of this genre, such as thinly clad Natives and their suggestive dances." Thus, this film is on this list for some of the tropes it doesn't have, which is very uncommon and noteworthy. Also of significance is that Langman recognized that these major sexualized tropes of South Seas cinema had been established in only the first few years of the South Seas film genre, during the early silent film era.

Rain (1932, United Artists)—Ø

Screenplay by: Maxwell Anderson. Directed by: Lewis Milestone.

This is the first talkie version of the famous story with Joan Crawford as Sadie Thompson, who epitomizes this genre's woman-with-a-questionable-past trope. Although not explicitly mentioned, Sadie is a prostitute recently exiled from Honolulu. In all "Sadie" stories, the wild and carefree Thompson is temporarily stranded in Samoa with sexually hungry U.S. Marines who longingly gaze at a rare and eligible white woman. Also stranded on the isle, until the next steamer passes through, is a strict and zealous Christian reformer (in this version played by Walter Huston) who despises Sadie, even though he internally lusts for her. The characters themselves lay the groundwork for a very sexual and dramatic environment: the zealous reformer rapes Sadie and commits suicide at the end.

But for the purpose of this filmography the focus here is more on the interracial couple, Joe Horn, an expatriate trader, and Sadie's innkeeper, along with his Native wife Ameena, who between them have a least three biracial children who are shown only in the beginning of the film. Also, at the end of that scene, there is only one quick shot comprising Joe and Ameena and only one of their children in Ameena's lap. This is the only shot of both interracial parents and at least one child. Ameena is played by Mary Shaw, an actress known not only for *Rain*, but also for *The Hurricane* (1937) and *The Tuttles of Tahiti* (1942). Shaw plays Polynesians in all three of these films. An observation should also be made about the lecherous behavior of the rank-and-file Marines towards the Euro-American Sadie. In most South Seas films, set throughout two centuries, the enlisted servicemen usually lust after young and fit Polynesian women, but the opposite is true here. Were these American servicemen tired of island Native women or just plain racist? *Rain* is based upon the classic short story by W. Somerset Maugham. Director Lewis Milestone has two Best Director Oscars and later co-directed 1962's *Mutiny on the Bounty*.

Rarotonga (1978, Acuario Films [Mexico])—✗∅
Screenplay by: Unknown. Directed by: Raúl Ramirez.

Rarotonga stars Mexican sex symbol Gloriella and the director himself, Raúl Ramirez. The movie is based on a popular Mexican comic book series published from the '50s to the '70s. The main character of the comics and film was named "Rarotonga," a Pacific Island jungle queen from Rarotonga in the Cook Islands. This character, in both the film and the comics, is a licentious woman who likes to entertain visitors to her island by dancing and romancing. All of the publicity shows a sensual character with little clothing; interestingly, Rarotonga wears an Afro wig. Perhaps Mexican moviegoers are not acquainted with the differences between Melanesians and Polynesians. (Cook Islanders are Polynesians and less likely than Fijians or Papuans, who are Melanesians, to have Afro style hair.)

A sequel to this sexploitation film was made in 1982 and titled *La Isla de Rarotonga*—or in English, *The Island of Rarotonga*. Raúl Ramirez starred in this later version, but it was directed and written by Alfedo B. Crevenna. The Mexican sex symbol Gloriella was replaced, in the second film, by a former striptease dancer and future Mexican movie star, Princess Lea (like Movita, adapting a Polynesian-like stage name). In the sequel, Princess Lea plays some kind of female sorcerer/island ruler and is nude in parts of the film. This film is a good example of Polynesian sexualized tropes also found in Mexican cinema.

Return to Paradise (1953, United Artists)—ʊ⏐⏐⏐✕Ø
Screenplay by: Charles Kaufman. Directed by: Mark Robson.

Gary Cooper falls in love with a South Seas Native woman in this movie derived from the *Mr. Morgan* chapter in the 1951 collection of James Michener's short stories also titled *Return to Paradise*. The film has an unusual plot involving two generations of interracial relationships. The first generation is when Cooper initially lands on a generic Samoan Island, where he is so mad at the local authoritarian European preacher that he decides to stay for a while to help balance out the situation with the Native population. He falls for brownface Texan Roberta Haynes, and they live together, with Haynes eventually becoming pregnant. Due to complications, Haynes dies after giving birth to a biracial baby girl. Cooper hands the baby to a trusted older Pacific Island couple and leaves the island distraught.

Years later Cooper returns, this time trying to be a more responsible father to his daughter, now in her late teens. All is well until a group of four American Naval officers arrive after Cooper rescues them from a plane wreck nearby. The problem is that a young captain is smitten by Cooper's half–Samoan daughter. Cooper is enraged by the fact that they have been seeing each other, accompanied by heavy kisses. Cooper rounds the four Americans up to ship them off to another port. He yells at the captain, and pops the essential question with the key title word: "Will you <u>return</u> after the war?" The captain is silent and looks away from Cooper.

Meanwhile, his daughter now hates the hypocritical father. Samoa-born Moira MacDonald, an 'afakasi (literally meaning half-caste) in real life, played Cooper's biracial daughter and received good reviews for her performance. The mother, Maeva, played by Roberta Haynes, also played a Polynesian named Mareva in *Hell Ship Mutiny* (1957). Haynes was the only faux, brown-painted Native, while many real Native Samoans had speaking parts with decent portrayals. Credited Samoan Indigenes included Chief Mamea Matatumua, Herbert Ah Sue, and Felise Va'a as the child Rori before he grew up to become editor of *The Samoa Times*. Mr. Ah Sue named a daughter after Roberta a short time later.

Twenty-six years after shooting *Return to Paradise*, Moira, now Moira Walker, returned to the big screen as the mother of protagonist

Sione in the film adaptation of Samoan novelist Albert Wendt's *Sons for the Return Home* (1979), lensed at Upolu and New Zealand. In that film, Moira, a generation older, is the mother of a young Polynesian man trying to find himself in the contemporary Pacific. Gary Cooper, who had recently won the Best Actor Oscar for 1952's *High Noon*, turned in one of his best performances in *Return to Paradise*, which was filmed in Western Samoa (now Samoa) on the island of Upolu. There is a "fale" (hut or cottage) named after Cooper at Aggie Grey's famed hotel in Apia. Mr. Cooper had stayed there while shooting this beautiful color classic.

Return has two Native First Kiss scenes a generation apart, from Cooper to Haynes, then from the U.S. captain to Cooper's daughter. The Canoe Greeting scene was tempered or subdued by the mentioned tyrannical preacher. The oppressive Bible thumper also regulated lagoon swimming and bathing. At the beginning of the film, a Native narrator describes an "island of chains," as young Native females are shown bathing in the lagoon, wearing a couple of layers of clothing: "Our young women once were proud of their bodies; now we're taught to be ashamed." Although not shown, but mentioned later in the film, a defiant Haynes utters: "Today we will not go to church. Today is for swimming in the lagoon." Besides the two Native First Kiss tropes, there is also the trope of couples running off to the jungle after a Sexualized Dance. There is also a sad and ingenuous Polynesian farewell scene. Lastly and most importantly, *Return* not only does not vanish a biracial parent couple, like most South Seas films do, but rather makes the Caucasian parent the lead role, while his Polynesian wife (even though she dies) is well-established in the first half of the movie. *Return to Paradise* is the first feature film adapted from a story by James Michener.

Revolt of Mamie Stover, The (1956, 20th Century–Fox)—✘

Screenplay by: Sydney Boehm. Directed by: Raoul Walsh.

Jane Russell, Richard Egan, and Agnes Moorehead co-star in a story about an aggressive woman with a questionable past (prostitute). The film starts with Russell, as Stover, who is driven by police out of San Francisco. She then lands in Honolulu right before World War II begins. In the aftermath of the attack on Pearl Harbor, she buys up land and soon becomes wealthy. She also now co-owns a hugely successful "gentlemen's club" that services thousands and thousands of servicemen going to and from the Pacific Theater. In the "gentlemen's club" or brothel, Russell does a sensual hula number. The provocative song with accompanying hula is "Keep Your Eyes on the Hands." Russell has four Hawaiian female hula dancers as backups (whose cellophane skirts reveal legs), and all contribute to arousing the U.S. soldier audience in an environment thick with male testosterone. There is a noteworthy and unusual Pearl Harbor attack scene lensed from a Honolulu civilian point of view because it dramatizes the air raid's impact on ordinary citizens living in the then-Territory of Hawai'i.

Like *The Sands of Iwo Jima* (1949), *Hell's Half Acre* (1954), *From Here to Eternity* (1954), and others, the setting is the World War II red light district of Honolulu, but here we also see Hawaiian women working in these clubs. Although a majority of the women who worked in Hawai'i's World War II Pacific sex industry were Euro-American, Polynesian and local Asian-American women were also an additional exotic commodity. Only in *The Sands of Iwo Jima* is it obvious that these women "entertainers" were prostitutes, but the word "prostitute" is still not mentioned in *Sands* and this film, partly to obey the Production Code and partly to protect the integrity of the U.S. soldier. Whether intentional or not, *Mamie Stover* closely mirrors the true story of a historical figure, Jean O'Hara, a real Honolulu prostitute of that era. At the end of the movie, Mamie gives it all away and returns to the mainland sadder and wiser. *The Revolt of Mamie Stover* was based on a novel by William Bradford Huie and mostly filmed on O'ahu.

Rewi's Last Stand (1940, Hayward Pictures [NZ])— ✗∅

Screenplay by: Rudall C. Hayward. Directed by: Rudall C. Hayward.

This drama/romance is based on a famous incident during New Zealand's Māori Wars of the 1860s. *Rewi's* was originally made as a silent picture in 1925, while the sound version was released in 1940. (AKA: *The Last Stand* was a shorter 1940 version for British release.) This is a must-see movie for Māori and everyone else. Similar to the Americans at the Alamo, the Māori "Last Stand" has the Natives being outnumbered six to one, but they would not surrender. The famous battle of Orakau Pa was the background to an interracial romance between a green, fresh recruit from England and a beautiful half–Māori/half–European young woman. They intermittently meet during the war and save each other. Director Hayward, a *pākehā* (British-New Zealander), was known to be fair in his portrayals of both the British and the Māori during their wars in the second half of the 19th century, showing viewpoints from both sides. This 1940 sound version was also balanced.

The interracial relationship in both versions of the film was significant in New Zealand and South Seas film history and to Hayward personally, because three years after *Rewi's* was released, the now legendary
New Zealand filmmaker married his Māori female lead in the film,
Ramai Te Miha (AKA Patricia Miller), and they made films together
until his death in 1974. Their romance mirrors that of the later Māori
filmmaker/actress Merata Mita and pākehā film director/producer
Geoff Murphy, who married and partnered in the film business after
meeting in the film production of *Utu* (1983). Fittingly for this tome,
Rudall Hayward's first job in the film business was painting Euro-New
Zealander women brown to play Māori on film.

Rhythm of the Islands (1943, Universal)—✗∅
**Screenplay by: Oscar Brodney, M.M. Musselman. Directed by: Roy
William Neill.**

This is a musical romance about two American men (Allan Jones
and Andy Devine) trying to sell a small plantation island in the South
Seas because of huge debts incurred in obtaining said island. They had
counted on cheap labor supplied by the Natives, but the Islanders will
not have any part of it, so the two Americans attempt to unload it on
other outsiders. To complicate matters, while the duo is about to hook a
rich tourist couple with a pretty daughter, fierce original Natives arrive
to reclaim their island. Eventually, the bad feelings blow over for all,
and two American couples are happily engaged at the end. Even though
the chief is the final judge in settling land deputes, he never rules that
the island is still owned by the Natives. Although the story takes place
during the height of World War II, there is no mention of the war except
in a note in the opening titles.

There are funny scenes in which the American owners (Jones and
Devine) trick tourists with brownface and Native costuming, also using
their African American servant and his friends (the Step Brothers) to
help entertain as Natives. A reverse interracial romance is avoided when
the daughter (Jane Frazee) of the rich couple, who entertains the idea of
buying the island, falls for the faux Native chief with a funny First Kiss
scene. She soon learns that the "Native" is an American (Jones), who is
in brownface as part of a scheme to sell the island. She somehow for-
gives him. Also, Jones and his partner Devine hire some Natives to be
part of the ruse, but an island Native female playing the part of Devine's
woman actually falls for Devine, and it was hard for her to give him
up, playing to the stereotype of "easy to get" and "hard to lose" tena-
cious Polynesian women. The pretty island woman, who is hooked on

the heavy-set, older, and not handsome Devine, wants to *honihoni* (kiss by nose rubbing) with Devine all the time. This island female is played by Acquanetta, known for "B-movie" jungle women roles. She was actually a part-Arapaho American Indian born in Wyoming with a Latina stage name playing a Polynesian. She was also known as the "Venezuelan Volcano." Only in Hollywood. Acquanetta similarly played a Polynesian woman in the classic sci-fi *Lost Continent* (1951), but in that film she was not so amorous but was nevertheless dressed in the ubiquitous, sexualized, short, tight-fitting sarong.

Ride, The (2003, Third Reef Pictures)—|||Ø
Screenplay by: Nathan Kurosawa. Directed by: Nathan Kurosawa.

Although sharing the same surname as Akira Kurosawa, Nathan is an American of Japanese ancestry from Hawai'i and is not related to that great Japanese director. This independent filmmaker and his semi-Indigenous film make for an interesting study. The subject matter and all major characters and actors are Hawaiian, except for one, the protagonist, who is a contemporary, pompous Euro-American world champion surfer who nearly drowns. When wiping out, he travels back in time. The arrogant surfer meets the famous and welcoming Duke Kahanamoku. In 1911 Hawai'i, Duke teaches the pretentious visiting surfer humility.

The American surf protagonist also meets and falls for a beautiful Hawaiian maiden, played by Mary Pa'alani. There is the trope scene in this film with Pa'alani and the hotshot American blonde surfer (Scot Davis) swimming in a lagoon and falling for each other. There is no nudity and no Native First Kiss, just Pa'alani and Davis swimming together underwater as many mixed-race couples do in this genre. Pa'alani swims in a full classical red sarong. This trope scene of interracial romance propagated by swimming together is commonplace in this South Seas film category, and this sequence is almost identical to a swim scene lensed 45 years earlier in *She Gods of Shark Reef*, complete with a blonde Euro-American male and a red-saronged Polynesian female. Sean Ka'awa plays Kahanamoku, while Hawaiians Weldon Kekauoha and Wil Kahele have important roles. There are also many minor roles played well by Hawaiians and other local Islanders.

Ride the Wild Surf (1964, Columbia)—✗Ø
Screenplay by: Jo Napoleon, Art Napoleon. Directed by: Don Taylor.

The beach party set of young actors—Fabian, Tab Hunter, Shelly Fabares, Barbara Eden, Peter Brown and Susan Hart—star in this film set in Hawai'i. California surfer Hunter falls for local *hapa haole* (half–Caucasian/half–Hawaiian) girl played by American black-haired dancer and actress Susan Hart, especially after her Sensual Native Dance at a beach luau. There are complications and objections to this interracial relationship, mostly from Hart's Euro-American mother. She apparently had a bad relationship with Hart's now dead Hawaiian father, and the mother does not want her daughter going through the same bad experiences. It doesn't make sense, as the biracial daughter raised in both cultures should be able to adapt to either of her cultures. As in *Return to Paradise* (1953), this film accounts for two generations of interracial relationships. The mother should be far more worried that Hunter is a surfer with no goals for the future, not that he is a Euro-American like she is. Compare *Ride* with *North Shore* (1987). Is the title a metaphor for Hunter's ride into a bicultural multiracial relationship? Island actor and stuntman David Cadiente has a part.

River Queen (2005, Weinstein Co. [NZ])—Ø

Screenplay by: Vincent Ward, Toa Fraser, Kelly Lyons. Directed by: Vincent Ward.

This is the story of a young Irish woman who immigrated to Aotearoa (NZ) during the Māori/British wars. It stars Samantha Morton, Rawiri Pene, Cliff Curtis, Temuera Morrison, Wi Kuki Kaa, Kiefer Sutherland and Stephen Rea. Morton is caught in the middle: her father is fighting for the British army, but she also falls in love with a Māori teen (who dies) and has a biracial son out of wedlock. *Queen* is in the tradition of New Zealand films that have balanced points of view showing both sides of the war, as in *Rewi's Last Stand* (1926 and 1940) and *Utu* (1983). *River Queen* continues this practice with the war in the background and personal interracial conflict in the foreground. In this case a young mother of Irish descent is fighting to find her now kidnapped biracial son. A couple of years later she finds her young son with his Māori relatives and the son has integrated well with his new culture and relations. A real struggle for the mother is when the war began, and she saw British soldiers from her world shoot at her son.

A love interest develops between the mother and the brother (Curtis) of her former lover, the son's Māori uncle. This being a New Zealand–based film, not an American one, miscegenation runs rampant throughout the film because it is centered on this mother and her half–Māori son. Surprisingly, there is a sexualized scene right before the big battle, when local chief Te Kai Po (Morrison) decides to have sex with another chief's daughter in a sequence with partial nudity. This angers the other chief, and right before the battle he and his army of warriors pull out. Another complication that most of these films demonstrate is that in New Zealand history, Māori were on both sides of the battle. Cousins were shooting at cousins. If the tribes were united under one leader, and not segmented, history in colonized New Zealand might have been very different.

Roughneck, The (1924, 20th Century–Fox)—none
Screenplay by: Charles Kenyon. Directed by: Jack Conway.

This silent romantic/adventure set in the South Seas stars Harvey Clark, George O'Brien and Cleo Madison. Widowed Madison is taken away by an evil captain, leaving her young son (O'Brien) to fend for himself. Twenty years later, O'Brien, now a man, catches up with them on a South Seas island and beats up the captain. Two South Seas tropes exist (even in 1924): scantily clad Native women (for silent era audiences) and an underwater shark attack. The story is based on novel by Robert W. Service.

Sadie Thompson (1928, United Artists)—Ø
Screenplay by: Raoul Walsh, C. Gardner Sullivan. Directed by: Raoul Walsh.

This first film version of the famous short story by W. Somerset Maugham starred Gloria Swanson as Sadie Thompson. This silent rendition was produced after the successful play of the same name and preceded two other successful film versions, *Rain* (1932) and *Miss Sadie Thompson* (1953). Sadie was a woman with a questionable past (a Honolulu prostitute) who is trying to get away from it all by heading to the Orient, but she is temporarily stranded in rainy American Samoa with a bunch of sexually starved American Marines and a zealous preacher (Lionel Barrymore), who hates Sadie and her carefree ways but he secretly lusts after her. At the end, Barrymore's character rapes Sadie and kills himself.

All these ingredients provide the basis for a sexually tense and dramatic story. Also in the story is an interracial couple who run the local general store and inn. The husband is an expatriate, Joe Horn, and his overweight, chain smoking, unattractive Native wife is named Ameena. Perhaps this is a lesson or warning—that marrying out of your race to a once-young, fit, beautiful Native will over time yield a very different-looking wife. In this version, Joe and his island wife show no biracial children, in line with other film iterations. Ameena is played by Latina Sofia Ortega.

Samoan Wedding (2006, South Pacific Pictures [NZ])—∅

Screenplay by: James Griffin, Oscar Kightley. Directed by: Chris Graham.

Wedding is a comedy about four Samoan young men, played by Oscar Kightley, Iaheto Ah Hi, Shimpai Lelisi, and Robbie Magasiva, who are banned from their best friend's wedding because of their past record of destroying other important community events with their immaturity and drunkenness. The film is set in the city of Auckland. Noted actors include Nathaniel Lees and Pua Magasiva.

While appearing to be an Indigenous film, there are nevertheless some incidents that seem out of place with that supposition. The main oddity here is the sexualized character of Kightley's beautiful cousin from the islands. It has been argued previously that a sexualized character or scene in an Indigenous film is not the norm, and it has been suggested to me that this film is a good case in point against this reasoning.

This may be a subcategory of Indigenous film that could be called the Diaspora Film or Indigene within a Larger Culture film that probably began with the 1979 adaptation of Albert Wendt's *Sons for the Return Home*, which also focuses on Samoans in New Zealand. Polynesians living in large Western cities such as Auckland, Honolulu or Los Angeles are living in a bicultural or multicultural world of their own traditions and those of the dominant majority culture (as well as possibly the customs, etc., of other ethnicities) surrounding them. The impact and influence by the dominant culture or neighboring subcultures might be indirectly changing their identities as Pacific islanders. Influences via popular mass media such as Western movies, television, newspapers, magazines, and social media can shape an individual. After a generation or two of diaspora, island life and island culture are being replaced by the dominant culture. Thus, ideologically, *Samoan Wedding* has subsumed more characteristics of Hollywood films than Indigenous Island films—even if it is made by Polynesians. Indigenous filmmakers in a diverse cultural setting should evaluate their message and style of filmmaking. Do they want to make an Islander or Hollywood type of movie? Their decision reflects who they are, despite skin color.

On the same note, in current times, influences from a dominant outside culture may impact an Indigenous story as in *Boy*, a 2010 film by

Taika Waititi. In that film, American pop culture has been absorbed into contemporary Māori culture as evident in the Michael Jackson-related scenes. In the bigger picture, outside influence has affected the contemporary Polynesian with regard to alcohol, modern monetary economics (poverty), processed foods (health), etc., resulting in Indigenous centered film of despair and hardship as in *Once Were Warriors* (1994). *Samoan Wedding* is AKA *Sione's Wedding*.

Savage Play (1995, Eaton Films [NZ])—Ø
Screenplay by: Alan Lindsay. Directed by: Alan Lindsay.

Starting as a New Zealand TV miniseries, this three-part work was later sold as one large film on tape about two generations of interracial relationships between Māori and British. *Savage* is based on a true story from the late 1800s, when the first New Zealand Native rugby team toured the UK for 17 months to play against various British teams. With their long hair and dark skin, they were quite the spectacle around the British Isles. Some Brits were surprised that the "savages" dressed in an English manner and spoke the Queen's English well. But that is the background story, with two personal stories in the foreground.

The first is a story of one of the Māori players (Peter Kaa), who worked hard to make the team for the secret, personal agenda of finding his real British father. His mother, played by Māori Rena Owens, hated her son's British father, and the idea that her son would leave to find him. The son's Māori chief, who is also his grandfather (Wi Kuki Kaa), supported his leaving for the love of the sport. The other storyline is this same biracial rugby player and the granddaughter of a British lord, who apparently sponsored the "Native" team's tour, fall for each other. The lord, although acting civilized, does not approve of the relationship, nor does Peter Kaa's mother back home. Compare this mother/son relationship to the mother/daughter relationship in *Ride the Wild Surf* (1964).

Seamen (1957, Herzog-Filmverleih [Germany])—Ø
Screenplay by: Gustav Kampendonk. Directed by: Wolfgang Schleif.

This South Seas adventure/romance from West Germany, starring Karlheinz Böhm and Claus Biederstaedt, was actually filmed in Tahiti. The film co-stars the beautiful part-Tahitian sisters, Maea Flohr as Rataha and Moea Flohr as Rarahu, with a part for Vahinerii as Tatü. The German auxiliary cruiser *Rheinstein* is assigned in the South Pacific during World War II, where the crew encounters an extremely friendly Polynesian isle. However, the *Rheinstein* makes a quick exit because of enemy ships in the area, stranding four German seamen onshore.

At first, the lifestyle is strange for the abandoned Germans, but soon they realize the sincere, loving hospitality of the Indigenes, especially the barely clad, young, fit Native women. One beautiful vahine sings a love song in German to one of the visitors in his bedroom, which begins an interracial relationship. The same American sexualized tropes of the Pacific Islanders are found in this German film. This film also contains the German legendary South Seas hit song "Der weisse Mond von Maratonga" ("The White Moon of Maratonga"). Although we tend to think of the French, British, Spanish and Americans as Oceania's main colonizers, *Seamen* reminds us of the colonial role Germany played in the "Südsee" prior to World War I in the islands of Samoa, Micronesia and Papua New Guinea. AKA: *Blaue Jungs* (original German title), *Amor en Tahiti* (Spanish), *Gli Amanti del Pacifico* (Italian), and Rarahu (French).

Shark Master (1921, Universal)—none
Screenplay by: George C. Hull. Directed by: Fred LeRoy Granville.

The fictitious Pacific Isle "Amanu" is where a shipwrecked American child turns into the island's white queen, played by Mary Collins, and bears a Caucasian child with a white castaway. However, his white former fiancée appears, so Amanu leaps into the sea where a shark (probably a great white) attacks her, but she is rescued by her white lover. Miscegenation is thwarted here again because the island queen is of Euro-American descent, as is the hero. It's either the sacrifice by jumping into shark-infested waters or the into-a-volcano trope. There is a difference because one has a chance of survival with the sharks—but there is no surviving after leaping into hot lava.

She-Devil Island (1936, Film Selectos [Mexico])— |||Ø
Screenplay by: Jorge M. Dada, Raphael J. Sevilla. Directed by: Raphael J. Sevilla.

What started out as a love story at a Mexican fishing village—with a side story of our fisherman hero washed on shore of an all-woman island—turned more into a sexploitation film after the American release studio (First Division) let loose its publicity department. The tile *María*

Elena was changed to *She-Devil Island,* and the art in various American posters was very sensualized, with many breasts laid bare. Plus, the tagline of this movie's poster reads: "With a Native Cast."

The descriptions of the film are only about the island scenes, ignoring the Mexican fishing village sequences: Drunken pearl traders invade an island of Amazonian-type beautiful women. There is nude swimming and Art Deco female Native wear. Although the setting of the island is vague, this film has all the trappings of a South Seas adventure with evil pearl divers on an island inhabited only by primitive, barely clad, fit young women, who swim nude. All are the tropes of a quintessential Hollywood South Seas film, but this time it is written and produced with the macho imagination of Mexico and sexualized even more by its American studio release partner.

She Gods of Shark Reef (1958, American International Pictures)—|||✕∅

Screenplay by: Robert Hill, Victor Stoloff. Directed by: Roger Corman.

Two very fit Euro-American brothers are shipwrecked on a Polynesian Isle inhabited only by women pearl divers. One of the brothers (the good one) saves a Polynesian girl from being a Shark God sacrifice because she broke the taboo of being with the other brother, who didn't care about her circumstances. The good brother takes the Polynesian maiden away, leaving behind the bad brother, who is killed by another shark while trying to rescue his stolen bag of pearls.

The island was called Banakai, and the underwater Mo'ai shark god was called Tangaroa (a major Polynesian deity). Roger Corman, the so-called "Pope of Pop Cinema," directed and produced this low-budget film on the island of Kaua'i. The local extras danced and sang in Hawaiian, while modeling clean sarongs furnished by Shaheen's of Hawai'i (a large, popular mid-century clothier of colorful Aloha-printed tourist attire), which was credited. Hawaiian canoes were used, as well as many local women from Kaua'i. Floyd Crosby—the first individual to win the Best Cinematography Oscar years earlier for the 1931 film *Tabu*—was the director of photography. The young Polynesian heroine was played by black-haired Lisa Montell, who in real life is an American of Polish birth. She dances a sensual hula, enticing the good brother. Even though the visitor was taboo, he and Montell also had trope scenes together of romantic Lagoon Swim and Native First Kiss. The poster of the film inexplicably has a blonde European woman being sacrificed. Do blondes sell more theater seats? Compare the swim scene with *The Ride* (2003).

Sinners in Heaven (1924, Paramount)—Ø

Screenplay by: James Ashmore Creelman. Directed by: Alan Crosland.

This silent film stars Richard Dix and Bebe Daniels as a British mail pilot and female friend who crash land off of a South Seas island. Perhaps taking a cue from Captain Cook, this couple of European descent poses as gods from the sky as a survival tactic, but a jealous Native woman exposes them as just humans. Daniels is rescued by another airplane, but cannibals shoot Dix with an arrow as he tries to flee towards the plane. Consequently, Dix is left behind. However, the pilot survives because he is saved and nursed by the same Native girl who'd exposed them. The Pacific Island woman is played by brownface American actress Betty Hilburn, and the Native chief is played by the very English Montagu Love, who played the European bad guy in *The Leopardess* (1923). Despite her newfound compassion towards him, our British hero does not forgive the Native woman and manages to escape and return to England alone.

Six Days Seven Nights (1998, Buena Vista Pictures)—✗Ø

Screenplay by: Michael Browning. Directed by: Ivan Reitman.

Harrison Ford plays a contemporary beachcomber-like character in and above the French Polynesian Islands. Ford has a job flying a small old charter plane where he meets romance and modern Asian/Polynesian pirates. An early scene foreshadows the plot's main location, as our hero couple (Anne Heche and David Schwimmer) meet in a swank Polynesian restaurant in NYC called Gauguin; ironically, in real life, it replaced a *Trader Vic's*. There, the boyfriend Schwimmer surprises his girl (Heche) with a trip for two to a small Society Island called Makatea (annoyingly pronounced Mac·a instead of Ma·ka throughout the movie). Once in Pape'ete, Tahiti, our couple are disconcerted to find their connecting charter plane to Makatea is a run-down antique. Here we meet Ford, the owner and pilot of the plane, as he and his mechanic frantically try to fix the plane for their scheduled takeoff.

Later, on Makatea, Heche gets a desperate phone call from her panicked boss (Allison Janney), who needs her back in Pape'ete for a fashion shoot, and the only way back is with cranky Ford on his rickety plane. When they finally fly back, Heche deliberately gets drunk to calm her nerves. Then a violent tropical storm suddenly appears and downs the plane on a little-known deserted island (which is a recurring South Seas cinema trope).

Meanwhile, Heche's fiancé Schwimmer is depressed because his girl left him for work in the middle of their dream romantic vacation. At the resort's Polynesian restaurant, where Schwimmer had already made reservations for two, he sits alone, surrounded by first and second honeymoon couples and plenty of tropical drinks. There he drowns his sorrows. Then the Polynesian entertainers hit the stage, and the lead dancer is mesmerizing in her sensual Tahitian dance. She wears a skimpy costume and is being accompanied by throbbing drumbeats. Schwimmer is suddenly floored by the dancer's beauty and sexuality. He doesn't know if she was glancing at him or others in the crowd. It seems to him that her desires are directed towards him and him only. In the meantime, while his fiancée literally crashes and fights for her life, the Polynesian dancer crashes into Schwimmer's hotel room for the evening, and Schwimmer has sex with the local Native.

This is a case of a Hollywood movie male fantasy that points out that the Polynesian Sensualized Dance trope and stereotypical licentious island maidens still persist in Hollywood film. The Sensual Dance trope continues, now being transmitted through the sexualized tourist industry on film. Ironically, the dance would have been even deeper in sensuality if the dancer could do the dance moves more correctly. Even though beautiful actress Jacqueline Obradors got the sensual stares down, her dancing was awkward. The dance is half the tempter's tool. Obradors is a Latina actress cast from Los Angeles who flew in early to the movie's Kaua'i faux French Polynesian locations to learn to dance Tahitian. *Six Days* includes early American film roles for Māori Temuera Morrison and Cliff Curtis as two of the movie's pirates. While Kaua'i looked good on screen substituting for French Polynesia, the lead Tahitian dancer looked uncomfortable. Both the location and the lead dancer were incorrectly represented.

Son of Fury: The Story of Benjamin Blake (1942, 20th Century–Fox)—ʊ|||✕Ø

Screenplay by Philip Dunne. Directed by: John Cromwell.

Cheated out of his sizable inheritance, Benjamin Blake, played by Tyrone Power, heads for the South Seas with John Carradine. They both jump ship near a Polynesian island, where Power quickly falls in love with a Native played by Euro-American Gene Tierney in brownface. Even though pearls are the goal for these visitors, Power can't get his mind off of Tierney.

Fury has the usual tropical trope scenes of the Lagoon Swim, Sensual Native Dance, luau feast, a small Canoe Greeting, and Native First Kiss, but, of course, Power goes Native. Carradine makes a poignant statement: "I was mad for riches, but I didn't know what they were; now I've found them and wisdom too." Carradine utters these words when he decides not to leave the new way of life he has encountered on the island. Power does leave to go back to England to clear his name but returns to Polynesia and to his Native love. Tani Marsh is a featured dancer, and the English characters are played by big name actors, including George Sanders, Francis Farmer, Elsa Lanchester, and Roddy McDowall as young Blake. All these noted actors, besides McDowall, played important island characters on other South Seas films. *Fury* is based on a novel by Edison Marshall

Sons for the Return Home (1979, NZ Film Comm. / Pacific Films)—ꓴ✗Ø

Screenplay by: Paul Maunder. Directed by: Paul Maunder.

This semi-autobiographical account of the life and thoughts of Samoan scholar and author Albert Wendt marks a pivotal moment in the evolution of South Seas cinema. This is an Indigenous film with the author's and main Samoan character's perspective. The film stars Uelese Petaia, Lani Tupu, and Malama Masina. The plot is about a young Samoan man (Petaia) born in the Samoan Islands but raised and educated in New Zealand, with a storyline about Western exploitation, colonization, racism, Polynesian diaspora and importantly, our main character's coming of age in terms of finding his identity.

Sons has good shots of outrigger canoes, greeting with leis at airport and Samoans dressed in lavalava (male wraps around the waist). A group of Samoans in their cultural dress and their custom of sitting on woven mats can be seen at the end of a modern runway as a contrast of cultures. Some racial themes including unwarranted late-night raids on Pacific Islander homes by New Zealand police of European descent and sex scenes with *pākehā* (Euro-New Zealander) girlfriend (Fiona Lindsay), who later hides Petaia in the bedroom when her pākehā friends come to visit. There are also scenes of a slap dance with new Māori friends, killing a pig as a young boy, and later making love to a pretty

Samoan young woman while a fire dance is performed outside the window, in the background. The main theme is of a man of two cultures accepted by none or who, at times, doesn't feel comfortable in either—a more general theme of Polynesian diaspora. Plus, there is a reverse interracial relationship, albeit insincere on the part of the Euro-New Zealander woman.

Of interest: the part-Samoan actress Moira Walker returns to the big screen as Petaia's mother for the first time since the 1956 British film *Pacific Destiny*, which was shot in Upolu, Western Samoa, and starred Denholm Elliott. In her motion picture debut, Walker played Gary Cooper's 'afa (half) Samoan daughter in *Return to Paradise* (1953). Also of note: early in his film career, Māori Lee Tamahori, who later became a director of New Zealand and Hollywood features (including 2002's 007 thriller *Die Another Day*), was the sound boom man in this film. A notable quote from *Sons* is when Petaia is asked by a pākehā how long the Samoan main character has been in NZ and the telling response is: "15 years but been in the region for a couple thousand." Based on the book of the same title also written by Albert Wendt, arguably one of Oceania's greatest men of letters.

South of Pago Pago (1940, United Artists)—ƆⅠⅡⅩØ
Screenplay by: George Bruce, Kenneth Gamet. Directed by: Alfred Green.

Victor McLaglen, Jon Hall and Frances Farmer star in this drama about an unscrupulous gang of American pearl traders on the uncharted isle of "Manoa." When his first mate raises a rifle at a hoard of innocent Polynesian canoes racing to greet the American ship, Captain Bucko Larson (McLaglen) comments: "Rifles are no good when you coming in, just for coming out." Trinkets are used to trade and to dive for, instead of the clichéd coins. Farmer is a Euro-American woman with a bar entertainer past, and Hall is the Native prince who sings and dances in the style of Hall's real-life Native Tahitian culture. Farmer finds sexy sarongs and finds love with Hall, and they marry. While on their honeymoon at the neighboring isle of Au Toa Toa, the rest of the American sailors steal pearls from innocent Polynesians, and the Natives rise up. Farmer, who originally was in cahoots with the evil gang, leaves Hall to get the bad Americans away from the island.

South has many genre clichés, including tropes of Canoe Greeting, Polynesian Sensual Dance, luau feast, Lagoon Swim with waterfalls, giant clam and a male god Pele's volcano on Au Toa Toa. Also credited are Los Angeles–based Polynesians Santini Puailoa and Al Kikume.

There are background stock shots of the Big Island of Hawai'i and a stage set for a tiki and worship area below the volcano. *South* is notable for its reverse Native gender seduction, one of the few films where the Indigenous lover is male, instead of the usual female. Farmer's character pays with her life for daring to have a romance with a brown man. Compare this film with *Pearl of the South Pacific* (1955).

South of Tahiti (1941, Universal)—✕∅
Screenplay by: Gerald Geraghty. Directed by: George Waggner.

Three unethical Americans, Brian Donlevy, Broderick Crawford and Andy Devine (as a character called "Moose"), try to steal a store of pearls from the Indigenous people of a beautiful, uncharted South Seas island, which has a Native princess named Melahi, played by Latina Maria Montez. Donlevy falls for Melahi, changes his ways and marries her in the end. A cast of "50 Sarong-clad Goddesses of Love" perform a strange fan dance. There are also many spotted leopards and a monkey (animals not endemic to Polynesia). While the women are dressed in the usual South Seas sarongs, the men are garbed in Southeast Asian attire, including turbans. This confusing mix of culturally incorrect South Seas costumes, customs and sets is typical of Universal Studios productions of the era. There are also a Samoan knife dance and a role for Al Kikume. The story is by Ainsworth Morgan.

South Pacific (1958, Magna/20th Century–Fox)—∪∅
Screenplay by: Paul Osborn. Directed by: Joshua Logan.

Rossano Brazzi, Mitzi Gaynor, Juanita Hall, Ray Walston, John Kerr and France Nuyen co-star in this classic musical set at a French-ruled Pacific isle during World War II but filmed on Kaua'i. The Rodgers and Hammerstein production has a well-known score, including the hits "Bali Hai," "Bloody Mary" and many more. Interestingly, the women playing Natives are Polynesian in looks and attire, but the actors cast as Islander men look and dress Melanesian. The island of Bali Hai has an even more eclectic concoction of Pacific cultures of the era, Polynesian, French Colonial, Melanesian, and Asian. Two of the main characters, Bloody Mary (Hall) and her daughter Liat (Nuyen), who live on the fictional island of Bali Hai, are Tonkinese or Vietnamese from the Gulf of Tonkin in the north of Vietnam, not Tongan Polynesians, as some people may think.

Racism at a Pacific paradise during wartime is the main theme of the film, which is a bold but true premise for its time. Gaynor (nurse Ensign Forbush) falls for the older Brazzi. The character Forbush, who is from conservative Little Rock, Kansas (where a real-life battle over school desegregation would be waged after World War II), finds out the French planter had already fathered two half–Polynesian children. She flees and decides to "wash that man right outa [her] hair," as her popular song puts it. To downplay and avoid the issue of miscegenation, the Polynesian mother, Brazzi's first wife, has died before the story begins, making her almost nonexistent. Eventually, Gaynor does overcome her prejudices, accepting the biracial children and the fact that Brazzi married and had children with someone other than a woman of European descent. However, John Kerr's Lt. Cable, who has been romancing Nuyen's Liat, does not prevail over his bigotry and symbolically pays for his racism with his life.

There is a Canoe Greeting trope. African American Archie Savage (his name is an ironic coincidence) plays a Melanesian Chief, as he did in *His Majesty O'Keefe* (1954). Juanita Hall was the first African American to win a Tony Award for also playing Bloody Mary in the Broadway production. Doug McClure and future Tarzan Ron Ely had bit parts. The movie is adapted from a successful Broadway musical of the same title by Richard Rodgers, Oscar Hammerstein II and Joshua Logan, who also directed the play. Both the play and film are based on the book by James A. Michener titled *Tales of the South Pacific.* By the look of the film and its awkward representation, Rodgers, Hammerstein and Logan (all from the Great White Way) had much more influence on the final look of the film than did author Michener, who was a World War II South Pacific veteran. The film is more of an adaption of the play than it is of the more realistic book version by Michener, and it shows.

South Seas Massacre (1974, Am. Natl. Enterprises [US/Philippines])—|||✗∅

Screenplay by: Tommy C. David, Leo Martinez. Directed by: Pablo Santiago.

Massacre stars Troy Donahue and Junero Jennings in a contemporary South Seas story with old and familiar Pacific plot elements. Modern-day pirates rob a cruise ship in the Pacific Ocean. Onboard, an armed cop and a fugitive he has long sought decide to jump ship handcuffed to each other. The two later wash ashore on an enchanted South

Seas island complete with peaceful and friendly Natives. The aforementioned pirates find the same island and claim it as a new base, and the Natives try to befriend them as well. Both Euro-American Donahue (the fugitive) and African American Jennings (the cop) find South Seas love with the island women. Donahue's romance appeared to be a long-term relationship, until his wahine gets killed by the pirates while trying to save Donahue.

There are First Native Kiss and nude Lagoon Swim tropes with a couple of twists. The pirates come upon a large lagoon and waterfalls only to frustratingly find nude Native men in and out of the water. Soon a pirate scout tells their disappointed and angry evil leader the nude wahine are in another lagoon. After a male gaze, the pirate men quickly attack the island women and rape and kill some of them, with some Native men trying to protect the women. Hence, the word "Massacre" in the title. The rest of the Native men shed their pacifism and kill off the pirates with the help of the two American visitors. Earlier, there are two Native Feast scenes—one with a friendly hula but the second with the Native women dancing a more seductive Tahitian tāmūrē, which greatly arouses the pirate men. Needless to say, all of the Pacific Islander characters, whether actors, dancers, drummers or extras, were played by Filipinos. This sexploitation film was first released in 1974 in the Philippines, where it was shot on location.

Stowaway, The (1958, Silver Films [Germany])—✗∅
Screenplay by: Paul Andreota, Ralph Habib. Directed by: Ralph Habib

European stars Martine Carol, Karlheinz Böhm, Serge Reggiani, Roger Livesey and Arletty appear in this movie filmed and set in Tahiti. The plot is about a man who settles in paradise but then inherits a lot of money from his uncle, and all of those characters who are now looking for him, both for good and evil reasons. A sub-plot follows a beautiful blonde, Lotte (played by French bombshell Martine Carol), who was a stowaway on a recent passing ship. She goes Native and becomes sexual like the local women; hence, this is a film with the sensual island trope as well as the trope of sensual Indigenous inhabitants.

Many of the *Stowaway* European cast and crew acted in the 1957 film *Seamen*, along with part-Tahitian co-star Maea Flohr. Other Tahitians had small roles in the film, including Charles Mauu, Teheiura Poheroa and Vahinerii Tauhiro. It is said the director paid more attention to the island scenery than to the cast, which includes the French superstar Arletty in two short scenes. Arletty's additional South Seas film credits include 1937's Polynesia-set but Morocco-shot *Aloha, le chant des iles* and Marcel Carne's 1945 classic *Children of Paradise*. Martine Carol was a pre–Brigitte Bardot sex symbol in Europe whose life parallels Marilyn Monroe's, with failed marriages and a suicide attempt, but in Carol's case, she fortunately survived. AKA: *Clandestina a Tahiti* (Italian title), *Le Passager Clandestin* (French), *Nachte Auf Tahiti* (German). Based on a novel by Georges Simenon, who wrote the immensely popular Inspector Maigret novels.

Tabu: A Story of the South Seas (1931, Paramount)—ʊ|||✕

Screenplay by: Robert J. Flaherty, F.W. Murnau. Directed by: F.W. Murnau.

This archetypal South Seas cinema classic stars Anne Chevalier as Reri and Matahi. A Native young man and his island princess girlfriend are suddenly forbidden to marry because she has been chosen to be a virgin bridesmaid of a local god and a *tabu* (taboo) is placed on her, making her forbidden fruit. Being young and in love, Reri and Matahi escape to a faraway island. There, the young man becomes a good pearl diver, but he doesn't understand the value of money and accumulates much debt. The two lovers are discovered by their Native priest, and in the early hours of the morning, the priest convinces Reri to return with him in his outrigger canoe. The young Matahi awakens, discovers his lover missing, and drowns in pursuit.

One thought-provoking plot quandary found in a few South Seas movies, such as *Tabu* or *Bird of Paradise*, is the fact that taboo Polynesian princesses are imperatively preserved to be a virgin sacrifice or bridesmaid to the gods; yet after losing their virtue, they are still sacrificed. Will the island gods not be offended? I guess not the god of profit or the studio gods of Hollywood. Additionally, in *Tabu* there are the usual tropes of vahines in a Lagoon Swim with a waterfall, Native Dances, luau feast, and sharks. *Tabu* is a semi-Indigenous-centered film because all major cast members are Tahitian, although the writer and director are not.

The issue in this film is with the only few topless vahine dancers; the semi-nudity appears ethnographic but, in reality, as in Flaherty's earlier *Moana,* it is staged. When both films were shot on location, Christianity had set in throughout the Pacific and the Indigene were covered up, so the director had to convince the women, their parents, and community chiefs to let a few of the women, not all, go topless. The excuse is to do a pre-contact period piece—but there is no consistency. These two films, although considered classics, set the stage for future unrealistic South Seas Native nudity in which only the young, fit and attractive are exposed. *Tabu* has an all-Native cast, including some half–Tahitians and a Chinese man. As in *White Shadows in the South Seas* (1928), Robert Flaherty started to co-direct then dropped out. Like *White Shadows*, *Tabu* was shot in glorious black and white at Bora Bora and both won an Oscar for cinematography. Floyd Crosby—father of David Crosby, of Crosby, Stills, Nash & Young, the popular American rock group—won the Best Cinematography Academy Award for his work in *Tabu*. Also Tahitian parts for Bill Bambridge, Hitu and Mehao.

Tahiti Nights (1944, Columbia)—|||
Screenplay by: Lillie Hayward. Directed by: Will Jason.

Jinx Falkenburg in brownface plays a island princess named Luana in this musical comedy featuring a novelty band, the Vagabonds. *Tahiti Nights'* tagline is "THEY MAKE WACKY WOO! THEY SING WACKY, TOO... ON THIS ISLE where love is everything but taboo!" The movie's musicians first appear in Honolulu wearing silly phony Native outfits. Later they sail for Tahiti because, we find out, the band leader (Dave O'Brien) is a fair-skinned Tahitian prince. Once at Tahiti, he finds out he's supposed to marry a Native princess (Falkenburg) from a neighboring island. O'Brien doesn't realize how beautiful the princess is, especially in her sexy sarongs. The prince and princess both separately protest the pending arranged marriage.

Similar to *Aloma of the South Seas* (1941), one day the princess sneaks out of her secure hut and takes a nude Lagoon Swim, where a monkey takes her clothes. O'Brien just happens to also want to swim in the same lagoon. Without knowing each other's identity, they fall in love. Again, this is just like *Aloma of the South Seas*, except that in *Aloma*, Dorothy Lamour's nude swim is unintended and due only to her sarong being caught on Jon Hall's fishing hook. All works out in the end for *Tahiti Nights'* lovers. Furthermore, an older vahine, brownface Euro-American Mary Treen, plays the stereotypical Mata (a female Native who wantonly desires white males). Mata relentlessly chases after one of O'Brien's American bandmates. There are parts for Los Angeles-based Polynesians Hilo Hattie, Satini Puailoa and Al Kikume, plus bandleader/ songwriter Harry Owens and His Royal Hawaiians.

Tahiti's Girl (1990, Opalo Films [Spain])—Ø
Screenplay by: Mariano Ozores. Directed by: Mariano Ozores.

Tahiti's Girl stars Vaitiare Hirshon Bandera, a mixture of many Euro and Polynesian races (Tahitian, Rarotongan, and Māori on the Polynesian side). In this story, Bandera is an anthropologist traveling to Madrid to open an Oceania Museum. On the initial trip, she hand-carries the centerpiece of the museum, a Tahitian fertility idol. The problem is that some smugglers have hidden their contraband in a fake tiki statue that looks identical to Bandera's idol, and in the airport in Spain they take the real god figure instead. Once in Madrid, she has a multitude of problems with the idol and with her local landlord, who wants to rent her an apartment by the hour.

Ozores is a veteran Spanish director known for his sexploitation films, which, for Ozores, means female nudity. The official movie poster has Bandera on a Tahitian beach wearing leis and the skimpiest bikini. She does not look like an archetypal anthropologist. In this type of film (sexploitation), she does not need to. Bandera also has a romantic relationship with her landlord's nephew.

Vaitiare has interesting South Seas cinema connections, including that her parents met on the 1962 *Mutiny on the Bounty* set, and both are part Polynesian. Also, Vaitiare was asked to play the lead female in Mel Gibson's 1984 *The Bounty*, but that did not come to fruition. She is also of Royal Rarotongan lineage through her mother. AKA: *Chica De Tahiti*.

Take a Chance (1933, Paramount)—|||Ø
Screenplay by: Buddy G. DeSylva & Laurence Schwab. Directed by: Monte Brice & Laurence Schwab.

Star James Dunn is forlorn over girl problems, but his co-star and roommate, Cliff Edwards (AKA Ukulele Ike), tries to give him advice by relating, to Dunn, one of his past stories. While Edwards sings and plays his ukulele, he reveals in song that, after being shipwrecked on a South Seas island, he was soon captured and scheduled to become the main dinner course for a tribe of Polynesians with fierce warriors. But in the imagination of Tinseltown, Edwards gets to display his ukulele talent before his demise. His flair with the ukulele impresses the Natives so much that not only does the tribe release him from his fate but also crowns him the king of the island, with the perk of picking as many island wives as he wants. Apparently, according to the song, that even includes married ones. His stereotypically subservient Native wives cater to Edwards' every need, including bearing many children.

At the end of this long flashback scene, we surprisingly realize Edwards has a wife and children back home on the continent. He suddenly misses them and takes off to return to his mainland family. His island wives cry at his departure. Despite the sadness and abandonment, it as though his Polynesian spouses and children are secondary to him, and the unfaithfulness to his first family is ignored. Male-dominated Hollywood displays its racism and sexism once again.

Tamahine (1963, MGM)—Ø
Screenplay by: Denis Cannan. Directed by: Philip Leacock.

Half-Asian Nancy Kwan plays a biracial Caucasian/Polynesian girl in this comedy. She goes to live with her proper, British boy's school headmaster uncle, and havoc ensues. She later marries the uncle's son. Even though Tamahine is half–Polynesian and raised halfway around the world, the two are still first cousins. Is this a racist construct making her any less related? There's some location filming on Bora Bora. Besides incorrect racial representation, the principal trope in this film is her carefree and liberated attitude toward the opposite sex.

This "fish out of water" film is an entertaining comedy because of the contrast between Tamahine's free spiritedness and the reserved, conservative nature of British private-school boys. How very unlike the rank-and-file crew of English ships of the early contact period between Europe and Oceania. However, British boys with a private school upbringing are likely to become the more reserved officers. Another trope in this feature is that Kwan runs around, at times even in the cold, in a short sarong and bare feet. Polynesians, especially by the 1960s, knew better. Moreover, the sexy appeal of her minimalistic clothes wreaks havoc on the campus of boys who are attired in conservative vests and ties. Kwan also dons a short sarong and plays a Polynesian in 1966's *Lt. Robin Crusoe, U.S.N.* The story of *Tamahine* is based on the book by Thelma Niklaus.

Tell It to the Marines (1926, Famous Players–Lasky/MGM)—Ø
Screenplay by: Richard Schayer (scenario), Joe Farnham (titles). Directed by: George W. Hill.

This silent film stars William Haines—and Lon Chaney in a rare non-horror role. An unusual South Seas film plot has Chaney saving fellow Marine Haines from a mob of Native men who are angry because he fell in love with a Native girl named Zaya. Usually, there is no Native resistance to a biracial relationship. Zaya (not close to a Polynesian name) is played by a brownface Euro-American (Carmel Myers), who sports an idiotic styled and inauthentic hairdo or wig, like many faux island females wore in silent movies. When we first see the Marines on the fictitious island, there are hurricane-type winds and rain, as there are in the Samoa-set *Rain* (1932) with U.S. Marines and Sadie Thompson. A South Seas island setting is only part of the *Tell* story. The characters also go to China to fight bandits, and Warner Oland (the Swedish actor who also went on to portray Chinese American Charlie Chan in a dozen-plus movies) plays another Chinese man, this time an Asian outlaw chief.

Through the Breakers (1928, Lumas Film Corp.)—Ø
Screenplay by: Harold Shumate (scenario), John Steele (titles). Directed by: Joseph C. Boyle.

This is a silent melodrama that involves an ocean liner, shipwreck, murder and suicide on a South Seas island. It stars Margaret Livingston and Holmes Herbert. Herbert works on a Pacific plantation where wife Livingston promises she'll join him, but soon after her arrival, the city-slicker wife can't take island living. She catches the next ship out— but not too far out, because the ship sinks, and Livingston lands back on Herbert's island. On shore, she observes a Native girl being killed by her Native boyfriend because she fell for Herbert. The Native then takes the woman's body out to sea in a canoe, where he buries her in the ocean and kills himself. After witnessing that incident, Livingston plays the good wife and stays loyal on the island. This is an unusual Polynesian film in which the Native man acts on his jealousies in the plot, although he takes the drastic, violent steps of murder and suicide. *Breakers* is based on a stage play by Owen Davis.

Tiara Tahiti (1962, Rank [UK])—ʊ|||✖Ø
Screenplay by: Geoffrey Cotterell. Directed by: Ted Kotcheff.

This comedy is centered on two British World War II veterans: James Mason, who is carefree and goes Native in Tahiti, and his former executive officer, John Mills, a stereotypically conservative, proper English gentleman. Mills is now a successful hotel executive, visiting Tahiti to begin the process of building a hotel on the island. The focus of the story is that both chaps have very different ideologies, because of which they despise each other. However, both being English gentlemen, they don't show it until the end.

The third important character in the story is Mason's Tahitian vahine, who is played by Mexican actress Rosenda Monteros. Monteros is full of Polynesian female tropes of sexuality: free, lascivious, unashamed of her nakedness, and having multiple sex partners. She has a nude bathing scene at a waterfall while the local French police stare. The Latina Monteros also has a young American lover, who works on passing yachts that need temporary crew members. Note the vast difference in persona Mason takes, while playing another Pacific character, Captain Nemo, in Disney's *20,000 Leagues Under the Sea*, eight years earlier. *Tiara Tahiti* also co-stars Czech-born Herbert Lom (who played Chief Inspector Charles Dreyfus in *The Pink Panther* film franchise) as Chong Sing. The film is based upon a book by Geoffrey Cotterell.

Treasure of Makuba (1966, PRC [US/Spain])—∅
Screenplay by: Jose Maria Elorriet. Directed by: Jose Maria Elorrieta.

Cameron Mitchell stars in this movie in which he searches for stolen pearls on a Polynesian island. Mitchell is reluctantly accompanied by three bad Americans who try to rape a Native girl and later kill the island chief. Mitchell saves the Native girl, who, in turn, stereotypically becomes devoted to him. Mitchell and the Indigenous girl (Latina Mara Cruz) are sentenced to death by Natives after the bad Americans blame the couple for their crimes. French police intercede to save Mitchell and Cruz from the lethal punishment of the Islanders. The police then help kill the bad outsiders. Here, the Colonial French are the heroes while the local Natives are inept, violent villains, and quick to judge. At the end, Mitchell stays on the island with his Native vahine. All of the Natives are played by Spaniards. AKA: *El Tesoro de Makuba*.

Tropic Madness (1928, FBO Productions)—∅
Screenplay by: Wyndham Gittens, Randolph Bartlett (titles). Directed by: Robert G. Vignola

Madness is a silent film starring Leatrice Joy, who, while sailing on her friend's yacht, finally finds her lost son on a South Pacific island. Earlier she had lived an extravagant lifestyle that caused her family to go bankrupt. Her former husband quietly slipped their son out to a South Seas island to be raised by a trader and kills himself after going mad—without revealing their son's location. Back on the island, a beachcomber-like or destitute doctor has a common-law Native wife, but he falls for Joy. Then the jealous Native wife convinces the local priest to sacrifice the newly found son in the volcano. The trader (George Barraud) saves the boy. Barraud declares his love for Joy, and, along with Joy's newly found son they, sail off together as a new family.

Tropic has South Seas tropes of volcano sacrifice, interracial romance, jealous Native female and the ubiquitous drunken South Seas beachcomber, who is ironically—and typically—also a medical doctor. Japanese actor Sôjin Kamiyama is in the cast. The story is by actor Ramon Romero.

Two Loves (1961, MGM)—none
Screenplay by: Ben Maddow. Directed by: Charles Walters

Two Loves stars Shirley MacLaine, Laurence Harvey and Jack Hawkins. MacLaine plays a conservative American teacher trying to find another approach to reach and teach her Māori students. In her efforts, MacLaine finds herself undergoing a full reversal in character, causing much concern for her supervisors and adult peers. The movie, set in New Zealand, is good in terms of drama, but the representation is amiss, with Nobu McCarthy (Japanese) and Juano Hernandez (Afro-Latino) playing Māori parts in this production shot in Californian. That said, this usually means racial misrepresentation in the actors' roles, possibly because of a scarcity of Polynesian actors in the area at that time, cost of travel and housing for a Pacific Island actor, or due to ignorance, lack of effort, and possible callous disregard by the filmmakers.

Again, this is dramatically decent, with good actors and acting, but *Two Loves'* insensitivity to Pacific Indigenous representation distracts from an otherwise worthy story. The major contrast in the earlier part of the movie is between the traditional MacLaine and the stereotypically carefree Māori of her surroundings. Perhaps it is this unfair characterization of Māori attitudes towards sex that motivated her later switch from a puritanical character to one of sexual permissiveness. Māori and others now know what Hawaiians have felt for years thanks to "Hollywood" versions of their worlds, though the sets and art direction made a worthy attempt.

The autobiographical novel by Sylvia Ashton-Warner was adapted for the screen by Ben Maddow, the uncle of MSNBC news anchor Rachel Maddow. In 1985, a New Zealand film version of this story entitled *Sylvia* was released, with Eleanor David playing the title character. *Sylvia* co-starred the noted English actor Tom Wilkinson and New Zealander Martyn Sanderson, who acted in 2001's NZ-made *Lord of the Rings* and directed the 1989 movie version of Albert Wendt's novel *Flying Fox in a Freedom Tree*, which was shot in Samoa.

Typhoon (1940, Paramount)—|||Ø
Screenplay by: Allen Rivkin. Directed by: Louis King.

Dorothy Lamour, Robert Preston and Coco the chimp co-star in this conventional "Sarong Girl" picture. Preston is exploring what he thought was an uninhabited island for a pearl diving company, but Lamour has been there for years. They meet and fall for each other. On the island, Lamour, Hollywood's reigning Polynesian queen of the sarongs, rescues Preston from a neighboring tribe. Then a series of disasters, including a giant fire, a tidal wave and a typhoon tie the couple together in a stronger relationship. Preston goes Native.

In the story Lamour's racial background is uncertain so as to not suggest an interracial relationship. This ethnic ambiguity is the same as with other Lamour films, in which she plays a Polynesian for the majority of a story, in dress and custom, and even island royalty, then the plot suddenly reveals that her character is Euro-American, leaving her free to cement a relationship with a lead male character of European descent. The producers get the best of both worlds—the exotic and erotic, barely-clad Polynesian-like love interest and a safe, same-race, sexual bond for 1940 audiences in an America where segregation was still widely practiced. *Typhoon* seems to be capitalizing on Lamour's 1937 hit *The Hurricane*. *Typhoon* also includes the Lagoon Swim trope. AKA: *South of Samoa.*

Up Periscope (1959, Warner Brothers)—Ø.
Screenplay by: Richard H. Landau. Directed by: Gordon Douglas.

In this World War II actioner, James Garner and Edmond O'Brien are "Somewhere in the South Pacific—1942," on both a Japanese-infested island and in a submarine based in Pearl Harbor. In Honolulu, officers hang out in a bar filled with sexy Hawaiian hostesses in cellophane grass skirts and leis. Alan Hale, Jr., later the captain in TV's popular *Gilligan's Island*, also co-stars. In the Honolulu bar, Hale is surrounded by Native beauties who stereotypically can't keep their hands off of him. When Hale leaves the bar, the wahines surround and grope Garner. *Periscope* is based on a novel by Robb White.

Up to His Neck (1954, General Films [UK])—ᗰ✕Ø
Screenplay by: John Paddy Carstairs, Patrick Kirwan. Directed by: John Paddy Carstairs.

In this UK comedy a lone British sailor, an older Ronald Shiner, is stationed on a South Seas island during World War II to guard supplies.

A few years go by, his navy forgets about him, so he goes Native, with most of the young Island women adoring him. Thus, the title "up to his neck"—with Native women, that is. Shiner settles down, picking a particular island female who is more his type (age) to become his partner. Ten years later the Royal Navy remembers him and returns, but he doesn't want to leave the isle. He ends up recovering a stolen sub and becomes a hero. There are Polynesian greeting, farewell, luau, and dance trope scenes. The film co-stars "black-haired volcano" Laya Raki (born in Germany to a European father and Javanese mother) as Lao Win Tan and accomplished actor and singer Anthony Newley. Laya Raki also played a sensuous Māori princess in *Land of Fury*, also in 1954. This is a remake of *Jack Ahoy* (1934), which did not have the Polynesian island and Islanders.

Utu (1983, Pickman [NZ])—Ø
Screenplay by: Keith Aderdein, Geoff Murphy. Directed by: Geoff Murphy

Māori Anzac Wallace stars in this critically acclaimed movie of a renegade British soldier who turns on the British army after witnessing the slaughter of his own village by English guns during the Māori Wars (AKA "Land Wars") period, circa 1870. Wallace vows revenge—or "utu"—on the British in this very dramatic and noteworthy film.

There is a scene where a pretty Māori young woman, a British captive, seduces a young British soldier with all the stereotypical charms of a sexualized Polynesian maiden, but in this case, she turns the trope on its head: it was all a ruse so she could escape. *Utu* is an early, almost Indigenous-point-of-view film by the Euro-New Zealand director/writer Murphy and is clearly a stellar example of a movie produced outside of the Hollywood studio system.

Utu also stars noted Māori director/producer/actress Merata Mita. Mita recalls being indignant at the director when she read for the role of a stereotypical libidinous Māori woman who only goes to bed with the hero to satisfy his lust before he goes back to war. The director, Murphy, was appalled at Mita's disrespect of his position and her straightforwardness. But Mita got her way with a more dignified character, and she and Murphy later were married, had children and partnered in a production company. Years later one can see the character Mita fought against in *River Queen* (2005). In that film, which also features many quality Māori thespians, a beautiful Māori daughter of an allied tribe's chief makes love to the hero chief (Temuera Morrison) right before his main battle with the British. Needless to say, in *River*

Queen the alliance was broken, and our hero chief battles the British alone with his tribe.

Wallaby Jim of the Islands (1937, Grand Natl. Films)—Ø

Screenplay by: Bennett R. Cohen, Houston Branch. Directed by: Charles Lamont.

Mamo Clark, George Houston, and Ruth Coleman co-star in this typical South Seas adventure set on the fictional isle of Raihoa. Wallaby is a skipper who loves the Natives, and they love him, especially Indigenous Clark, who loves him romantically. An evil German trader forces the Natives to dive for pearls in deep water while he tricks Wallaby into leaving the island. Wallaby figures out what is really happening and returns to save the day.

Wallaby sings as well as he fights. Of the many characters listed, the only Polynesian credited is Mamo Clark, even though others have speaking parts, including Al Kikume and James (Kimo) Spencer. Sarong-clad Mamo is at times stereotypically relentless in her pursuit of Houston. At the end, Houston's commitment to the Native Mamo is still questionable. This is a typical American South Seas film in which a European can suddenly control the whole island and its inhabitants, and a lone American can save the Indigenous, arguably an unconscious projection of Pacific power politics—a colonial trope that Pacific Islanders are defenseless and need America to save them. *Wallaby's* story is by Albert Richard Wetjen. AKA: *Spoilers of the South Seas.*

Weird Woman (1944, Universal)—none

Screenplay by: Brenda Weisberg, W. Scott Darling. Directed by: Reginald Le Borg.

This horror film, with an insulting title, stars Lon Chaney, Jr., Evelyn Ankers as Ilona Carr and real Polynesian Hanna Kaapa as Laraua. Chaney plays a professor who returns from a Pacific Island vacation with a Euro-American bride raised by Natives who belong to a spiritual order of some kind. There is no interracial marriage per se, as our island bride is either European or of Euro-American origins (to avoid a miscegenetic marriage). *Weird* has lots of inappropriate Hawaiian dancing and singing to a very fictitious island god and many Hawaiian background players. Chaney also has a very jealous Euro-American ex-girlfriend who goes mad, spreads rumors that his bride is a voodoo priestess, and then commits a series of murders so she can blame them on the new island bride. Why is the woman from the island with a Polynesian-style sensibility considered "weird" and not the delusional mass-murderer Euro-American ex-girlfriend? The bride worships an idol and thinks the deaths are caused by a curse until her rational husband destroys her relics of Native rituals and protection. He then solves the case like any all-American hero would. *Weird* is based on a novel entitled *Conjure Wife* by Fritz Leiber, Jr.

What the Butler Saw (1950, Hammer [UK])—∅
Screenplay by: Edward J. Manson, A.R. Rawlinson. Directed by: Godfrey Grayson.

In this UK comedy, a British earl retires following long years of service governing a South Seas island. After he returns to England, he finds that an island princess shipped herself over to the British Isles by hiding in the earl's freight. Her reason for stowing away in the shipment was because she is in love with the earl's butler. The earl tries to return her but fails. The princess is played by Latina-looking and sounding, but very British born and raised, Mercy Haystead. As in *Tamahine* (1963), the island princess has an aversion to wearing many clothes. But this trope is magnified in this film because Haystead goes totally nude in a scene of a formal reception for the princess. Apparently in the princess' culture, the more formal the occasion, the less one wears. Once again, the Western heterosexual male imagination runs wild.

Interestingly, the title, *What the Butler Saw*, is a known saying that refers to a famous 1860s trial and later a pornographic Mutoscope title—both simply referring to a butler peeking through a keyhole. Later, the term "what the butler saw" indirectly referred to some kind of female nudity and how men voyeuristically view it. The title of this particular film, as well as Polynesian sexual tropes, surely had the same intent of marketing sex to attract the male audience. I should say that Henry Mollison, who plays the butler Bembridge, was not a voyeur, nor did he take advantage of the island princess, but behaved as a proper English gentleman, calmly and patiently assisting Haystead in her cultural adjustments. Here again, one finds the social and age imbalance between a young Islander of royal lineage romantically involved with an older European of the working class—as if, in the Western world, this is the proper balance: a mature, commoner, white male is equal to a beautiful, young, Islander of Polynesian chiefly status. It is an American or European ethnocentric racist construct or the superior white race concept.

When Time Ran Out... (1980, Warner Brothers)—∅
Screenplay by: Carl Foreman, Stirling Silliphant. Directed by: James Goldstone.

Paul Newman, Jacqueline Bisset, William Holden, Red Buttons, Ernest Borgnine, Burgess Meredith, James Franciscus, Barbara Carrera, Pat Morita, Shelly Winters and more co-star in a blockbuster produced by the "Master of Disaster" Irwin Allen. This time the subject or source of the catastrophe is a volcano set 1,000 miles from Fiji on the fictional island of Kalaleu. There, a developer builds a high-end resort with the island's volcano as an attraction—but that brilliant plan backfires when, at the Grand Opening of the hotel, the volcano violently erupts and threatens the whole island.

A Hawaiian influence is discernible in the Native inhabitants, probably due to filming on location on the Big Island of Hawai'i. One Native named Iolani is played by Latina Carrera (who also portrayed the Polynesian title character in the 1988, Fiji-shot, Samoa-set, TV mini-series *Emma: Queen of the South Seas*). Iolani is a hotel executive who has an affair with the developer Franciscus, who is married to Nikki, played by the beautiful actress Veronica Hamel. For some Hollywood-fabricated men, a gorgeous wife is not enough. *Time* was purposefully filmed on the Big Island of Hawai'i, where there are active and dormant volcanos and lava-covered fields, all used in the filming. Compare *Time's* escaping volcano scene with the one in *The Devil at Four O'Clock* (1961). *Time* is based on upon Gordon Thomas and Max Morgan Witts' novel *The Day the World Ended*, which was also the original title of this star-studded movie. Co-screenwriter Stirling Silliphant also wrote the 1978 O'ahu shot and set TV mini-series *Pearl*, co-starring his wife, Tiana Alexandra-Silliphant.

Where the Pavement Ends (1923, Metro)—∅
Screenplay by: Rex Ingram. Directed by: Rex Ingram, Alice Terry.

This dramatic silent feature is about an affair between a young South Seas island chief named Motauri, played by Latino Ramon Novarro, and Matilda (Alice Terry), daughter of a prejudiced missionary portrayed by Edward Connelly. This is an early film showing the beautiful and natural world of a Polynesian island being destroyed by zealous and bigoted Europeans. Despite a fierce storm and violence with a jealous American bar owner, these travails do not deter Novarro and Terry from finally consummating their relationship.

Soon afterwards, they both settle in Novarro's hut, but unexpectedly, the young chief sneaks out and nonsensically leaps to his death over a large waterfall. In an alternative script ending, demanded by the studio, it is discovered that Novarro is of European descent, with a tan, and not Polynesian after all, so he happily travels to England to marry the pastor's daughter. Both endings are inexplicable, except to obviously avoid miscegenation or the marriage and the possible birth of a multi-racial child in this saga of reverse interracial love. Originally the project was a story that revealed the prejudices of the Europeans, but instead it ends up being an example of racism in America in which Jim Crow and segregation were still widely enforced.

This rare South Seas plot in which a Polynesian male has a relationship with a Euro-American female can perhaps be attributed to the rare co-direction of a female director. The co-star Alice Terry was also one of the first female co-directors of a major studio film. Her husband, Rex Ingram, a major silent film director, was the other half of the directorial team. They made fifteen films together, even though she was not always credited onscreen as a director, as Terry was not credited as such in *Pavement*. This is one of the many examples of sexism by the male Hollywood establishment. John George, born Tufei Fithela in Aleppo, Syria, played a Polynesian servant named Napuka Joe. *Pavement* is set in 'Uvea (Wallis Islands) but was shot in Cuba and Miami. AKA: *The Passion Vine*. Adapted from a novel written by John Russell.

White Flower, The (1923, Famous Players/ Paramount)—✗Ø

Screenplay by: Julia Crawford Ivers. Directed by: Julia Crawford Ivers.

Flower features the same cast and lead actress, Betty Compson, as the 1922 *The Bonded Woman*. But this time, Betty plays Konia, a biracial daughter of a plantation owner. Compson falls in love with the newly arrived pineapple manager (Edmund Lowe), but his fiancée from the States follows.

Compson's Native suitor, David Panuahi, played by Euro-American Leon Barry in brownface, tells Compson to have the *kahuna* (priest) put a curse on the plantation manager's betrothed. Barry's real intention is to show that Rutherford would pay more attention to his ailing fiancée, and thus his devotion to his future wife would end Compson's interest in him. Barry's plan works. Compson then asks the kahuna to lift the sickness curse out of respect for the relationship of the American couple. Her internal conflict of the heart drives her to want to jump into a volcano, but the lifting of the curse means Lowe's fiancée is well, freeing the plantation manager to choose the direction of his true heart. He finds Compson in the nick of time before she leaps. Love and happiness then abound.

Flower was supposedly shot in Hawai'i but definitely shot on a soundstage with tropes of a luau, hulas and surfing scenes. It is a lost film that dramatizes a very uncommon interracial love quadrangle in a South Seas movie, and uncommonly, Maui Kaito plays a female kahuna. While in the real Polynesia it is not unusual for a woman to be accepted as a powerful spiritual person, whether in life or in legend, it is uncommon for women to wield such power or position in a Hollywood South Seas picture. Kahunas, even ones with the nickname, are stereotypically males on the big screen. The '60s "California Beach" films almost always seemed to have a character with the appropriated

The White Flower (1923, Paramount Pictures). In *The White Flower* silent film star Betty Compson as Konia (pictured here) dances a seductive Hollywood hula. Compson plays a half–Hawaiian daughter of an American plantation owner. She stereotypically falls for the new American plantation manager played by Edmund Lowe, and she is determined to get him. The difficulty here is that Lowe's fiancée follows him soon afterwards on another ship. Besides the South Seas tropes of the Seductive Dance and the Kahuna Curse, there is also the Sacrifice into a Volcano cliché, but in this case, it is a self-sacrifice or, some would say, suicide. American lobby card (11" × 14").

nickname "Kahuna," who was always a wiser, older male surfer. Referring to a female Kahuna in *Flower*, perhaps with the combination of a powerful Hollywood actress and an atypical female director of note (who also wrote the script), one should not be surprised. Compson as Konia has a sensualized Hollywood faux hula dance that embarrasses the white women in the room but certainly not their husbands. Cinematographer James Van Trees is the director's son.

White Heat (1934, Pinnacle Productions)—|||Ø
Screenplay by: James Bodrero, Lois Weber. Directed by: Lois Weber.

Heat is a complicated romance involving a prejudiced American sugar planter who deplores his fellow neighbors of European descent for marrying Native women. The planter also deplores Indigenous women who flirt with him. One night, in a drunken stupor, the planter falls for a wahine, Leilani, who was bathing in the nearby ocean. They move in together, and she serves him loyally until he goes to the mainland and marries a Euro-American socialite. Leilani is heartbroken while the new wife is now on the island. The socialite quickly becomes bored and flirts with a Native man, then has an affair with a rich American former boyfriend who sails in on his yacht. Who is the licentious woman in this film, the Polynesian or the Euro-American?

Heat is notable for true location shooting in Hawai'i with many bit parts played by island residents—Nani Palsa, Kolimau Kamai, Kamaunani Achi, Nohill Kaumu—all of whom are credited. The lead wahine, Leilani, is played by a Latina, Mona Maris. *Heat* is a pentagon of interracial love. Note: Lois Weber was another early female director, considered to be one of the most important in American cinema history. This is possibly why our Polynesian heroine is presented with a more balanced or realistic depiction, as compared to other females of different races in this story, plus the early use of a female of European descent flirting with Native men. In the 1930s, this was very bold, to say the least. Unfortunately, this lost film was Lois Weber's final and her only talkie. The original story is by James Bodrero. AKA: *Cane Fire.*

White Shadows in the South Seas (1928, MGM)—ʊ|||✗Ø
Screenplay by: Ray Doyle, Jack Cunningham. Directed by: W.S. Van Dyke, Robert J. Flaherty.

At first, this archetypal South Seas cinema classic is set on a Polynesian Island already settled by Europeans and Americans. There, an alcoholic doctor, played by Monte Blue, is irritated by the greed, injustice, introduction of ill health, promotion of vices, and the exploitative treatment of the Natives by local members of his European race. In retaliation to Blue's bad attitude towards them, the settlers knock the doctor out, tie him to the deck of a newly quarantined ship, with its diseased and dead crew members still aboard, and set him adrift. Normally, a deadly ship of this nature is towed far offshore and burned with all its contagious contents, including human remains. Fortunately for Blue, the burning does not take place with the unconscious doctor bound on deck. Somehow the non-mariner Blue survives, and he lands upon an island of Polynesians untouched or influenced by Euro-American culture—except that Natives speak English for the Hollywood camera in what was MGM's first talking picture.

On this new island, many Pacific Island tropes appear. There are the inevitable scenes where Blue spots nude Native females swimming in a lagoon. Later goes Native and marries the chief's daughter (half–Latina Raquel Torres), whose name—Fayaway—is derived from Herman Melville's archetypal 1846 novel *Typee*. There is also tiki worship, an island luau feast, an unintentional Sensual Dance by a taboo Native princess (Torres), and a Native First Kiss scene.

Blue becomes greedy for Native pearls, but after some serious reflection, he comes back to his newly adopted Native senses. Then the large white sails of a European ship appear (white shadows). Aboard is an evil German trader whom Blue knows and despises. Blue fails to convince the innocent Natives to stop the Canoe Greeting, to avoid the strange ship and the cheap temptations of the trader, and to send the ship away. The now-furious doctor is killed by the evil European captain in his attempt to prevent the foreigners from interacting with the Natives. Eventually, what was a virgin isle becomes, like the first island of the film, filled with Native exploitation and vice, in other words another paradise lost.

Considering the historical fact of the near genocide of the Polynesians by introduced diseases and with the recognition that Covid-19 can be spread by an asymptomatic person, one contemplates the possible horror if Blue inadvertently transported the deadly disease from the ship to an island filled with innocent Indigenes with no inherent antibodies for foreign viruses. Fortunately, *White Shadows* is a fictional account from decades past, and the writer and original audiences of this film had no common understanding of the term *asymptomatic transmission*, which probably accounted for many deaths of Polynesians in actual Pacific history.

White Shadows was shot in Papeete, Tahiti, and, as previously noted, was MGM's first sound film. It was directed by Robert Flaherty, and then by W.S. Van Dyke, and the discerning eye can see the clash between Flaherty's more documentarian style and Van Dyke's more Hollywood approach. Clyde De Vinna worked as the director of photography, winning an Oscar for *White Shadows'* superb camerawork. Van Dyke and De Vinna were frequent collaborators, specializing in ethnographic-type, docudrama-like films shot in far-flung "exotic" locations. Mexico-born Torres was one of the first Latinas to play a Polynesian and portrayed Ilanu in 1931's *Aloha*. *White Shadows* is derived from a famous book with same title written by Frederick O'Brien.

Wild Women (1918, Universal)—✗∅
Screenplay by: George Hively. Directed by: John Ford.

Harry Carey stars in this silent movie with a huge dream sequence (almost the whole movie) involving a castaway cowboy, a pretty Hawaiian princess, and an aging Hawaiian queen, all on a South Seas isle. In the beginning of the movie, Carey and his pals are celebrating after winning a rodeo. They go to a San Francisco café which has hula dancers. Carey then dreams he and his pals land on the shore of an island of hula dancers where the queen kidnaps Carey and forces him to marry. Thus, there is a stereotypically aggressive Native female in this story contrived by John Ford and Harry Carey. Miscegenation is circumvented here because it was all just a dream. Data for this film shows the director as Jack Ford. The legendary director John Ford switched to his real first name, going from Jack to John in 1923. Renowned for directing Westerns, Ford also helmed many similar type films set in Oceania, and *Wild Women* may be Ford's first stab at South Seas cinema.

Wings Over the Pacific (1943, Monogram)—∅
Screenplay by: George Wallace Sayre. Directed by: Phil Rosen.

Brunette Inez Cooper is featured in this story of a U.S. veteran's peace and quiet being shattered as two pilots, a German and an American, shoot each other down over "his" Pacific Island at the beginning of World War II. Pretty Miss Cooper plays the half–Polynesian daughter of the U.S. veteran who bought the isle from a friendly local chief. Of course, the American pilot gets the pretty biracial Native at the end and marries her. In the story, the Native warriors and Americans form an alliance to defeat the Germans and invading Japanese. Polynesians Santini Puailoa, James Lono and Hawksha Paia were credited. Pacific language or languages are spoken in this World War II action film set in the Pacific Theater, where the enemies are at first Nazis, not the Imperial Japanese. There is the typical erroneous racial representation of a Polynesian woman so as to justify a relationship between the Euro-American male and a fair and imagined beautiful island female.

Woman There Was, A (1919, Fox)—Ø
Screenplay by: Adrian Johnson. Directed by: J. Gordon Edwards.

Vamp actress Theda Bara played Princess Zara on a South Seas island where a handsome missionary arrives. There is romance but also bad luck because of a typhoon and her accidental death. The semi-distraught missionary goes home and marries his girlfriend of European descent. This is no paradise. Zara's untimely demise avoids the issue of miscegenation.

This early silent, filmed in and around Miami, Florida, is full of misrepresentation. The inauthentic location is usually a base for erroneous representation by virtue of its distance from the real South Pacific. Although there are sand and coconut trees, the similarities end there. Many of the supposedly Polynesian Natives are played by African Americans and Euro-Americans in brownface. The costumes, grass hut architecture, and names are all off base. Many South Seas cinema tropes occur in this early silent: pearl diving, human sacrifice, island princess as the love interest of a Euro-American protagonist and a large natural disaster, in this case a typhoon. As with most South Seas cinema plots, there is no accountability for a disloyal Euro-American male who temporarily abandons his girl back home.

Women of Pitcairn Island, The (1956, 20th Century–Fox)—Ø
Screenplay by: Aubrey Wisberg. Directed by: Jean Yarbrough.

This B-picture imagines life on remote Pitcairn Island eighteen years after the mutiny of the HMS *Bounty*. The mutineers stumbled upon and then took refuge on this very isolated island in the southeast Pacific. The movie is a far-from-factual account about the strong and determined Tahitian women survivors of the *Bounty*'s mutinous crew and their mixed-Polynesian offspring. In this story, shipwrecked pirates fight over a bag of pearls. There are very adult themes with widowed Native women and their mature looking teenaged children. The pirates also want the beautiful part-Polynesian young daughters in a bad way. While showing the empowerment of Native women in this story is important, it seems for the producers it was equally important to show the barely clad handsome and muscular male and beautiful female teenagers from the island. All the Native characters on Pitcairn, who in reality are of a mixed Tahitian and English lineage, are represented by Euro-Americans and a couple of Latino actors, many with a light brownface body make-up. Based on a novel by Aubrey Wisberg.

Conclusion

Possible New American Enlightenment

Hollywood has always been a Euro-American masculine industry, and this fact is reflected in the vast majority of its films. American cinema narratives that are set in a foreign land or colony are almost always American-centric, and the protagonists are almost always, especially in South Seas cinema, American males. In the majority of these Pacific Island films, as Indigenous filmmaker and scholar Vilisoni Hereniko aptly put it, "Pacific Islanders merely provide colorful background in tropical settings, which to those who live in cold industrial countries, are the equivalent of an Eden or Paradise."[1]

Generally, the only instance in which Pacific Island characters have a major role in these American films is when they play submissive love interests in interracial affairs with the Euro-American male heroes. More of these Polynesian parts are portrayed either by Latinos or brownface Americans. The few actual Polynesians who act in these films do an admirable job, such as Mamo Clark and Al Kikume,[2] but why more Polynesians are not cast in these films remains a mystery. Two possible reasons could be that the Pacific Island talent pool is very small, with few experienced Native actors—or just a case of lazy or culturally ignorant and insensitive casting. With the onset of quality island-made Indigenous Pacific Island films comprising very good and fresh Indigenous actors, Hollywood filmmakers should be more secure in casting Polynesian talents with camera experience.

American producers, directors, and film studios normally don't take chances with inexperienced Pacific actors, but one has to note a couple of occasions when filmmakers cast first-time Polynesian actresses, Jocelyne LaGarde (Tahitian) and Keisha Castle-Hughes (Māori), who both received Oscar nominations for their debut performances. Also noteworthy is that Castle-Hughes was only 13 years old when nominated for Best Leading Actress, by far the youngest, in 2004.

Castle-Hughes was in *Whale Rider* (2003) and LaGarde co-stared in *Hawaii* (1966). Both surpassed immense challenges, besides being inexperienced. For Castle-Hughes, her age; for LaGarde, she did not know English. She spoke French and Tahitian and held her own opposite the great thespians Max von Sydow, multi-nominee for Oscars, Emmys, and Golden Globe awards; Richard Harris, two-time Oscar nominee; and Julie Andrews, Academy Award winner.

Regardless of the past use of Latino and brownface thespians and the later use of Asian-Americans and other Asians as Polynesians, I also see a recent thread in faux Polynesian representation in contemporary American film, which I call the "White Polynesian." For example, Hawai'i has been subject to more than 100 years of colonial occupation. Hollywood is now rationalizing that many part-Hawaiians have blended racial bloodlines and that filmmakers can take advantage of this by casting Euro-Americans as Euro-Polynesians, or American actors with 100 percent European ancestry as Polynesians with little indigenous blood. Early examples of this practice can be seen in *Tahiti Nights* (1944) and *Call of the South Seas* (1944), in which American actress Janet Martin plays an island queen with only one-eighth Polynesian lineage. No brown body makeup is needed. As long as the bloodline is announced in script and dialog, one can get away with this dubious concept.

The 1990 South Seas satire *Joe Versus the Volcano* had a whole island full of Polynesian, Jewish and Druid mixed inhabitants. The casting of speaking parts and background players in Hawai'i was simplified with an almost "anything goes" attitude in terms of ethnic appearance. More recently, George Clooney and all his cousins on film were ⅛ Hawaiian, while his daughters were ¹⁄₁₆ Hawaiian in the acclaimed *The Descendants* (2011). As a result of this concept, all of these aforementioned roles in *Descendants* were portrayed by pure Euro-Americans. In *Aloha* (2015), as with mega-star Clooney in *Descendants*, Euro-American and current Hollywood A-lister Emma Stone played Allison Ng, who is of ¼ Hawaiian, ¼ Chinese and Swedish lineage, with a total look of unadulterated blonde European ancestry.

Hollywood producers get to cast their "big money draw" American players with European racial backgrounds without many repercussions on representation. In the current vernacular, the term for the use of Euro-Americans playing other races in Hollywood films or Euro-Americans playing the hero in a foreign setting is "whitewashing." Ridley Scott's 2014 *Exodus: Gods and Kings* is a notable example, with many ancient Hebrew and Egyptian characters portrayed by actors of European ancestry, such as Christian Bale and Sigourney Weaver.

Furthermore, with regard to more opportunities for Polynesians playing themselves in American films, there is an irony in Hollywood that there are major Polynesian or part-Polynesian actors in Hollywood who have never played a prominent Polynesian role. For example, stars Keanu Reeves and until recently, Dwayne Johnson. Also, many fine Polynesian actors, especially from New Zealand, including Islanders from the diaspora or Native Māori, find themselves cast as sci-fi characters because of their unfamiliar looks, or many are covered in prosthetics so completely that no one can recognize them. Hawaiian Jason Momoa has acted in fantasy and science fiction series and features, including *Stargate: Atlantis*, *Game of Thrones*, *Aquaman*, and *Dune*. Dozens of seasoned Polynesian actors can be found in mega blockbuster film series such as *Lord of the Rings* or *Star Wars*, but most are unrecognizable and certainly not playing Polynesians.

Then there is the Polynesian "thug" stereotype, in which actual Polynesians are used but their parts have little dialog, just the flexing of masculine muscle. This now-common stereotype can be found in television and movies. Examples of these Polynesian thugs in cinema are 1994's domestic violence drama *Once Were Warriors*, the surf films *North Shore* (1987) and *Blue Crush* (2002), and most recently, Polynesians as organized crime thugs can be found in the 2018 film *Den of Thieves*. Unfortunately, even when playing a stereotypical character, female Polynesian actresses are not considered for these parts, because after all, it is a male stereotype.

Fortunately, a few good Polynesian actors have come up in the Hollywood ranks by getting their starts acting in the New Zealand or Australian film industries, some even by playing Polynesians in Pacific Island films. A good case in point are the Māori actors from *Once Were Warriors* (1994), Cliff Curtis and Temuera Morrison,[3] who have done well in American films playing non–Polynesian roles. When they do play themselves as Māori, they have to return home to act in New Zealand–based productions. Most recently, Australian director George Miller cast two actresses, one of Māori and European descent (Megan Gale) and one of Chinese, Māori, Cook Island, and European descent (Courtney Eaton), in major roles in the popular Australian- and American-produced film *Mad Max: Fury Road* (2015). Both delivered excellent performances, especially Gale as the Valkyrie, while the younger Eaton is a new up-and-comer in Hollywood. Both played generic human survivalists in post-apocalyptic worlds. What are the odds that they will have Pacific Island parts in future American cinema? With new Polynesian actors emerging out of Indigenous independent film, and many Polynesians actors in the current Hollywood talent pool (coming out of Hawai'i, New Zealand, Australia and from the Polynesian

Diaspora), why are the "Emma Stones" still cast in contemporary American South Seas cinema as Polynesians or part-Polynesians?

After some backlash for the racial misrepresentation in *Aloha*,[4] the young and now enlightened Emma Stone admitted to some errors of judgment in taking this role. From the online Australian source *news. com.au*, here are some quotes from an interview with Stone:

> "I've become the butt of many jokes," says Emma Stone, referring to her most recent role in the rom-com *Aloha* in which she was grossly miscast as a half–Asian character [*sic*].
>
> "I've learned on a macro level about the insane history of whitewashing in Hollywood and how prevalent the problem truly is. It's ignited a conversation that's very important," she acknowledges. (The movie was an unmitigated flop with a budget of $US37 million and took in a mere $US23 million worldwide at the box office).[5]
>
> "There's a lot of conversation about how we want to see people represented onscreen and what we need to change as a business to reflect culture in a clearer way and not in an idealized way. There are some flaws in the system," she says. "My eyes have been opened in many ways this year."

With this statement by Miss Stone, that this issue has "ignited a conversation that's very important," more questions need to be asked. While it is not only refreshing to hear the acknowledgment of an error and new awareness gained by a new generation of Americans, the first question is: Will others admit that this erroneous practice of "whitewashing" from Hollywood has been happening for many decades? Also, will this current conversation be sustainable enough to effect real change in racist practices in American cinema? Hopefully, this discussion of racism, found throughout this book, can continue and can be broadened to cover other racist practices found throughout the history of American film.

Some recent notable events have to be mentioned here. Both mega-actor Dwayne Johnson and hugely popular actor Jason Momoa have large Polynesian tattoos, embracing and proudly signaling their Polynesian heritage, regardless of the costly time and money to cover them for various non–Polynesian characters they play; when one reaches a certain level of stardom, much of this extra cost is overlooked. In the following two films Dwayne Johnson displayed his real Polynesian tattoos, playing Samoan characters. In *Be Cool* (2005) Johnson played a Samoan thug but with a twist—despite his daunting, conventionally manly appearance the character was very feminine in nature. At the end Johnson had a dream come true by performing onstage the Samoan fire knife dance and showing off his real Samoan tattoos in all their glory. Johnson's part was not a leading role in this film, but as mentioned, more recently, the #1 box office actor Dwayne "the Rock"

Johnson can now influence the direction of stories in his films. In 2019's *Fast & Furious Presents: Hobbs & Shaw* Johnson not only establishes his character as Samoan, but also, the second half of the film is set in Samoa, where his Polynesian family helps fight the bad guys. Many Polynesians had roles in this film because of Mr. Johnson's influence.

In 2017 Hawaiian Jason Momoa starred as the classic DC comic book character Aquaman in *Justice League*. The co-director of *Justice League*, Zack Snyder, must have taken some criticism for casting a Hawaiian actor to play the part of blond Euro-looking Aquaman of comic book fame. Not only did Snyder defend his decision, but he took advantage of Momoa's Hawaiian background, not only using his own Polynesian tattoos but augmenting them more onscreen. In addition, Māori actor Temuera Morrison plays his earthy Polynesian father in the solo *Aquaman* (2018) movie to explain Aquaman's new Polynesian appearance and his Pacific Island tattoos. So far, the audiences love Momoa's portrayal and Snyder's explanation of Aquaman's background. Hopefully these are signs of a Hollywood turnaround.[6]

Also fueling this possible turnaround is the huge hit *Moana* (2016) by Walt Disney Studios. Although animated, this film, with some inaccuracies and stereotypes (Herman), shows much promise in the reversal of erroneous representations and greater cultural sensitivities by a major Hollywood studio. Combining negative criticism about the overuse of the "white" princess character, as in recent Disney films such as *Tangled* (2010) and mega-hit *Frozen* (2013), plus the success of the franchise *Lilo and Stitch* (2002–2006) movies and TV series, Disney responded with *Moana* in 2016, which was previously planned but moved up a year to answer the criticism. The critical backlash against the Disney white princess has spurred a new enlightenment and sensitivities in at least one major Hollywood studio. Hopefully others will follow suit. With two Polynesian-themed shorts, *Lava* (2015) and the charming old-fashioned cartoon *Mickey Mouse in Kuʻu Lei Melody* (2016), along with the rich, culturally laden Mexican-themed film *Coco* (2017) and the successful African-centered *Black Panther*, Disney has set the bar for more diversity in American film. This is true not only in stories and casting but also in Indigenous music. The last two films, as well as *Moana*, brought in huge profits for the studio.

On a very significant side note, two young Polynesian singers/actresses had their singing talents recognized with back-to-back Academy Award nominations for the Best Achievement in Music Written for Motion Pictures (Original Song). Both Pacific Island actresses were able to perform their movie signature songs live onstage at the annual Oscar ceremony in front of millions of viewers worldwide. First, then-sixteen-year-old Auliʻi Cravalho sang "How Far I'll Go" from *Moana* at the 2017 Oscars presentation. The following year (2018) Keala Settle sang "This Is Me" from *The Greatest Showman* (1917) and was given a standing ovation by the star-studded audience. Miraculously, we later heard Keala Settle had a mini-stroke one week before her memorable performance. The song, with Keala Settle as the principal singer, did win a Golden Globe for Best Original Song in 2018, although not an Oscar. There is no more diverse a cast than in a film with many roles for circus oddities, formerly known by the politically incorrect term "freaks." Miss Settle played an overweight, brown, bearded woman, receiving recognition for her acting and many accolades for her singing. It was Auliʻi's first film. It was Keala's second: she had played a movie bit part beforehand—but she did have Broadway experience. Keala also has Polynesian tattoos, and they were very noticeable during her Oscar night performance. She was proud to wear them and obviously did not attempt to cover them up.

When 15-year-old first-timer Miss Cravalho was cast in the title role in *Moana*, she was billed ahead of veteran mega-star Dwayne Johnson, who played the Polynesian demi-god Maui. An analysis of *Moana* and its differences from Polynesian legends reveals the following: it is the story of Polynesia, albeit with historic holes filled with legends and myths, but they are of Polynesian origin, not emanating from the imagination of a Euro-American writer sitting at a desk far from the Pacific Isles. Some of the plot is an amalgamation or balance of similar Indigenous stories from various Polynesian cultures. The producers and directors traveled extensively throughout Polynesia to get the proper feel firsthand of the islands, their inhabitants and their cultures. These same responsible people used a cultural board filled with academic and culturally sensitive Polynesians as advisers. Even though animated, the voice cast was predominantly made up of Polynesians from various Pacific Islands, including Māori Temuera Morrison and Rachel House. The parents of Samoa-born, New Zealand–raised Opetaia Foa'i are from Tokelau and Tuvalu. He was one of the animated film's songwriters, along with *Hamilton* creator Lin-Manuel Miranda, who is of Puerto Rican descent. Importantly and as mentioned, the impact on younger, impressionable American children was positive, without the recycling of past tropes. It displayed a new and positive outlook towards another race and culture with education and some insight moving towards authenticity.

Although a princess, Moana, the main female character, was not lavished with material wealth and servants, bestowing a non-entitled tone on her character. Moana was an empowered female role, not sexualized but determined and willing to learn and try her best for the benefit of others—all good characteristics for any viewer to emulate. One important character flaw was the very overweight appearance of the demi-god Maui. He looked like a stereotypical big Samoan of today. In pre-contact Polynesian religion, Maui was a physically fit, strong character, not obese. Maui was a legend from the pre-contact era with a healthy fish and taro-based diet, not a product of today's diet of canned, fatty, processed foods.

I'm not saying this film was perfect, but as a whole it is a huge turn-around in terms of sensibility, hopefully for a new, more diverse and accepting Hollywood—and possibly for a new American enlightenment. As far as the subject of Polynesians is concerned, it is an inflection point that would likely make the late Walt Disney proud, because regardless of his reputation or generational attitude toward others, it is well established that his history and relationship with the peoples of the Pacific was very positive.[7] Hopefully, *Moana* signals a new, sustainable, divergent Hollywood, one that would make Pacific Islanders proud, as well as others from the diverse peoples of the world.

Polynesian Vocabulary
of Interest

This selective glossary provides definitions and origins relevant to usage within the text. Some words may have additional meanings or origins.

'Afa popa'a (Tahitian). Two words: half and white or biracial.

'Afa kasi (Samoan). Two words, literally meaning "half-caste." A modern mix of words with English origins.

'Akaloa (Hawaiian). Laughter + much.

Ahmi-Oni (Invented). Fictional Hawaiian Island from the film *Song of the Islands,* derived from the two Hawaiian words *'ami* and *'oni* (see separate entries).

Ahu (Rapanui). Usually a flat, stone-paved platform surrounding or in front of a sacred tiki or mo'ai.

Aloha (Hawaiian). Goodbye, hello or love—*better*: empathic compassion.

Aloha 'oe (Hawaiian). Two words, good-bye, hello or love and to you, singular.

'Ami (Hawaiian). Hula move with hip revolutions.

'A'ole (Hawaiian). No.

Aotearoa (Māori). New Zealand.

Ari'i nui (Tahitian). Big chief or king. Two words: royal or chiefly lineage and big or grand.

Auē or *Auwē* (Various). Extreme sadness, hurt or wailing.

Fafine (Samoan). Woman.

Fale (Samoan). Hut or house.

Fefine (Tongan). Women.

Hale (Hawaiian). House, hut or (modern) building/

Haleakaloa (Invented). Fictional Polynesian island in the film *Donovan's Reef* derived from the two Hawaiian words *hale* and *'akaloa* (see separate entries).

Haole (Hawaiian). Any foreigner, more specifically and at times in a derogatory manner, a white person or Caucasian.

Hapa haole (Hawaiian). Two words: Half and foreign or half-foreign/half–Hawaiian or biracial.

Hui (Hawaiian). group, association, organization of people.

Hukilau (Hawaiian). Literally, *huki* pull + *lau* ropes or a drag-net, combined into a single word meaning a community activity of pulling a large net together on shore with the whole village sharing the catch. Commonly found throughout Polynesia.

Kahuna (Hawaiian). Priest, expert.

Kama'aina (Hawaiian). Literally, child of the land. Modern usage: an established Islander of any race.

Kanaka (Hawaiian). Person or people. Modern slang: person of Polynesian ancestry.

Kāne (Hawaiian). Man or male.

Ki'i (Hawaiian). Image or replica of ancestors, deity or man. *Ti'i* or *tiki* in other Polynesian cultures.

Kumu (Hawaiian). Master or teacher.

Lanai (Hawaiian/English). Modern: outside lounging area such as a terrace or large porch.

Lani (Hawaiian). Sky, heaven or heavenly, spiritual.

Lava (Samoan). Simple men's wrap around waist.

Maha 'oe (Hawaiian). Two words: rest, visit or vacation and to you (singular).

Mahalo nui (Hawaiian). Two words: thank you and big.

Maha'oi (Hawaiian). To act imperti-nently.

Malo (Hawaiian). Simple loincloth for males.

Manu (Various). Bird.

Manu'a (Samoan). Injury; also, a small Samoan island group. Tui Manu'a (Kingdom of Manu'a) or Manu'a tele (the great Manu'a) was a powerful Samoan Dynasty that ruled central Polynesia for many generations. Manu'a is sacred to both Samoan and later Tongan empires. Manu'a is said, in legend, to be the origin of Poly-nesia.

Manulani (Fictional). The name of the plantation in the film *Dia-mond Head*. Two Hawaiian words: *manu* and *lani* (see separate entries).

Maoli (Hawaiian). Native or of Indig-enous blood.

Māori (Māori). Indigenous person of Aotearoa.

Mo'ai (Rapanui). Large stone image associated with Easter Island.

Mu'umu'u (Hawaiian). Polynesian full-cover dress designed by early missionaries.

Na'auao (Hawaiian). Knowledge.

'Ohana (Hawaiian). Family.

'Omoo (Marquesan). Rover or to wander between islands.

'Oni 'Oni (Hawaiian). To move, stir or wiggle.

Pākehā (Māori). Euro-New Zea-lander.

Papālagi (pl.) or *Pālagi* (s.) (Samoan). Non–Samoan or of Caucasian race.

Pareu (Tahitian). *Pa'u* (anc.), *Pareo* (mod.). Simple women's wrap with Polynesian design prints.

Rapa Iti (*lit.* Little Rapa). (Rapanui). A small Polynesian inhabited isle in the Bass Group of French Poly-nesia.

Rapa Nui (Rapanui). Big Rapa (lit.), Easter Island, as opposed to *Rapa Iti* (see above).

Taboo (English). Forbidden or prohibitive. Modern derivative of the word *tabu*, which is of Polynesian origins.

Tāmūrē (modern and world known, of Tahitian origin). 'Ori Tahiti or Tahitian dance of fast hip movements. This famous dance evolved from the previously missionary-abolished dance 'upa'upa in the 1800s. The Tāmūrē started during World War II and has been used to entertain tourists for decades. Of today's four traditional Tahitian dances, the Tāmūrē is akin to the 'ōte'a dance.

Tapu or *tabu* (Tongan, Tahitian, Māori). Taboo, forbidden or sacred. *Kapu* in Hawaiian.

Tattoo (Various Polynesian). A design on skin by pigments. Origins: *tatu* (Marquesan), *tatau* (Samoan, Tahitian) *kakau* (Hawaiian).

Tiki (Māori) Engraved wood or stone image of man. See *Ki'i* above. Various Polynesian origins.

Vahine (Tahitian). Women.

Wahine (Hawaiian). Women.

Chapter Notes

Chapter 1

1. There are general differences between Pacific films and South Seas cinema categories, and the knowledge of the distinctions among these categories are important to this publication. Pacific film is a broader classification of films about the Pacific and set in the Pacific, including several film types such as documentaries, ethnographic films, travelogues, Indigenous shorts and feature films produced in Hollywood, Europe, Asia and within the Pacific itself, such as Indigenous Pacific films. South Seas cinema describes a narrower genre of commercial films set in Oceania and produced by modern global economic-base counties typically found outside of the Pacific. This category includes all popular moving picture types including TV commercials, music videos, animated cartoons, episodic TV/cable or streaming programs, theatrical features, short films, plus web-based productions. A main emphasis is that films from this genre are written and produced by the people from the "West," usually with Euro-American or European-centered main characters or written with an American or European perspective. Indigenous Pacific films, on the other hand, relate to films also set in the Pacific, but which are written, produced, directed and acted predominantly by Indigenous Pacific islanders. The significant difference between these genres is the perspective of the story: a Native Islander point of view versus a Hollywood or outsider perspective. Also of note is a more recent and related film category which I call Polynesian Pop Pictures, mainly American-produced films that are set outside of the Pacific but that have scenes or sets that are influenced by Oceanic cultures. For example, a movie with a residential luau or a scene inside a Polynesian-themed restaurant or tiki bar.

2. Major resources used are Larry Langman's book *Return to Paradise*, the "Pictures" database in southseascinema. org, access to the South Seas Cinema Society's (SSCS) private database, records of the U.S. Copyright office, *IMDB* movie database website, *New York Times* movie review archive, plus many more minor sources.

3. Data from the "Beach of Fame" page, "Oscar Winners and Nominees" section of the southseascinema.org website.

4. Read *American Masculinities: A Historical Encyclopedia*, edited by Bret Carroll under the heading "Hollywood."

Chapter 2

1. The first film version of the *Bounty* story, titled *Mutiny of the Bounty*, was an Australian/New Zealand production released in 1916. It was co-written, produced and directed by Raymond Langford. As of this writing this film does not exist, but a handful of official stills of the movie do exist. According to the photos and other readings, the film was shot in Rotorua, New Zealand, using Māori as Tahitians and Rotorua as Tahiti. A still shows supposedly Tahitian women, in Māori dress, acting very close and friendly with the *Bounty*'s men. This still is a greeting scene or part of one that

takes place on the shore. Even in this photograph, it is apparent that the trope of the "sensual, friendly female Native" existed in 1916. Main sources (with stills): Helen Martin and Sam Edwards' *New Zealand Film 1912–1996*. Auckland: Oxford University Press (p. 26). Additional information can be found in Norman Douglas's article "The Perennial Cinematic Voyage of Bligh, Christian and HMS *Bounty*" (1982) and Greg Denning's 1996 book *Performances*.

2. The Production Code of Conduct was a voluntary intra-industry or self-regulatory conception used to keep the federal government out of the private dealings of the U.S. film industry. The Hollywood Code of 1930 was signed not only by major production studios but also by major theatrical venues. So, at this point, Chauvel's *In the Wake of the Bounty* was not bound by the indecency factor of the Code because his was a foreign production company and not a signatory to the Production Code. Nevertheless, *Wake* could never have had a huge general release because the theater chains, found in major markets, could not show his film, being bound by the rules set for them by the American Production Code. Chauvel would then have had to go to individual, small, independent theater houses and negotiate each exhibition location separately. Exposure and profits would be minimum. See also Olga Martin's 1937 *Hollywood's Movie Commandments: Handbook for Motion Picture Writers and Reviewers* and *Hollywood's Censor: Joseph I. Breen and the Production Code Administration* (2009) by Thomas Doherty.

3. Marlon Brando's second wife Maria Castaneda was born in Mexico. She was professionally known by her single stage name Movita, supposedly because the roles for ethic brown-skin women at the time were the popular South Seas movies. She was one of the female leads on the 1935 *Bounty*. Ironically, just after she and Brando separated in 1962, her ex set out to star in a new *Mutiny on the Bounty* on location in Tahiti, where he eventually married his real-life Tahitian female lead, Tarita. For more readings on this subject see David Thompson's biography of Brando titled *Marlon Brando* (2003).

4. Mamo Clark's discovery was credited from a *Los Angeles Times* article, dated Dec. 20, 1986. Although typecast as the Polynesian lead female on many Polynesian films, the late Mamo Clark made a semi-career out of Hollywood South Seas movies, even with the indignities of the film business and prejudices of the Euro-American dominated film industry. Case in point: after *Mutiny*, Mamo starred in a serial titled *Robinson Crusoe of Clipper Island* in 1936. Although the co-star of the film, Mamo Clark's name is listed on the credits underneath the featured dog and horse of the movie. The two animals not only had fewer lines than Miss Clark (tongue in cheek), but more importantly, much less screen time.

5. For additional reading on this subject, see David E. Stannard's *Before the Horror: The Population of Hawai'i on the Eve of Western Contact*. Stannard's book argues that the Hawaiian Islands' population before the arrival of foreigners was much larger than previously estimated, highlighting Westerners' devastating impact. Stannard's book also references other sources on the subject.

6. A contemporary term meaning hidden objects on screen (TV, film or video games). These objects could be intentional for commercial reasons or simply practical jokes on the part of the production crew. A few of these Easter eggs end up on the cutting room floor, if caught by an editor. However, a few, because of their current popularity, are featured in special shorts as extras on a DVD, to the thrill of the person who placed an Easter egg and sees it survive the final cut. With today's video discs and the pause button on streaming video services, many Internet sites are devoted to finding and sharing Easter eggs on screen. Having worked in the film industry for 25 years, I have been in involved in placing a few eggs directly or indirectly on set.

7. This immensely interesting historical occurrence, unfortunately, is not found in any American film. One has to speculate that since this story is centered on a woman, her story is of a lower priority in a male-dominated film industry. The same influential Hollywood Euro-American male dominance may account for the absence of the

Captain Cook story. This hugely important and popular account is also not portrayed in American film. I posit that it is because Captain Cook, a male hero of the Caucasoid race, did not have any known Indigenous romances or dominate the Polynesian Hawaiians. Rather, he was defeated and killed by them. Euro-American Hollywood shies away from this kind of failure of a member of their supposedly superior race, with few exceptions. Unfortunately, this omission damages the psyche of the other race involved, the Polynesians. The absence of stories in which Polynesian people defeat outsiders is widespread in American media and creates a false impression that Polynesians are a weak, inferior, and unsuccessful race.

8. The "ethnographic reality excuse" is also referred to by contemporary social scientists as the "ethnopornographic gaze" (Hansen, Christian, Catherine Needham, and Bill Nichols). Further discussion on this subject follows in Chapter 3.

9. This article can be found in the book *Bittersweet: Indigenous Women in the Pacific*. Edited by Alison Jones, Phyllis Herda, and Tamasailau M. Suaalii.

10. Social activist and feminist bell hooks, born Gloria Jean Hopkins, does not use capital letters in her pen name.

11. The theory that a Hollywood film centered on a Polynesian cast is a formula for failure for an American audience is not founded on fact. The historically successful and critically acclaimed films *Moana: A Romance of the Golden Age* (1926), *Tabu* (1931), and *The Hurricane* (1937) were all centered on Polynesian characters and actors. As for a possible current lull in Polynesian-centered American films, which is common after any story's financial failure (i.e., *Rapa Nui*), Hollywood tends to stay away from any similar subjects for an undetermined period. Needless to say, the time for new Polynesian-centered American films arrived with the 2016 release of the Disney animated film *Moana*. This film did have critical and financial success. Disney also has had box office success with what turned out to be a *Lilo and Stitch* franchise, but that story, also animated, is co-centered on a young Hawaiian girl

who lost her parents and a fierce and dangerous or misunderstood alien.

12. For example: "Kaala, the Flower of Lanai" is found in King David Kalakaua's book *The Legends and Myths of Hawai'i* (Kalakaua), and "The God of Love" is found in the book *Hawai'i Island Legends: Pele, Pikoi, and Others*, which is edited by Mary Kawena Pukui. (Pukui 1983)

Chapter 3

1. Further readings on the cinematic gaze of interest: Norman K. Denzin's *The Cinematic Society: The Voyeur's Gaze* (1995); Ann E. Kaplan's *Looking for the Other: Feminism, Film and the Imperial Gaze* published in 1997; the 2004 book by German feminist writer Isabelle Fol, titled *The Dominance of the Male Gaze in Hollywood Films: Patriarchal Hollywood Images of Women at the Turn of the Millennium*; and the pioneering essay *Visual Pleasure and Narrative Cinema* (1975) by Laura Mulvey.

2. Quote from the writings of Whitehead and Sigal: "Or to put this more pointedly—is the anthropological project inherently pornographic? In one sense, the answer is clearly yes, if 'pornography' is here understood as the production and circulation of representations that invite sexual response. After all, ethnographers are persons in a cultural context and arrive at their 'field-sites' as fully equipped sexual, even violent beings. The cultural meaning of anthropology itself is in this way part of the epistemological heritage of colonialism" (Whitehead & Sigal, p. 4). Hansen, Needham and Nichols write, "Pornography is part of a larger discourse of sexuality and the organization of pleasure, and ethnography is part of a larger discourse of science and the organization of knowledge. But our culture makes ethnography (science) licit knowledge and pornography (sexuality) illicit, carnal knowledge. Ethnography is a kind of legitimated pornography, a pornography of knowledge, giving us the pleasure of knowing what had seemed incomprehensible. Pornography is a strange, unnatural form of ethnography, salvaging orgasmic bliss from

the seclusion of the bedroom" (Hansen, Needham, Nichols, p. 210).

3. This information and data are taken from Reynolds and Price's book *Rapa Nui: The Easter Island Legend on Film*.

4. Interestingly, the film *The Bounty* (1984) was also a financial failure despite its revered story, popular and award-winning cast, and high production values. It is possible *The Bounty's* failure was due to the same theory of a "GP" rating and an audience that was also unaware of the gratuitous nudity and adult sexual content.

Chapter 4

1. I use the early Americanized term "hula hula" in this context to distinguish this popular faux Hawaiian dance, mostly found on the North American continent of the early 20th century, from the authentic hula dance originating in the Hawaiian Islands and practiced today.

2. From the private data files of the South Seas Cinema Society.

3. From an educational video by Dr. Sut Jhally on Orientalism in which Edward Said is interviewed on camera. In the chapter labeled the "Repertory of Orientalism," Said states, "...there seems to me that there was a kind of repertory of images that kept coming up, you know (e.g.) the sensual women... and the more I looked the more I saw that this was quite consistent with itself. It had very little to do with people who had actually been there and even if they had been there, there wasn't much modification. In other words, you didn't get what you would call realistic representations." Later, talking about movies, Said pronounces: "There is a handy set of images and clichés, you know, not just from the newspapers and television but from movies." Pacific historical anthropologists Margaret Jolly and Serge Tcherkézoff further discuss this theory in the book *Oceanic Encounters: Exchange, Desire, Violence*, in which they write: "The new evidence that will be presented here suggests that the Western construct of Polynesian societies as island paradises, where sexual freedom

was the norm in adolescence and where young girls and young women were sexually accommodating, must be radically revised. This is a construct largely built, as we shall see, on the male fantasies and Eurocentric misreadings of early French visitors to the region, and then revisited and recycled from the same masculine, Eurocentric perspective in centuries to come" (p. 115). Also, Paloma Fresno-Calleja reiterates this theory in her 2012 article "Revised Spectacles: Literary Transformations of Hollywood's Pacific Narratives," in which she states, "...representations generated in these multiple imperial centers have been endlessly recycled in neocolonial and global discourses such as advertising, tourism and cinema" (p. 265).

4. Correction by author of quote, writer and film critic Ed Rampell. The original quote from the documentary *Hula Girls: Imagining Paradise*, written and produced by Trevor Graham.

5. Found in the Internet encyclopedia *Wikipedia* under the heading "Motion Picture Production Code." http://en.wikipedia.org/wiki/Motion_Picture_Production_Code#Decline_of_the_Production_Code

6. These television commercials are found via access to the South Seas Cinema Society private database.

Chapter 5

1. Some references for this metaphor can be found in "Imagined Islands: White Shadows in the South Seas and Cultural Ambivalence" (p. 99) by Jeffrey Geiger, in *The Invention of Delores del Rio* (p 26) by Joanne Hershfield; in Michael Sturma's book, *South Sea Maidens: Western Fantasy and Sexual Politics in the South Pacific* (p. 3); and *Securing Paradise: Tourism and Militarism in Hawai'i and the Philippines* by Vernadette Vicuna Gonzalez (pp. 7, 28).

2. This is, of course, from the total body of South Seas films of record as of this writing. More films may be discovered at a later date, which will, of course, change the percentages, but it would not change the reality of a minuscule number of American titles with women of

European descent having love relationships with Polynesian males.

3. Quote found on page 115 from the book *Rex Ingram: Visionary Director of the Silent Screen*, written by Ruth Barton.

4. Also noting this practice of Hollywood's using Latinas and brownface and using term *Hollynesian* are Patty O'Brien, in her book *Pacific Muse: Exotic Femininity & the Colonial Pacific* (p. 235), and James C. Desmond in *Staging Tourism: Bodies on Display from Waikiki to Sea World* (ch. 5).

5. Sweet, Frank W., *A History of the Minstrel Show* (2000) (p. 25).

6. *White Shadows in the South Seas* (1928) and *Bird of Paradise* (1932) are good examples of this taboo Native woman trope.

7. The rule is found in Section Six: PARTICULAR APPLICATIONS, Part II: Sex, Number 6. Miscegenation (sex relationship between the white and black races) is forbidden.

8. From the book *Pre-Code Hollywood: Sex, Immorality, and Insurrection in American Cinema, 1930–1934* by Thomas Patrick Doherty (p. 47).

9. Since the airing of *Gauguin the Savage* in 1980, research was needed for the appropriate censor board of the day. The current TV ratings board, the TV Parental Guidelines Monitoring Board, with its television ratings, along with its TV Parental Guidelines, is responsible today for monitoring and rating TV programs in the United States. It was started by an Act of Congress in 1996 and the FCC. For further information read the Wikipedia entry "TV Parental Guidelines" at http://en.wikipedia.org/wiki/TV_Parental_Guidelines and "Exploring U.S. History 'Regulating Television'" at: http://chnm.gmu.edu/exploring/20thcentury/regulatingtelevision/

Chapter 6

1. There are many writings about this "Tiki" or Polynesian Pop culture in America and other "Western" countries. Important works on this subject are: *The Book of Tiki* and *Tiki Pop* by Sven Kirsten, *Smuggler's Cove* by Martin Cate, and *Mai Kai* by Tim Glazner. Interestingly,

Sven Kirsten in *Tiki Pop* formulates throughout the book that the modern Tiki popular culture was created essentially in Hollywood, using prop masters, set designers, set craftsmen, and other creatives from the film industry to help create the South Seas illusions in American Tiki establishments. Also, the titles and images from South Seas movies influenced this American pop culture. American imaginations of the South Seas by Hollywood spread to a whole new realm.

2. To be fair, some Māori claim that the ceramic mugs representing Māori tiki images were created earlier than American mugs in 1949 by New Zealand's Crown Lynn. The first American tiki mugs were created in 1955 by Bob Bryant of Tiki Bob's in San Francisco. Earlier tropical mugs (non-tiki) were coconut and pineapple fruit ceramic mugs from Don the Beachcomber in 1941 and the Hula Girl drinking bowl in 1947 by Trader Vic's.

3. A good documentation and further readings of this exhibit can be found in the 2014 book *Art Deco Hawai'i* published by the Honolulu Museum of Art.

4. In this film, there is evidence how the "Hula Hula" of vaudeville evolves into "Wicky Wacky Hula" of Tin Pan Alley. The two beautiful Blane sisters in the plot were recruited from vaudeville not only because of singing and dance talents but also because they had sex appeal or great legs for the hula skirts.

5. A sarong is a simple female wrap from Indonesia. The word sarong is widely used throughout Hollywood plots and comedic jokes. More appropriate to the theme of this book is the word *pareu*, which is the Tahitian word for a women's wrap. It is very similar to the sarong but was created separately. Interestingly, both were hip wraps only until Westerners arrived and influenced both places with Christian morals. The simple differences are the printed designs and the material used. Polynesians used bark from the mulberry tree while the Indonesians use woven fabric. The latter was much more durable and practical, which is why Hollywood designers and modern Tahitians use that material since the first Western trading ships passed through the Pacific Islands. In most Polynesian

languages, including Tahitian, the wrap is called *pā'ū*, which evolved, in Tahiti, to *pareu* and now *pareo* is a more popular form of the word.

6. The song may be found on Sepia Records ©2004. It is titled *Dorothy Lamour—Queen of the Hollywood Islands*. Other songs of significance on this CD, a mix of Hawaiian and Hollywood popular tunes, are "My Little Grass Shack," "Hawaiian Hospitality," "Lovely Hula Hands," "The Moon of Manakoora," "Aloha Oe," and "Pagan Love Song." One song, "Moon Over Manakoora," was made famous by Lamour as a track from the South Seas film classic *The Hurricane* (1937). Dorothy Lamour visited Hawai'i many times, acquired many friends there, and learned many songs and some hulas.

7. A mu'umu'u (muumuu) is a common dress worn throughout Polynesia. It is a full covering dress with Polynesian prints. Originally designed by missionaries for the Natives to cover up, it is still used today for Indigenous women as well as tourists. It can be worn by women of all shapes and sizes; thus, an older and larger Dorothy Lamour would wear one.

8. Besides the writings of Ethan de Seife, Dorothy Lamour's autobiography, *My Side of the Road*, is a good read for anyone wanting to know more about the Queen of South Seas Cinema.

Chapter 7

1. Hotel Street is the main street of Chinatown in Honolulu. The streets and sidewalks have a reputation for prostitution.

2. *Taboo*, a commonly used word in English, originated in Polynesia. It is a derivative of the word "tapu," or, in Hawaiian, "kapu." The meaning for all its word variations is the same—prohibited.

3. Search https://en.wikipedia.org/wiki/From_Here_to_Eternity

4. Donna Reed had the title role for the popular ABC TV series *The Donna Reed Show* (1958–66). Ms. Reed won a Golden Globe as the Best TV Star for this series and was nominated for four Emmy Awards. She also won a Best Supporting Actress Academy Award as a prostitute for *From Here to Eternity*.

5. Jean O'Hara was a real WWII-era prostitute in Honolulu who had real issues with the military and local authorities. Her small but informative book was self-published because no publisher, back in that day, would touch a prostitution story or back someone (especially a woman) who bucks authority. I was fortunate to read a genuine copy of this rare book.

Chapter 8

1. Other TV show examples are *Green Acres* (1965–71), CBS, in the episode titled "Guess Who's Not Coming to the Luau"); *Pee-Wee's Playhouse* (1988), CBS, in the episode titled "Luau for Two," which featured a contest for a Hawaiian dinner for two; *I Love Lucy* (1951–57), CBS, in an episode titled "Ricky's Hawaiian Vacation"; on children's TV in *Sesame Street* (1969–present), PBS, season 9, episode 24); *The Flintstones* (1960–66), ABC, in an episode titled "Hawaiian Escapade"; *Goof Troop* (1992–93), DISNEY TV in an episode titled "Wrecks, Lies & Videotape"). This list is from the South Seas Cinema Society's database.

2. Movie examples of "The Hawaiian War Chant" appear in: *Moonlight in Hawai'i* (1941) featuring the Merry Macs; *Ship Ahoy* (1942), and *Song of the Islands* (1942). Television examples include: *Colgate Comedy Hour* (1950–55), NBC; *The Muppet Show* (1976–81), CBS; *The Adventures of Ozzie and Harriet* (1952–66), ABC; *The Liberace Show* (1952–69), SYN/GUILD FILMS; and *The Lawrence Welk Show* (1955–1982), ABC, featuring the Lennon Sisters.

3. While this book focuses on Polynesians and the Polynesian Islands, a short note about Hawai'i-born actor of Japanese descent James Shigeta is of value. A tall, handsome, talented actor with an amazing voice, James Shigeta struggled to find consistent work in Hollywood, even after the success of the seminal film *Flower Drum Song* (1961). Though stars in the film, Shigeta and Miyoshi Umeki, are actors of Japanese ancestry playing Chinese roles, the film had a huge success breaking barriers to Asian-centered stories and characters in a popular major

film. Unfortunately, with similar Hollywood barriers broken in the film classic 1935 *Mutiny on the Bounty*, these barriers still endured in Hollywood. Another connection of note for South Seas cinema and *Flower Drum Song* is the African American actress Juanita Hall, who played a Vietnamese woman in *South Pacific*. That stereotype image carried on to *Drum Song* as Hall played a Chinese woman.

4. Claiming to be the world's tallest atoll, the all-cliff island was for years stripped of its phosphate rock, along with any tropical foliage above the mines. It is now considered an environmental disaster. Today, years after the mining companies have left, the once-bustling industry on the tropical island is nearly abandoned. With just a few dozen former Polynesian workers, Polynesian practices of ancient sustainability and mother nature, there is surprising hope that the island will return to its former beauty despite the many scars underneath the newly rebounding tropical forest.

5. From Vernadette Vicuña Gonzalez's book *Securing Paradise: Tourism and Militarism in Hawai'i and the Philippines.*

6. From my own experiences filming in Hawai'i for 25 years as a member of the Directors Guild of America, I've witnessed the generosity of the travel industry towards the film industry until it all stopped in the late 1970s. Since then, high demand for tourism in Hawai'i has been consistent; therefore, there is now no need for comp locations, rooms and vehicles so there is no need for this exchange for the free publicity a film would generate. Now, the tourism industry in Hawai'i competes for high-paying film crews that take many rooms on a long-term basis—not comp rooms but discounts for large-group, long-term boarding.

7. Of course, Covid-19 has altered this ritual even more.

8. Quote taken from the article "Lovely Hula Lands: Corporate Tourism and the Prostitution of Hawaiian Culture." PDF Retrieved from: https://journals.lib.unb.ca/index.php/bl/article/view/24958.

Chapter 9

1. There have been protests of note by Pacific Islanders over Euro-American film representations, but the instances are few. Three events come to mind: Samoans picketing a big theater in Honolulu over the false depiction of Samoa in the film *Hurricane* (1979). *Hurricane* was filmed in Tahiti using Tahitians as Samoans and Tahitian culture as Samoan culture. "The Rock," half-Samoan Dwayne Johnson, was scheduled to play Hawai'i's King Kamehameha—but many small protests in the news and Internet by a few Hawaiians against that idea created negative buzz, and as of now that film proposal has been scrapped, although a new version with Johnson is in the early stages of development. Finally, a British writer/director and his non-Indigenous producers, who lensed the independent movie *Princess Ka'iulani*, wanted to title the film *The Savage Princess*, but amidst much small but persistent protest against the title in the local Hawai'i news and on the Internet, the negative campaign finally worked, and the title was changed.

2. Taika Waititi, a Māori from Aotearoa, had been writing, directing and starring in New Zealand films for over a decade before his breakout film *What We Do in the Shadows* (2014). In fact, his early short *Two Cars, One Night* (2003) earned Waititi (known earlier as Taika Cohen) a Best Live Action Short Film Oscar nomination. His directing and co-starring in *Thor: Ragnarok* (2017) elevated Waititi into Hollywood's A-list with high demand for him as a director, writer and actor. In 2021, he had parts in two big hits, *Suicide Squad 2* and *Free Guy*, both released within one week of each other.

3. A must-read for Indigenous Pacific filmmakers is "Cultural Translation and Filmmaking in the Pacific" by Vilsoni Hereniko. It is informative and valuable because he writes of his own experiences making Indigenous Pacific films.

Conclusion

1. Found in Hereniko's article "Representations of Pacific Islanders in Film and Video" (p. 1).

2. Al Kikume was a Hawaiian who is relatively unknown but acted in over 70 films between 1933 and 1958, or 25 years in Hollywood, according to the IMDB website. Of course, he acted in many South Seas cinema titles, a rare case of a Polynesian playing a Polynesian.

3. Actually, Temuera Morrison did play a quasi-Polynesian character in the American film *Couples Retreat* (2009), which was set in Tahiti. The problem was that Morrison's character wears Southeast Asian outfits complete with an Islamic Indonesian Kufi hat.

4. Since the release of the film *Aloha*, there has been an online backlash against the actress Emma Stone cast as a ¼ Hawaiian, ¼ Chinese character. Much of the backlash came from the Asian-American community. The famous director of the film, Cameron Crowe, publicly apologized for the misrepresentation. He further stated that the character was based on a real life, red-haired, Anglo-looking ¼ Hawaiian, ¼ Chinese person. Ironically, the author of this book is a red-haired, Anglo-looking ¼ Hawaiian, ¼ Chinese person.

5. To link to this web news article, see "Staff Writers" in the "Bibliography" section of this book.

6. What must be mentioned here is that other Polynesian actors will play—or are or were in consideration to play—internationally known superheroes. Dwayne Johnson played Black Adam in a 2022 DC film, and Keanu Reeves is always in official (not rumored) consideration to play different characters in the Marvel Universe. Young Māori actor Julian Dennison plays Firefist in *Deadpool 2* (2018) and may return to the role in possible future works. Finally, Megan Gale was cast, fitted and trained as Wonder Woman in the George Miller directed *Justice League: Mortal* (2008) before its last-minute cancelation by Warner Bros. just days before the commencement of filming.

7. There is evidence of a strong cultural respect for Polynesia by Walt Disney. It is well known that after long hours of work establishing the success of his studio, Disney finally took a necessary break and vacationed in Hawai'i in 1934. His personal respect for and admiration of the islands started then. According to Disney Historian Jeff Kurtti, before he left the islands on his first of many visits to Hawai'i, Disney promised to produce a Hawai'i cartoon. Disney released the beloved *Hawaiian Holiday* in 1936. Disney also personally produced the Academy Award-nominated short *Samoa* (1956), as well as many other South Seas films, and personally wrote *Lt. Robin Crusoe, U.S.N.* (1966) under his pen name Retlaw Yensid (Walter Disney spelt backwards). The most critical evidence of this admiration, and the least known, is a new-found fact that Disney visited the Lalani Hawaiian Village in Waikiki. Disney was fascinated by the village and the concept of recreating the past in order for visitors of all ages to learn and enjoy. The Hawaiian Village by George Paele Mossman, among other things, helped to inspire Disney to create the Disney Parks (Glasner). George Mossman and Walt Disney became good friends. In his first park, Disneyland in Anaheim, California, Walt Disney personally oversaw the development of the Tahitian Market Place for the grand opening and soon afterwards, the Tahitian Terrance and the Enchanted Tiki Room. Mr. Disney also insured that the first version of the "It's A Small World" ride in his park had a dedicated "South Seas" room with dolls representing many cultures of Polynesia and the Pacific. All future "Small World" attractions in other Disney Parks would also include South Seas representation. Soon afterwards and just before his death, Disney imagined a Tiki Bar in the future EPCOT. The Polynesian Village Resort was built as envisioned by Mr. Disney for the opening of Walt Disney World in Orlando, Florida. It was one of the two first Disney Hotels.

Bibliography

Agnew, Vanessa. "Pacific Island Encounters and the German Invention of Race." In *Islands in History and Representation*, edited by Rod Edmond and Vanessa Smith, 81–94. London: Routledge, 2003.

Andrade, Carlos. *Hā'ena*. Honolulu: University of Hawai'i Press, 2008.

Arista, Noelani. "Captive Women in Paradise 1796–1826: The Kapu on Prostitution in Hawaiian Historical Legal Context." *American Indian Culture and Research Journal* 35, no. 4 (2011).

Bailey, Beth L., and David Farber. *The First Strange Place: Race and Sex in World War II Hawai'i*. Baltimore: Johns Hopkins University Press, 1994.

Barclay, Barry. *Our Own Image*. Auckland: Longman Paul, 1990.

Barrow, Terence. *Captain Cook in Hawai'i*. Norfolk Island: Island Heritage, 1976.

Barsam, Richard Meran. *The Vision of Robert Flaherty*. Bloomington: Indiana University Press, 1988.

Barton, Ruth. *Rex Ingram: Visionary Director of the Silent Screen*. Lexington: University Press of Kentucky, 2014.

Brawley, Sean, and Chris Dixon. "'The Hollywood Native': Hollywood's Construction of the South Seas and Wartime Encounters with the South Pacific." *Sites* 27, no. 19 (1993).

_____. *Hollywood's South Seas and the Pacific War: Searching for Dorothy Lamour*. New York: Macmillan, 2012.

Brown, Caroline. "The Representation of the Indigenous Other in *Daughters of the Dust* and *The Piano*." *NWSA Journal* 15, no. 1 (2003): 1–19.

Calder-Marshall, Arthur. *The Innocent Eye: The Life of Robert J. Flaherty*. London: Allen, 1963.

Campbell, Russell. "Prostitution and Film Censorship in the USA." *Screening the Past* 2 (1997).

Carroll, Bret (Ed). *American Masculinities: A Historical Encyclopedia*. New York: Moschovitis, 2003.

Cate, Martin, and Rebecca Cate. *Smuggler's Cove*. Berkeley: Ten Speed Press, 2016.

Chappell, David A. "Shipboard Relations between Pacific Island Women and Euroamerican Men 1767–1887." *The Journal of Pacific History* 27, no. 2 (1992): 131–149.

City of Honolulu. "Prostitution in Honolulu." Report prepared and published by the City, 1944.

Dening, Greg. *Mr. Bligh's Bad Language*. New York: Cambridge University Press, 1992.

_____. *Performances*. University of Chicago Press, 1996.

Denzin, Norman K. *The Cinematic Society: The Voyeurs Gaze*. Thousand Oaks: Sage, 1995.

de Seife, Ethan. "What's Sarong with this Picture? The Development of the Star Image of Dorothy Lamour." *Senses of Cinema* 22 (2002). Accessed March 22, 2015. http://sensesofcinema.com/2002/female-glamour-and-star-power/lamour/.

Desmond, James C. *Staging Tourism: Bodies on Display from Waikiki to Sea World*. University of Chicago Press, 1999.

Doherty, Thomas. *Pre-Code Hollywood: Sex, Immorality, and Insurrection in American Cinema, 1930–1934*.

New York: Columbia University Press, 2013.

———. *Hollywood's Censor: Joseph I. Breen and the Production Code Administration.* New York: Columbia University Press, 2009.

Douglas, Norman. "The Perennial Cinematic Voyage of Bligh, Christian and HMS Bounty." *Pacific Islands Monthly* 53, no. 1 (1982): 11–14.

Edmond, Rod. *Representing the South Pacific: Colonial Discourse from Cook to Gauguin.* Cambridge University Press, 1997.

"Emma Stone: 'I've become the butt of many jokes.'" July 13, 2015. News.com.au. Accessed November 27, 2015. https://www.news.com.au/entertainment/movies/new-movies/emma-stone-ive-become-the-butt-of-many-jokes/news-story/2e5e0d18ec600f5ed4d1c6dc605c8cf9.

Fol, Isabelle. *The Dominance of the Male Gaze in Hollywood Films: Patriarchal Hollywood Images of Women at the Turn of the Millennium.* Hamburg: Diplomica, 2004.

Fresno-Calleja, Paloma. "Revised Spectacles: Literary Transformations of Hollywood's Pacific Narratives." *Journal of Postcolonial Writing* 49, no. 3 (2012): 265–277.

Geiger, Jeffrey. *Facing the Pacific: Polynesia and the U.S. Imperial Imagination.* Honolulu: University of Hawai'i Press, 2007.

———. "Imagined Islands: White Shadows in the South Seas and Cultural Ambivalence." *Cinema Journal* 41, no. 3 (Spring 2002): 98–121.

Glazner, Tim. *Mai-Kai: History and Mystery of the Iconic Tiki Restaurant.* Atglen: Schiffer, 2016.

Gonzalez, Vernadette Vicuña. *Securing Paradise: Tourism and Militarism in Hawai'i and the Philippines.* Durham: Duke University Press, 2013.

Graham, Trevor, dir. *Hula Girls: Imagining Paradise.* 2005; Sydney, AUS: Electric Pictures. VHS, color (with b&w sequences).

Hansen, Christian, with Catherine Needham, and Bill Nichols. "Pornography, Ethnography and the Discourses of Power." In *Representing Reality: Issues and Concepts in Documentary*, edited

by Bill Nichols, 201–28. Bloomington: Indiana University Press, 1991.

Hayes, Michael. "Sexualising Pacific Island Women." *Sites* 36 (1998): 22–43.

Heimann, Jim. *Hula: Vintage Hawaiian Graphics.* Köln: Taschen, 2003.

Hereniko, Vilsoni. "Cultural Translation and Filmmaking in the Pacific." Paper presented at University of Hawai'i at Mānoa International Symposium *Folktales and Fairy Tales: Translation, Colonialism, and Cinema*, Honolulu, September 23–26, 2010.

———. "Representations of Cultural Identities." In *Tides of History: The Pacific Islands in the Twentieth Century*, edited by K.R. Howe, Robert C. Kiste, and Brij V. Lal, 406–434. Honolulu: University of Hawai'i Press, 1994.

———. "Representations of Pacific Islanders in Film and Video." *Documentary Box* 14 (1999): 18–20.

Herman, Doug. "How the Story of Moana Holds Up Against Cultural Truths." Smithsonian. December 2, 2016. https://www.smithsonianmag.com/smithsonian-institution/how-story-moana-and-maui-holds-against-cultural-truths-180961258/.

Hernán, Vera, and Andrew M. Gordon. *Screen Saviors: Hollywood's Fiction of Whiteness.* Lanham: Rowman and Littlefield, 2003.

Hershfield, Joanne. "Race and Romance in 'Bird of Paradise.'" *Cinema Journal* 3 (1998): 3–15.

———. *The Invention of Delores del Rio.* Minneapolis: University of Minnesota Press, 2003.

hooks, bell. *Black Looks: Race and Representation.* Boston: South End Press, 1992.

Hopkins, Jerry. *The Hula* (2nd edition). Honolulu: Bess, 2011.

Hunt, Terry L. "Rethinking Easter Island's Ecological Catastrophe." *Journal of Archaeological Science* 34 (2007): 485–502.

Hunt, Terry, and Carl Lipo. *The Statues That Walked: Unraveling the Mystery of Easter Island.* New York: Free Press, 2011.

Hudgins, Morgan. *Mutiny on the Bounty* [adapted from 1962 movie]. New York: Random House, 1964.

Imada, Adria L. *Aloha America: Hula*

Circuits Through the U.S. Empire. Durham: Duke University Press, 1912.

IMDb (Internet Movie Database) home page. Accessed March 2, 2015. http://www.imdb.com/?ref_=nv_home.

Jhally, Sut, dir. *Edward Said on Orientalism.* Northampton: Media Education Foundation, 1997. DVD, color.

Jolly, Margaret. "Lascivious Ladies, Beasts of Burden, Voyaging Voyeurs: Representation of Women from Cook Voyages in the Pacific." Paper presented to the Ninth David Nichol Smith Memorial Seminar, University of Auckland, New Zealand, August 24–28, 1993.

———. "Desire, Difference and Disease: Sexual and Venereal Exchanges on Cook's Voyages in the Pacific." In *Exchanges: Cross-cultural Encounters in Australia and the Pacific,* edited by Ross Gibson, 187–217. Sydney: Museum of Sydney and Historic Houses Trust of New South Wales, 1996.

———. "From Point Venus to Bali Ha'i: Eroticism and Exoticism in Representations of the Pacific." In *Sites of Desire, Economies of Pleasure, Sexualities in Asian and in the Pacific,* edited by Lemore Manderson and Margaret Jolly, 99–122, notes, 303–306. Chicago: University of Chicago Press, 1997.

Jolly, Margaret, Serge Tcherkézoff, and Darrell Tryon. *Oceanic Encounters: Exchange, Desire, Violence.* Canberra: Australian National University E Press, 2009.

Kalakaua, David. *The Legends and Myths of Hawai'i.* Honolulu: Mutual, 1990.

Kamakau, Samuel M. *Ruling Chiefs of Hawai'i.* Honolulu: Kamehameha Schools Press, 1961, 1992.

Kaplan, Ann E. *Looking for the Other: Feminism, Film and the Imperial Gaze.* New York: Routledge, 1997.

Kristen, Swen A. *The Book of Tiki.* Koln/Los Angeles: Taschen, 2000.

———. *Tiki Pop.* Koln/Los Angeles: Taschen, 2019.

Kurtti, Jeff. "The Wonderful World of Walt: Aloha and Mahalo Walt Disney." 2018. https://ohmy.disney.com/insider/2012/07/16/the-wonderful-world-of-walt-aloha-and-mahalo/.

Langman, Larry. *Return to Paradise: A Guide to South Sea Island Films.* London: Scarecrow, 1998.

Larsen, Annegret, and Dale F. Simpson, Jr. Comment to Rull et al. (1913). "Challenging Easter Island's Collapse: the need for interdisciplinary synergies." *Frontiers in Ecology and Evolution* 10, no. 3389 (2014): 56.

Limbrick, Peter. *Making Settler Cinema: Film and Colonial Encounters in the United States, Australia, and New Zealand.* New York: Macmilllan, 2010.

Lutz, Catherine, and Jane Collins. "The Photograph as an Intersection of Gazes: The Example of National Geographic." *Visual Anthropology Review* 7, no. 1 (1991): 134–149.

MacDougall, David. "The Visual in Anthropology." In *Rethinking Visual Anthropology,* edited by Marcus Banks and Howard Morphy. New Haven: Yale University Press, 1997.

Malo, David. *Hawaiian Antiquities.* Honolulu: Bishop Museum Press, 1951.

Manley, Brian. "Moving Pictures: The History of Early Cinema." ProQuest Discovery Guides, 2011. http://www.csa.com/discoveryguides/discoveryguides-main.php.

Martin, Helen, and Sam Edwards. *New Zealand Film 1912–1996.* Auckland: Oxford Press, 1996.

Martin, Olga. *Hollywood's Movie Commandments: Handbook for Motion Picture Writers and Reviewers.* New York: W. H. Wilson, 1937.

Mawyer, Alexander Dale. *From PŌ to AŌ: A Historical Analysis of Filmmaking in the Pacific.* Master's thesis, University of Hawai'i Honolulu, 1997.

McGee, Tom. *Betty Grable: The Girl with the Million Dollar Legs.* Lanham: Welcome Rain, 2009.

McInnes, Dick. *Dorothy Lamour: My Side of the Road.* Upper Saddle River: Prentice Hall, 1980.

Merriam-Webster 1828–2020 online dictionary. Accessed April 17, 2020. https://www.merriam-webster.com.

Moorehead, Alan. *The Fatal Impact.* New York: Harper & Row, 1966.

"Movie" section of online movie search from the newspaper archive and other sources. *New York Times.* Accessed March 2, 2015. http://www.nytimes.com/pages/movies/index.html.

Mulvey, Laura. "Visual Pleasure and Narrative Cinema." *Screen* 16 no. 3 (1975): 6–18.

O'Brien, Patty. *The Pacific Muse: Exotic Femininity & the Colonial Pacific.* Seattle: University of Washington Press, 2006.

O'Dwyer, Carolyn. *Pacific Orientalisms: South Seas Discourse and Colonial Cultures.* PhD dissertation, University of Melbourne, Australia, 2001.

O'Hara, Jean. *My Life as a Honolulu Prostitute.* Honolulu: self-published, 1944.

Papanikolas, Theresa, and DeSoto Brown. *Art Deco Hawaii.* Honolulu: Honolulu Museum of Art, 2014.

Poignant, Roslyn. *Oceanic Mythology.* London: Hamlyn, 1967.

Preiss, Kathy. *Cheap Amusements: Working Women and Leisure in Turn-of-the-Century New York.* Philadelphia: Temple University Press, 1986.

Pukui, Mary Kawena, and Samuel H. Elbert. *Hawai'i Island Legends: Pele, Pīkoi and Others.* Honolulu: Kamehameha, 1983.

———. *Hawaiian Dictionary:* Revised and Enlarged Edition. Honolulu: University of Hawai'i, 1986.

Rennie, Neil. *Far-fetched Facts: The Literature of Travel and the Idea of the South Seas.* Oxford: Clarendon Press, 1995.

Reyes, Louis, and Ed Rampell. (1995). *Made in Paradise, Hollywood's Films of Hawai'i and the South Seas.* Honolulu: Mutual, 1995.

Reynolds, Kevin, Tim Rose-Price and Diana Landau. *Rapa-Nui: The Easter Island Legend on Film.* New York: Newmarket Press, 1994.

Sahlins, Marshall. *Islands of History.* University of Chicago Press, 2003.

———. *How Natives Think: About Captain Cook, for Example.* University of Chicago Press, 1995.

Said, Edward W. *Orientalism.* New York: Random House, 1978.

Salmond, Anne. *Aphrodite's Island: The European Discovery of Tahiti.* Berkeley: University of California Press, 2010.

Schmitt, Robert C. *Hawai'i in the Movies, 1898–1959.* Honolulu: University of Hawai'i, 1990.

Scott, Helen Christine. *Race and the Struggles for Cinematic Meaning: Film Production Censorship and African American Reception 1940–1960.* PhD dissertation, Harvard University, 2007.

Silva, Noenoe K. *Aloha Betrayed: Native Hawaiian Resistance to American Colonialism.* Durham: Duke University Press, 2004.

Smith, Barnard. *European Vision and the South Pacific, 1768–1850: A Study in the History of Art and Ideas.* Oxford: Clarendon, 1960.

Soares, Andre. *Beyond Paradise: The Life of Ramon Novarro.* New York: St. Martin's Press, 2002.

"Shows-Feature Films." South Seas Cinema Society. Accessed March 2, 2015. http://www.southseascinema.org/shows.html.

Stannard, David E. *Before the Horror: The Population of Hawai'i on the Eve of Western Contact.* Honolulu: Social Science Research Institute, University of Hawai'i, 1989.

Stella, Regis Tove. *Imagining the Other: The Representation of the Papa New Guinean Subject.* Honolulu: University of Hawai'i, 2007.

Sturma, Michael. *South Sea Maidens: Western Fantasy and Sexual Politics in the South Pacific.* Westport: Greenwood, 2002.

Sweet, Frank W. *A History of the Minstrel Show.* Palm Coast, FL: Backintyme, 2000.

Tamaira, A. Marata. "From Full Dusk to Full Tusk: Reimagining the "Dusky Maiden" Through the Visual Arts." *The Contemporary Pacific* 22 no. 1 (2010): 1–35.

Tcherkézoff, Serge. *First Contacts in the Polynesia, the Samoan Case (1722–1848): Western Misunderstandings about Sexuality and Divinity.* Canberra: *Journal of the Pacific History Monographs.* Christchurch, NZ: Macmillan Brown Centre for Pacific Studies, 2004.

Thomas, Nicholas. *Islanders: The Pacific in the Age of Empire.* New Haven: Yale University Press, 2010.

Thompson, David. *Marlon Brando.* New York: Dorling Kindersley, 2003.

Trask, Haunani-Kay. *Lovely Hula Lands: Corporate Tourism and the*

Prostitution of Hawaiian Culture. 1991, accessed April 19, 2015. https:// journals.lib.unb.ca/index.php/bl/ article/view/24958.

————. *From a Native Daughter: Colonialism & Sovereignty in Hawai'i.* Monroe: Common Courage, 1993.

Van Trigt, Judith. "Reflecting on the Pacific: Representations of the Pacific and Pacific Island Women in Five Dominant Cinematic Texts." In *Bitter Sweet: Indigenous Women in the Pacific,* edited by Alison Jones, Phyllis Herda, and Tamasailau M. Suaalii, 93–108. Dunedin: Otago University Press, 1998.

Vasey, Ruth. "Foreign Parts: Hollywood's Global Distribution and the Representation of Ethnicity." In *Movie Censorship and American Culture* 2nd ed., edited by Francis G. Couvares, 223.

Amherst: University of Massachusetts, 2006.

Whitehead, Neil L., and Peter Sigal. "Ethnopornography." Academia.edu. Accessed March 29, 2015. https:// www.academia.edu/169099/Ethno pornography.

Williamson, Robert W. *Essays in Polynesian Ethnology.* New York: Copper Square, 1975.

Wilson, Rob. *Reimagining the American Pacific.* Durham: Duke University Press, 2000.

Wood, Houston. *Displacing Natives: The Rhetorical Production of Hawai'i.* Lanham: Rowan & Littlefield, 1999.

Wyeth, Leonard. "Tin Pan Alley." Acoustic Music. Accessed March 23, 2020. https://acousticmusic.org/research/ history/musical-styles-and-venues-in-america/tin-pan-alley/.

Index

Numbers in **bold italics** indicate pages with illustrations

Index 273

Λ